The Atlantis Hypotheses

By

Raymond S. Hislop

Shield  Crest

© Copyright 2009 R. S. Hislop

All rights reserved

This book shall not, by way of trade or otherwise, be lent, re-sold, hired out, or otherwise circulated without the prior consent of the copyright holder or the publisher in any form of binding or cover other than that in which it is published and without a similar condition including this condition being imposed on the subsequent purchaser

ISBN: 978-0-9558557-4-0
MMIX

Published by
ShieldCrest,
UK: Aylesbury, Buckinghamshire, HP22 5RR
USA: Morrisville, NC 27560
www.shieldcrest.co.uk

CONTENTS

PREFACE

THE OLD HYPOTHESIS

1. Maat
2. Super communicate
3. < Real Aliens >
4. Communication
5. Contact
6. Technology
7. The Contradiction in Terms
8. Options and Super Communicate
9. Through the Mists
10. YH2UH
11. Contradictions
12. Visions and Reality-More Contradictions
13. The Overthrowing of Apep.
14. The "One" God
15. Misunderstandings
16. The Lord The Krystyesus
17. The Risen Lord
18. The Two Rs
19. Strange Books
20. RA

THE NEW HYPOTHESIS

21. Finding Atlantis
22. Keeping Atlantis
23. Threatening Atlantis
24. Atlantyon Galactic Physics
25. < Atlantyon Galactic Physics >
    Hieroglyphs in < THE NEW ATLANTIS >
    Includes two technical drawings and
    TWO STYLISED STAR CHARTS
    <<<< BARRED SPIRAL COMBINATION GALAXY >>>>

PREFACE

THE OLD HYPOTHESIS
and
THE NEW HYPOTHESIS

I have divided this text into three. There is this Preface and then there is the Old Hypothesis and the New Hypothesis. Essentially that is a style matter.

The Old Hypothesis was completed by me around 2004 and while offered at that time for publication, with a slightly different title, which was refused, I was not aware of some serious deficiencies in it. While I had intended that the text which comprises the Old Hypothesis would be retained here substantially unadjusted and with its original preface, given the New Hypothesis, and the < UNDERSTANDING > and Science in it, I have had to make several substantial adjustments and to remove the original preface and indeed to adjust this PREFACE as of this date.

I have made reference in these texts to the journey made across the Atlantic Ocean by the individual Thor Heyerdahl and his boats Ra1 and Ra 2. I was given that book as Geography prize in my final year at school before going to University to study Law.

Like the boat built by Thor Heyerdahl and called Ra 1, I had thought that with the Old Hypothesis I had all the relevant information. If The New Hypothesis is read before the Old Hypothesis is read, it should clearly be seen that there are number of glaring errors even in the now revised Old Hypothesis . In many respects it is like the first Ra 1.

When writing the Old Hypothesis I was not aware of the significance and the importance of the correct understanding of Atlantis. I had originally mentioned Atlantis only to be highly critical of the story. Unfortunately, like Heyerdahl, I had not appreciated that Atlantis is FUNDAMENTAL to the DESIGN as is the < AT LAN TY K > Ocean. Without that < ADVANCED UNDERSTANDING > then like the rope tensioner on Ra 1, these HYPOTHESES are INVALID and will SINK . Indeed I have had to make substantial revisions to the New Hypothesis to ensure scientific accuracy; particularly with the < ATLANTYON GALACTIC PHYSICS >. And that includes the requirement that I must have in this < TEXT > Three < CORRECT > < STAR > names from < STARS> in Three Specific System Galaxies.

Although it may not appear so to "Scientists" the New Hypothesis is VERY TECHNICAL and CONTAINS MUCH SCIENCE, particularly the < Applied Metaphysics > or < ATLANTYON GALACTIC PHYSICS > as it may otherwise be called. This is not just any Applied Metaphysics. It is done to a < PARTICULAR STYLE > and has a number of < SPECIFIC REQUIREMENTS > and <<< UNDERSTANDINGS >>>, including SPECIFICALLY the <<< SPORTING >>> program with its large and stylized EXERCISE STICKS [AdSY's] and <<< HIGHLY STYLISED HEADPIECES >>>.

That means that this text it is suitable for study in Applied Metaphysics classes and those familiar with such, including those at <<<< Hermarut >>>>, will immediately spot what are otherwise apparently very odd or unusual parts of the text. They are there for a SPECIFIC reason; particularly in the New Hypothesis.

In respect of the Old Hypothesis, where something looks odd or out of place, I would recommend a look at the New Hypothesis for clarification. Although the pages are numbered, that is not required in many of the < Applied Metaphysics > works. The < SPORTING > program is a material part of the Science, for technical physical reasons, and that was not known nor fully appreciated, both when writing the Old Hypothesis and indeed in the initial text of the New Hypothesis completed by 8 January 2009. The revisions were carried out up to 8 May 2009 and this new title added as of 11 May 2009. The < TIME > element in these adjustments and the noting of them is required. While it may explain some inconsistencies in the Old and New Hypothesis, there are still inconsistencies which in certain respects are examination questions to assess the level of understanding. Currently there is virtually no understanding of the < GRAVITY STICKS > which I call < AdSY's > .The understanding of them is fundamental and that discloses the level of development of the < Footstool > population. The current level is not even at ONE PANEL, but this text is suitable for those who understand up to THREE PANEL. Indeed Three Panel is required because of the < GALACTIC CONNECTIONS >.

Likewise the working of and the < POSITIONING > of the < AdSY> < HEADPIECES > both on and off the < WORKING and SPORTING AdSY >. The AdSY's and headpieces are essentially keys for < COMBINATION + TIME LOCKS > which < MUST > be operated in the < CORRECT LOCATIONS > and < SEQUENCE >. This is often referred to as a < FEET > exercise. This is all to do with a REAL FEELING referred to as <<< HOSTING >>>. That is again explained in the New Hypothesis.

The use of the Chevrons is to highlight the particular scientific understanding of < Applied Metaphysics >. While at a reading level they can be ignored the intention is to draw attention to the < SPECIFIC > and < TECHNICAL > nature of the words. The are mostly used in the New Hypothesis and where they occur in the Old Hypothesis are evidence of a material revision or note which I considered had to be added. The use of Four Chevrons usually indicates a place. One, two or three chevrons usually indicate an individual. The use of one chevron can indicate also only one Galaxy whereas three would indicate at least Three Galaxies.

In keeping with the New Hypothesis when referring to Biblical text I have to be strict. The KING JAMES VERSION HAS TO BE USED. In the Old Hypothesis I used the Good News Version, and while that is suitable, from a style point there are

HIGHLY TECHNICAL and SCIENTIFIC TIME POINTS which means that I MUST INSIST on the KING HY ME VERSION. If another version is used, a COMPARISON should be made of the King James Version. The reason for the King HY ME version is < TECHNICAL > at < ADVANCED > and < ULTRA > levels. It relates to < SPECIFIC and DESIGNATED TERRITORY > and < BOUNDARY MARKERS >.

I have used Chevrons because my knowledge of The Atlantyon language is < RESTRICTED > and again I regard that as < TECHNICAL > from a scientific point of view. At this date a mixture of ATLANTYON and ENGLISH words with TONE CONTROLS (often shown by a stylized spelling) and the chevrons will adequately convey the accuracy of the text. The use of <chevrons> and the number of them is <COMPLEX > in the < Applied Metaphysics > context.

Technically this is a < CLOSED FOOTSTOOL > and the one chevron indicates that basic understanding. That basic understanding was given in the < AGP TY ON > Hieroglyphs and drawings. The use of Three Chevrons is much more advanced and the use of the Three Chevrons indicates certain < TECHNICAL > matters are being considered in this text. In simple terms it whether the < GALACTIC LINKS > can be re-established and the Three Chevrons indicate that it is for at least < THREE GALAXIES > to have a say in that matter. Unless they agree < CONTACT > will NOT be re established. In that connection the < GALAXIES > have specific names in < ATLANTYON > and these I have used < WITH PERMISSION >. The same applies to the < STAR > Names.

Where the text shows four chevrons and it is clearly not a place, their use indicates a serious problem or concern. When talking of tone controls it is like "accents" and "dialects" but not exactly the same.
Thus the < STAR > names in particular have a < SPECIFIC > use. < HYT GHARVYK BY AT RUTH > for example is a particular Blue White Star in < THRENS >. That Galaxy is

known currently at this < FOOTSTOOL > as M 31. M 104 also has an < ATLANTYON > name and that is given in the Technical Specification. Beyond M 104 is another < HIGHLY SECURED and HIDDEN GALAXY COMBINATION of the BARRED SPIRAL and SCULPTED TYPE >. It has < TERRITORIAL MARKERS > on this < FOOTSTOOL > identified by names such as < THOR > and < THUN >. The prefix < THOR > is a < STAR > and individual identifier while < THUN > is a place name. That should highlight how easy it is to wrongly pronounce names. The < STAR > names with place names MUST BE CORRECTLY PRONOUNCED and USED . < ATLANTIS > for example is a < STAR and PLACE and STYLE NAME > and MUST be correctly identified as this entire < FOOTSTOOL> with its < SPECIFIC POPULATIONS >. The use of the word "planet" or "earth" or even "human" immediately discloses a WRONG SCIENTIFIC UNDERSTANDING of the GALACTIC SCIENCE.

Likewise the Blue white which is associated with the place names must be known by its CORRECT NAME. In the text I have used variations, but in this preface, the < THUNDER > is < DELIVERED > and < RECEIVED > for the < STAR is ANGRY > with what it finds at <<<< ITS TERRITORY >>>>. It is not recommended to be on the wrong side of a Blue White Star.

With < APPROVAL > and < CONSENT > I use the name < THOR ARRAN ARGHAARTH > . The < HEADPIECE > is dark blue, light blue and gold < BARRED SPIRAL + SYFERT SCULPTED >. White TRIPLE and GREY CORDED SPORTING. These < Headpieces > made of Balsa type wood, when inserted into the sporting headband, give the appearance of a < THORN >. Since they relate to < THREE GALAXIES > they might be correctly described and referred to as a "Crown of Thorns!"

<<< WHITE TRIPLE AND GREY CORDED HEADBAND and TRILBY >>>
<u><<<< FORMAL AT FURIOUS ANGER >>>></u>

This concept of the stars being < LIVING > is a < FUNDAMENTAL > of the < APPLIED and ATLANTYON GALACTIC PHYSICS > and is something the Stars are quite capable of making < PERFECTLY CLEAR > as both the Hypothesis texts should clarify.

Examination questions in < Applied Metaphysics > and < Atlantyon Galactic Physics > at < Advanced > and < Ultra > can be set using this text and I am satisfied that < SPORTING > can be taught. Since Advanced deals with ACTUAL ALIEN CONTACT, there are many <<< TECHNICAL POINTS >>> which are not appropriate for this work, which is intended as <u>an introductory and public text</u>.

While ACTUAL ALIEN CONTACT would be considered by many to require VARIOUS GOVERNMENT APPROVAL that is NOT TECHNICALLY CORRECT. In that connection the United Nations is NOT a Suitable Organization to deal with the Aliens detailed in the New Hypothesis. That is < TECHNICAL > because notwithstanding the UN name and its < AT LAN TY K > location it is likely to be viewed as situated in < NOT PROTOCOL > territory. The same applies to the UN at Geneva but not had it been at < THUN > which is < PROTOCOL >.

Essentially it is the <u>ENORMOUS GALACTIC CIVILISATIONS</u> who set the agenda since they are far more advanced and they view this as one of <u><<<< THEIR FOOTSTOOLS >>>></u>. That is NOT a DETAIL as the New Hypothesis should make clear. And it is THEY who VET potential visitors and determine what are < <u>THEIR PROTOCOL COUNTRIES.</u> >

While many of the Countries of the European Union are indeed Protocol for the purposes of ALIEN CONTACT there are STRICT BOUNDARY MARKERS <u>IN TIME</u>. In the NEW HYPOTHESIS TEXT and in the technical drawings section I have tried to clarify the PROTOCOL TERRITORIES and the TIME ZONES.

One of the main purposes of this text is to DEMONSTRATE a CORRECT UNDERSTANDING of this ADVANCED SCIENCE and that required me to offer it for publication. Without the NEW HYPOTHESIS TEXT AVAILABLE there the will be NO COMMUNICATION and NO CONTACT AT OFFICIAL LEVEL with these particularly powerful INDIVIDUALS and THEIR GALAXIES.

Their <<< TY >>> Officials, including such as may be <<< TRANSITING >>> can assess for < PROTOCOL COMPLIANCE > or < OTHERWISE >and they are likely to <<< INSTRUCT WITHDRAWAL >>> where such individual is threatened, particularly if it is done at Government level.

Their <<< FUNDAMENTAL PROTOCOLS >>> on <<< JUSTICE and MEDICINE >>> MUST BE MET BEFORE any meaningful contact with other Galactic Footstools will be permitted. And the time periods can be hundreds and thousands of years.

They ARE LIKELY TO WATCH EVENTS particularly as televised locally, such a football matches and other large sporting events to satisfy themselves that their STYLE REQUIREMENTS ARE MET.

The Main ASSESSMENTS will be taken at < STAR > level and it is only when the < SYSTEM and SEQUENCED STARS > are satisfied at < STAR > level that PROTOCOLS ARE AGREED TO THEIR REQUIRED LEVEL and MAY SAFELY BE EXCHANGED that this ADVANCED GALACTIC CONTACT can be contemplated.

Essentially it is a < STAR MATTER > and it is the Local < STAR > which has to be < COMPATIBLE > and with its species.

I CANNOT EMPHASISE ENOUGH AT A SCIENTIFIC LEVEL, the IMPORTANCE OF SAFE PROTOCOLS. This is a MOST MATERIAL POINT, particularly on MEDICINE and JUSTICE MATTERS as I have tried to make clear in this text and in the NEW HYPOTHESIS.

<<< AMEN >>>   <<< AM >>>   <<< RTUR >>>

It is a FACTUAL Matter on which the < SEQUENCED GALACTIC STARS > take their own assessment.

The cover photograph is taken from Tenerife looking towards La Gomera. It is relevant to this text in that the view would be similar to that on Threns in M 31 Galaxy looking from the Atlantyon Island of Dal across to the island where the <<< TYEM AM >>> one of the < THREE AMENS > of M 31 Galaxy has a large Palace. The view is adjacent to where his Ambassador to the Atlantyons has a residence on Dal Island.

<<< TSUTRAN KYDRAN AD KURALAKYS LLOFOTTYEN FVRECKRAN >>>

<<< AM >>>   <<< RTUR >>>   <<< AMEN >>>

THE OLD HYPOTHESIS

1
Maat

"A large Library will not assist in understanding unless it works are of the highest quality, while a few works of quality may be of greater benefit than the biggest library."

The library at Alexandra was burnt to the ground. Christian zealots were behind such because it was regarded as "decadent". How many libraries would be burnt today for exactly the same reason? Such action I would say lacks "enlightenment".

And yet I am a child of the Christian tradition. Can I appreciate what life was like for revolutionary thinkers like Galileo, and the threats he had to endure from a "Christian Church"? I can't. That is the simple answer.

I may look at the old "Egyptian civilizations" like those of King Tut, but in many respects they are alien to me. Their theology is also alien. Given the gap of thousands of years I am able to write this text, whereas at the time of Christ that would probably not have been possible. Indeed, even earlier, it may have been necessary to mask "alternative" thinking so as not to upset religious sensitivities. Some things do not change!

Does that in part explain some of the inconsistencies with the Old Testament and Genesis and Exodus in particular? Was there a desire to convey the information, but being unsure of it, it had to be presented in a different form? Or was it that there was a desire to eradicate the past, and to present as real that which was in fact fiction?

It is my suspicion that the latter is indeed the case. Some recent writings which I have read tend to suggest that is the case. It is the proof which is difficult. Thus this hypothesis.

Akhenaten and his "Aten" religion may indeed have been the prime mover with the foundation of the "monotheistic" faiths of this day. But where did he get that from?

As I understand it he got it from an obscure cult of "Ra" and it is with that that I begin with this Hypothesis. For the Hypothesis is that the metaphysics is that the Universe did NOT begin with a big bang, and is not going to end with a "big crunch" but rather that it is the product of a kind of metaphysics, which is capable of starting IN THE MIDDLE, and thereafter continuing without limit of TIME!

Quite a difficult concept that! And it is made the more difficult when the received wisdom of this time would prefer a mathematical solution rather than a "hypothesis."

It is convenient for many to say there is no "God". While others take issue with the "Name of God" and with the theories which they seek to enforce.

I say seek to enforce, for much of religion is concerned with power and the domination by the minority of the many. Many are made to suffer to provide the pleasure and security for the few.

The enlightenment of western Europe in the 16 and 17 centuries did much to assist the poor, but it was not without a price. Human blood sacrifice of the many in France, to name but one. The "United Kingdom" was not much better given that it was more united in a common name than with a common people. The 18 Century was not very pleasant for many in Scotland and Ireland. Transportation and exodus to strange new lands which they then required to develop.

Yet an enlightenment in the 19 century brought development in the fields of medicine as people struggled to understand the realities of the body and how it works. Much was learnt, and much of benefit.

Then we had the 20 Century and appalling barbarity, particularly in what was once an enlightened Germany. Why? What was gained by such barbarity?

In essence nothing. And in addition much was lost. It not easy to see what is lost, because much of that is with the ideas, and they are more intangible. As we enter the 21 Century, I might wonder what has been learnt from that last century.

On the surface western society has learnt much, but like Byzantium before it is under attack, and it groans from the weight of even more rules than even Byzantium could have devised.

There are also forces at work which would seek to undo the enlightenment and turn the light to darkness. These are not forces of enlightenment, but forces of utmost barbarity. The word "evil" springs to mind.

Violence is easy, peace is not. Peace is difficult. If violence is used to maintain peace, the result may simply be to lose the "peace".

The real question surrounds the word "truth", and it is perhaps highly significant that Pilate asked of Christ, "And what is truth?" and then did not wait for an answer. Indeed I might say that if he had to ask the question at all, and he himself did not provide the answer, then he was not capable of knowing Truth!

In old Egyptian times the concept of "truth" was referred to as "Maat" and there was the individual of that name. Now thousands of years later as I ponder over that thinking, I wonder just exactly what was meant. For Pilate's concept of truth, the idea of his audience and indeed many modern concepts of it, including scientific ones ARE NOT MINE. That should be apparent from the New Hypothesis and the chapters on < ATLANTYON GALACTIC PHYSICS >. That is a technically challenging subject for University study, and with this text I have tried to make it accessible to those who wish some insight, but who do not wish to study the subject at University level.

In essence the Egyptian Hieroglyphs, particularly the pictorial drawing contain MUCH advanced science, and deal VERY MUCH with the < UNDERSTANDING > of Truth. <u>It does not change. It is factual</u>. It can be dressed up in such a way that it is disguised, but the principal behind it cannot be changed. If it is changed it is not truth. It may become "dogma" but that is not truth. It may be a comfort to many. "Repeat the mantras" and while you may feel better, if in them there is not an element of truth, they will mean little.

I suspect it was to see some of that Science that a young carpenter took his wife and son to Egypt, and where that carpenter or his son might have been given a small piece of balsa wood to repair by an Egyptian NY TY R, not appreciating that in Atlantyon form that it was a NY TY R, and when repaired watched him as he moved it like a small fan, as if performing a technical dance. It is that highly stylized piece of balsa wood which might be called the "Headpiece on the Staff of Ra" and the technical dance, is just that. I call it < Applied Metaphysics Sporting > and it is done for health reasons and for highly technical reasons as well.

When I now look back to the Legends of Ra and of the old Egyptians and their hieroglyphs I no longer wonder, but rather have a fairly accurate idea of what they actually saw and what where they trying to say? Their strange concepts and ideas were indeed influenced by the NY TY RA and it was the technical difficulty in grasping what the NY TY R were trying to say and their detailed knowledge of the structure of the Universe which led to those strange and some times apparently ridiculous ideas. Their concept of the universe was that it was a strange and dangerous place populated by dangerous and mythical beings. In fact a FAR MORE ACCURATE understanding that the current convenient "big bang theory" which proceeds with evolution and has spawned the monster of a tax grabbing global warming. A SERIOUSLY FLAWED understanding of the Universe!

It is the Volcanoes and the Crust cracking which show the REAL MECHANICS of this < FOOTSTOOL > at work!

The technical expression can be said as: - "The Truth is obvious. It is so obvious that it can only be seen with difficulty, but it is seen by all, all the time. That is why it is the truth."

How does that tie in with "maat"?

I change Maat to "MaTT". And I do that because of super communicate. And once I change it to MaTT, and use the super communicate, with the Atlantyon Galactic Physics, I know exactly why he said < "I am the way the truth and the life" >. Pilate does not understand but the INDIVIDUAL before Pilate is now a < VISIBLE INVISIBLE >. In a split second, the man who was taken down to Egypt as a child now knows what he saw there and WHO he saw there! And in a further split second the < VISIBLE INVISIBLE > is "apparently gone".

For the purpose of this Hypothesis *as revised* I choose to call him "Ra". He is not an individual and yet he is. He is "Trinity" and to that extent "MATT" is "One of his personifications". It is a small personification, as disclosed by the hieroglyph, but also a MASSIVE ONE. He is a < GALACTIC INDIVIDUAL >.

Even now some 2000 years after the event Rome does not appreciate the < FURIOUS ANGER > of <<<< THAT INDIVIDUAL >>>>.

I have revised a large part of this text to this point, because as originally written the < VISIBLE INVISIBLE > concept is clearly not understood. Having written the New Hypothesis, that aspect has to be accommodated, even here, and that I have now done. But I am not going to substantially review the remainder of the Old Hypothesis but instead try to keep in mind the concept of the < VISIBLE INVISIBLE >. As I said in the Preface there are substantial technical errors in Old Hypothesis text. These errors are the examination questions in the < APPLIED METAPHYSICS CLASS >.

Maat is usually shown with one feather headdress, which brings me to the feathered crown of Egyptian Pharaohs. It also takes me to the "feathered plumed and painted serpent" that is "Kwetlskoatels", and that despite the Egyptian "serpent gods".
    Truth as such is not the province of just this world, big as it is, but rather of the whole universe, which include many < VERY LARGE and EXCEPTIONALLY POWERFUL GALAXIES >. VERY LARGE indeed.
    In the story of Ra after the fight with Isis, Ra is seen to depart into the heavens. I might say he departed to a distant planet in a far distant galaxy. With the means to travel there he is "gone" in the sense that he is not here. But that does mean that he does have the capability to watch! And he is still very much real, despite comments from "earthly voices".
    To have the capability to travel in the stars is beyond even the most powerful country in the world today. Even with a combination of the three most powerful counties on the world, and populations of thousands of millions, they can barely struggle to put a man on the moon! And in certain quarters there is disquiet at even that, and suggestions that the moon missions were "faked". Now while I do not consider the moon mission to have been faked, I am nonetheless concerned that there should be ANY suggestion to that effect! I would regard such as easily scorched, since the "truth" is obvious. But that is exactly

where those disputing that take issue. Why are the photographs taken from the moon showing those grids?

However there is a "truth" in the moon rockets, and in the current space program which is not quite so obvious, and yet is. Those in charge of it have been careless with human life, and have lost a number of their astronauts.

While this may be seen in certain quarters as "an acceptable price for progress" that is far from the truth. And with such attitudes regretfully it will not be possible to make progress into deep space. It will not be possible to develop the super light speed communications and super light speed craft necessary for such.

Science fiction may indeed be that, as it discloses by its failure to accurately deal with the advanced science that the local population have not reached the required level to "communicate" let alone travel in deep space. In that connection the "style" of the Aliens and their dialogue is VERY RELEVANT. There are a NUMBER OF TECHNICAL SCIENTIFIC POINTS which MUST be shown to be clearly and ACCURATELY understood!

Serious < STAR > travel is not fiction to those who are capable of that. That although thousands of years old, is really what the legend of Ra says! It also says they will ONLY SHARE that ADVANCED TECHNOLOGY with their FRIENDS!

Andromeda star system is 2.2 million light years distant. It is not possible to say here if they are using super light speed travel. And what of all the other galaxies? The story of RA states PLAINLY that we are NOT the first civilisation to reach for the stars. Again a < HIGHLY TECHNICAL POINT >.

Kwetlskoatels may have looked on as Atahualpa was attacked by the Spaniards. It was a long time ago, and he is now regarded as irrelevant. But if he was a < VISIBLE INVISIBLE > Rome has just done AGAIN through one it officials yet a further human blood sacrifice!

South America is Christian. But is it? The people so brutally treated have not forgotten their old traditions. However, even before the first Christian arrived they may have lost what it was all about. For it is part of this hypothesis that what Kwetlskoatels was opposed to was "human blood sacrifice".

Those who deal with South American archaeology may disagree, and the evidence of human blood sacrifice is there, but watch. Appearances can be deceptive.

France was and is a "Christian country" but its use of the Guillotine would earn it a title of a country which worshiped human blood sacrifice. I am certain that those who were involved with that would not have seen it in that light, but that is exactly what it was. And the difficulty is that once that is done, it may take 3 or 4 generations to remove the "blood lust".

As I look around the world today I see the blood lust writ large. How is it to be defeated? With weapons ? Yes, but first with wisdom.

The King of Heaven is often referred to as the King of creation. That is an important description. It is the power of creation which is important. I can burn a book, and indeed that may be necessary where it tells "untruths", but it can take a very long time for the understanding to be reached.

Currently we have in the "word wide web" a large library, but it will not greatly assist with progress, because its works are not of the highest quality! I do not here refer to certain images, which though distasteful are none the less real. No of greater concern are the myriad pages (which I would not even bother to look at) which contain erroneous and deliberately hurtful information. Such are "bad" or "evil" if they deliberately set out to attack peace, to upset the balance which may be said to be in the Universe.

The "www" is a mechanical and electrical device. It is therefore possible that a massively powerful galactic civilization may already have access to the "www" simply by dialing into it. With its super light capacity, there is no means to check its presence, and it may, even as I type be absorbing the material it finds.

The "seti" [Search for extra terrestrial intelligence] program may be the limit of our technology, but that is not going to take us far if those we are trying to contact are shielding their presence from us, and communicating super light.

The hieroglyphs of Egypt do not speak to me, in much the same way as Atahualpa said to Cortez about the Bible. The difference is that I am a small individual, and I am searching for truth, not seeking an excuse for war and human blood sacrifice!

The story of Ra and Maat and the boat of millions of years in which he travels is interesting. It is as though in super communicate it is trying to say something which the words, the hieroglyphs, do not convey. And yet unlike English (or Roman text as I refer to it)(in my case Acanthus font),the hieroglyphs do say something else.

That for RA incorporates the sun disk.

That would be appropriate for I might refer to him as the Lord of Hydrogen Fusion.

[I have to insert here that it is < STAR PLASMA > which is the correct reference. In writing this, I am very much like Heyerdahl with Ra 1. I am using the best technology (science and teaching that I have been given), which is unfortunately almost entirely wrong (in a Universe and Galactic context). Like Heyerdahl look to these revision, mostly shown in < Chevrons> and in Bold as RA 2 and as though a NY TY R or Atlantyon had actually cast his or her eyes over this text as revised. It is a bit like the Professor of Applied Metaphysics complaining as he reads this text to himself that I have not got the correct grasp of what I am talking about. With this insertion, such Professor should know that I do. For thousands of years, many have been trying to understand and claiming to have the correct knowledge. This is a genuine attempt to CORRECTLY explain the reality in a scientific context with the correct understanding and style. Thus the examination questions.]

In short letter form I might use the letters YHUUH. Now note here the variation from YHWH. But then "W" is simply "2 U" The reference is there to "water" which is H2O.

I can write it then thus YH2UH. That means that like Chinese I introduce a tone control. It could be that H2U is simply a description of a particular kind of water; that which is used for hydrogen fusion. But if I allow that Ra and YHUUH are one and the same figure, what has been going on?

What then if Moses and Akhenaten are the same individuals ? Or even if they are not the same individual, Moses story does take place in Egypt. Let me suppose that Akhenaten went out to try and discover what this religion of his fathers was about. What happens if he discovers an important and carefully shielded ancient mystery, a mystery of great power ; of a lost civilisation destroyed by a flood! The Atlantyon myth? No, the Ra story.

But the flood which was alluded to was an "earth crust desplacement", and was caused by a very angry RA, who was irritated that his sacred name had been violated. Is it small wonder that Moses asks,

Exodus 3 at verse 14 [GNB p 61] "What is his name? So what can I tell them?"

It is a very tart reply given by THE I AM, who says; "I am who I am. This is what you must say to them. The one who is called I AM has sent me to you".

Now I read that in an English text. What is important is what, in hieroglyphic speech, Moses would actually have said. The real words are vital.

Not Hebrew words, but the spoken words of Moses, the Egyptian Prince. And here the phonetic sound is very important. Current scholars of ancient Egypt, who are also fluent in its language could doubtless try to tell me what, in their view, would have been said. But what it actually sounded like, may have differed. After all with the lapse of time in Egyptian society, it is possible that the name of the "I AM" individual had changed.

However the super communicate remains in the English text. It discloses that the comment is made by an individual who simply has to say, "I am".

In that sense, and for the purpose of this hypothesis, Ra does not have to say he is Ra. That is obvious. That may arise because of some form of TONE of dress or perhaps because, if looked at, he may have on his clothes a name, which if it could be read, says just that:-

Revelation 19, verse 12. "He had a name written on him, but no one except himself knows what it is".

Is that not akin to the "Secret name of Ra?"

That passage at verse 11 talks about "heaven open".

Now I am probably fairly certain that current received Christian theology will have that as a vision of John. And indeed it may be just that. But care has to be taken, for John may have been allowed to see what in fact can happen!

Current science fiction film might indeed talk of a "stargate" and even that series pointed the finger at RA. What it did not contemplate, and what the story of Ra as told by the Egyptians alludes to, is the reality of an individual who travels around the heavens; the universe in current language. If that is the case, then there may be a star gate which is capable of being "opened" as John suggests. His vision is then more real than, thus far, it has been given credit for. Yes it is complicated, but that complication may be necessary. It may be for reasons of security.

Again the name of the boat of Ra. "The boat of millions of years."

The distance to Andromeda is 2.2 million light years. That means that at the speed of light it would take 2.2 million years to reach it. To reach it in one year it is necessary to have a vehicle capable of travelling at "millions of years"

Now, I write the words in English but the meaning is the same.

The idea has "super communicated". And I suspect, as it *was intended to do.*

2
Super Communicate

This is arguably one of the most difficult chapters. I am particularly reluctant to write it, or to explain it.

Acts 2, verse 6. "When they heard this noise, a large crowd gathered. They were all excited, because each one of them heard the believers speaking in his own language."

And at verses 8 to 12, "how is it, then, that all of us hear them speaking in our own native language? We are from Parthia......Mesopotamia....from Egypt.......from Rome....from Crete and Arabia-yet all, of us hear them speaking in our own languages about the great things that God has done. Amazed and confused they kept asking each other; "What does this mean?"

At verse 13 it reports that others made fun of them saying, "These people are drunk!"

Super communicate at work, in verses 8 to 12. With verse 13 thrown in to hide part of the power. For what is talked about is real power!

While checking of that text with which I am familiar, I found a passage from Ezekiel at Chapter 37 and marked by me with a note in a script which I write the letters which spelt the word "messenger".

Chapter 37 of Ezekiel is the one about the Sovereign Lord asking Ezekiel to prophesy to the bones and to bring them back to life. A very powerful individual this "Sovereign Lord".

The words of Ezekiel are interesting. At chapter 20 God is reminding the "prophet" and "Israel" that he "revealed" himself to his people in Egypt and promised to bring them to a land rich and fertile, the finest land of all(verse 6). Today modern Israel would not qualify as such, but on close inspection the United States would. After all outside Israel it probably has the largest "Israel" people living there. And there they wield considerable influence.

When super communicate is used, the words do not necessarily mean what they say, since they may be transposed in time and in written language.

Thus from a pulpit in the United States the passage from Ezekiel may be quoted, but entirely miss the super communicate aspect, because it is not something easily "understood" or appreciated. Instead it is likely to be taken "historically", which is not in the context and with the meaning intended by "The Sovereign Lord."

Super communicate is not easy to understand. I need to move the spelt "Ezekiel" back to its super communicate, which is to take it in part to its phonetics.

ES E KY EL.

Now what that then means to me is, "It is HE, the" I could write it slightly differently. Like the Spanish, "ES", third person of the verb To be. That designates it clearly as "THE I AM". Spanish is akin to Latin, possibly its closet relation as to the phonetic sound. Thus Spanish is a super communicate vehicle, and that I even with my limited knowledge of that language can understand.

Now the next letter is "E" At the moment I am not sure what that stands for. The "EL" at the end again immediately takes in the Spanish "EL" meaning "The".

The letters "KY" are straight super communicate, and I would translate them as "third person singular, He"

That leaves me only the "E" to translate as super communicate.

At this point I leaf my way through Ezekiel. I am trying to understand what I am writing, conscious that I am working with a very special text. It is like a code breaker trying to make sense out of the apparently random letters of a code. But as a code breaker knows the apparently random letters are not that. So I know that within this super communicate are words of real power. For that reason they have been guarded for centuries; for thousands of years. And they may be guarded yet for thousands of years.

As I read the press and listen to those who are searching through computers, I am conscious that I must be careful with the super communicate. How much can I release? Is the use of the word "Ky" as "he" too much? Is my difficulty in writing about it also too much information? As a language I say it pre dates, Latin, Greek, Chinese, Hieroglyphs, Summerian. A language which is thousands upon thousands of years old. The language of super communicate?

I view the "two letter combinations." I use super communicate as a device, like tool used in the understanding of super communicate.

I have seen no evidence of the existence of the super communicate language written in a form as I would understand it. Except that the letters "YHWH", which I would re write as "YH2UH" to make them super communicate, then says to me, "The Lord of Hydrogen fusion, the Lord of Light".

Now as soon as I use the term "Lord of Light" it fits in nicely with "Ra",and with "Aten" and with the concept of an individual.

However at Acts 7, verse 48 .

Immediately I see in it the specific words of super communicate, "THE MOST HIGH GOD"

I would write these in super communicate as "DTT" Am I allowed to write that?

Verse 48 says, "but the Most High God does not live in houses built by men; as the prophet [Isaiah 66, vs 1-2"] says, the Lord says:-

"Heaven is my throne, and the earth is <u>my foot stool</u>. What kind of house would you build for me? Where is the place for me to live in? Did I not myself make all these things."

It was Stephen who was speaking these words to the people and they did not like what he said so they stoned him. A human blood sacrifice I would say. An unacceptable practice. And in both respects, although written in English, I use a super communicate element in my words. My use of the words "human blood sacrifice", not as just that but to any form of ritualised murder, whether done by a private individual or by a state, is to super communicate them.

I have been brought up in the Christian tradition, but it has not been by a dogmatic faith, but rather one which tries to do things according to the "Spirit". It is not for me to determine the time, to let my words be seen. It is for THE I AM THE.

Again my use of the words, "The I AM The" is my attempt to super communicate the reality, as opposed to a fiction or a hypothesis.

Now for thousands of years Egypt and its Gods have had a very bad press. In many respects that is because of the text of the Good News. The recent suggestion that the Pharaohs may have written the Bible, sheds a different light on that. And the efforts to show a link between the Hebrew and the hieroglyphs, does indeed shed some light on a very dark and mysterious period of Egypt's history and the Pharaoh, known as Akhenaten, and his son Tut ankh amun. [Text added at this point: <u>The correct spelling and sound MUST end with <<< AMEN >>></u>].

I would take the view that such efforts merely assist me with this hypothesis, for there are still many unanswered questions.

While I am reasonably comfortable that there may be a direct link between Hebrew and the hieroglyphs, and an element of "back engineering" that, in my view and in terms of this hypothesis does not go far enough.

For super communicate purposes, "D" and "T" have similar sounds. I would not refer to Thoth as such but as "Ta HA Ty" which is to strictly super communicate it. In that word, the ""Ta" would be a short form of <<< Taydaranakushton >>>. That I might have to break down to "Tay DA R An a Kush T On" Is it a coincidence that there was once a kingdom of "Kush", in much the same way as there was once a "Maya"?" Ta ha Ty" and "Dahouty" are similar in sound, but is only with reference to the super communicate that the correct pronunciation as Ta HA Ty would be appreciated.

In certain respects the super communicate is like a "mnemonic". And it may be that much of the ancient texts, although not yet appreciated, take that form!

As I understand it Tahaty would be the old Egyptian name for "Thoth" who was then transposed to Hermes and Mercury. By the time he had arrived at Mercury, the super communicate had been lost, except perhaps for him in his capacity as "winged messenger". It may also be maintained (without appreciating the significance) in the "shape shifter" aspect of the "metal" mercury!

Again, the super communicate is maintained in that designation. For I would say that "Ta Ha Ty is indeed the winged messenger of Ra, friend of Ra; as he is sometime described."

To have as part of a hieroglyph, Ta H a TY over the seated figure, which is in fact one of the representations of RA (in terms of this hypothesis) simply serves to confirm in the super communicate, of the protection by the Ta Ha Ty of the figure of MaTT. In that capacity, as truth MaTT is the small representation of RA; of Ra in the fragile human form; of a form which could easily be taken as might be described of Christ himself. Of the concept of God with us.

Acts 7 at 48 would tend to suggest that "god" cannot be contained within a small area but that deflects away from a reality where the King of Heaven can appear as "just a little man". The figure of MaTT.

I look at the first line of Chapter 8 of Acts and I shake my head. I am not long returned from the island of Malta, where Paul spent some time. But, before he arrived in Malta, and prior to his conversion on the Damascus road, Saul as he then was, is reported in chapter 8 verse 1 as having approved of his [Stephen's] murder.

Acts is interesting in that it does try and super communicate, although as Stephen did point out, Vs 51, "How deaf you are to God's message" At verse 53 he says: "You are the ones who received God's law that was handed down by angels-yet you have not obeyed it."

The super communicate here is that the "words" were "handed down" from heaven but were NOT obeyed. What is causing the problem?

The answer is in the love of rules over the Spirit which is for Peace.

Thus Leviticus with its rules, is NOT likely to be the word of God. It does not, in my view, Super communicate. And if that is tried, it would come out as the words of MAN.

El VY TY Kus, is to break it down to the super communicate. The difficulty comes with the word "Kus", which is not itself a super communicate word and I suspect that it has not been correctly written. Given that I suspect there is no super communicate input. That should not come as any surprise. El Vy and TY are all "capable of" super communicate, but the last word should clearly be super communicate if all is to super communicate. If, in an effort to make it super communicate, I sub split it to "K us", it becomes "of Us" in the English sense of the word "Us", so that its wordage is then; "These are the rules we want". Which is exactly the criticism that Stephen makes of the religious leaders of his day.

In many respects that is the criticism that Christ also makes of the desire to follow rigid rules.

Today one of the best examples of the application of rigid rules is probably to be found within the Parliamentary systems and their "justice systems". Most modern societies would make the rules of the Pharisees of Jesus day pale into insignificance!

And as I look at the European convention "rights" I am reminded of that old adage; "the route to hell is paved with good intentions".

The strict application of Acts of Parliament has a long history in this Country [United Kingdom], which is far from Glorious, and some of it has been horrific.

Given that they are Acts of Parliament, they fall neatly in the "Leviticus " pit. It is what we want! No Spirit in the "Rules", but just simply what the "people want"!

3
< Real Aliens >

"The truth is obvious. It is so obvious that it can only be seen with difficulty, but is seen by all, all the time. That is why it is the Truth"

That phrase is a fundamental concept to the Understanding of Peace. It is easy for me to say, but to record it is difficult. There is a resistance from the words to allow them to be written.

When Pilate asked the question of Christ, it is the reply which could have been given. But what was the point? By asking the question, and in the way he does, he demonstrates, that he has no need of the answer.

Now as I write it is 2003 AD, but the words have been with me for 20 or 30 years. A very short time in the scheme of 100's, 1000's or millions of years!

Today we search the heavens for Extra terrestrial life, and many are probably of the view that there is nothing out there, and that humanity is alone.

That I would dispute.

Some would say there is no evidence of any "alien intelligence" reacting with this planet. That I would also dispute. It may not be obvious, nor quite as expected, but the evidence is there.

Where did the old Egyptians get all these gods with their animal heads from? Did they just make them up? I suspect that while they made up a number of them, some of the individuals, (who are not gods but "messengers") have a <u>very real basis in fact</u>!

And the fact that certain of these fictitious gods were elevated to a high level, caused a particular irritation with one individual in particular, who was and is most definitely an "extra terrestrial".

"Heaven is his Throne, Earth his footstool". In that context, Earth is where he chooses to "put his foot", to walk among humanity. The concept of God with us. But it is all a little more tricky than that. Take for example the Ibis headed figure of "Thoth"; the Ta Ha TY as I call him. He can "shape shift". That means that he can appear "just like one of us". That means he can be present just as an ordinary individual!

However, if the "shape shift" is effective, the individual is in all respects human and can be easily damaged. The only difference is in the mental capacity! The mental capacity of those who are able to shape shift is considerably more advanced than those who are not able to do such!

The story of Ra is thousands of years old. In essence it is lost at the mists of time, when the ancient Egyptian religion started. It has two forms. One is the story of how Isis set a trap for Ra and the serpent bit him. The story is told in Genesis, but with the Mask of the "Adam and Eve" instead of the "Osyris and Isis". The serpent which bit Ra still gets a very distinctive mention, but the offence is hidden. And Ra's anger is hidden, except that Osyris and Isis are put out of Eden. And in terms of this hypothesis Eden is well hidden, partly as a result of an Earth crust displacement which causes one massive flood, and partly by miles of solid ice!

At the time of Ra, thousands of years ago, he is the "Star" figure. And certain of the old Egyptian gods are referred to as "star" figures. If those who are regarded as "star" figures are separated from those which are not, then a division is made between those who were "gods" BEFORE Egypt and Egypt's gods, which are merely monuments of stone!

It is a distinction I must make as part of this hypothesis, and it is one which, if it is accurate, will assist to lift a veil which has been placed over the planet for thousands and thousands of years. A question remains. WHY?

The answer I consider to be quite simple.

Ra, while feeling comfortable with some of his creation, wanted to make creatures in his own image. That is after all what the text of Genesis says; GNB p 5, Chapter 1, vs 26; "and now we will make human beings. They will be like us and resemble us.......So God created human beings, making them to be like himself".

I take Genesis to be super communicate, so I watch the word carefully.

G NY SY IS. What do I make of that, "God, Voice, Peace, People" is how I would translate the words in super communicate. Immediately I am conscious that I am translating very sacred words and I have to be careful, particularly with, NY SY and IS. Because "IS" is to be found in Israel, NY and Sy is to be found in Sinai, and in a specific order.

Who wrote Genesis? Some have suggested it was Akhenaten. Others have suggested different interpretations. The religious authorities would have it as "God given".

Certainly both Isaiah and Jesus are critical of Jewish authorities who had NOT observed the word of God.

I read Exodus 19. I am concerned, particularly with the references to "blood sacrifice" at verse 12. If people cross a line they are to be put to death. That causes me considerable concern.

I look for and find the story of Abram and the proposed sacrifice of Isaac. [Genesis 22]

The context of that is that at that time, individuals like Abram would have felt that they required to sacrifice their most precious possession, their sons and daughters to appease a violent, powerful and angry god. So in essence Abram is put to the test. I am comfortable with the angel instructing Abram NOT to hurt his son, [verse 12] then lying on the altar, but NOT with the comment about not keeping back his only son.

In essence the human blood sacrifice did not take place. Now note a detail in verse 5 of Chapter 17 of Genesis. In that Abram's name is changed to AbraHAm. That may seem simply like a bit if window dressing, since the pronunciation does not change much, but in super communicate terms it is a massive change. It incorporates "HA" which is massively important. If I translated that as to meaning, I would say, "of light", so that by adding that to his name, Abraham is being accepted for "having seen the light". That position is checked out with the proposed sacrifice of his son. If he does sacrifice his son he is NOT of the light and the use of him as a foundation of the people is worthless. As it turned out he did NOT sacrifice his son (because according to the text by the intervention of the angel) and is therefore acceptable in HEAVEN's terms.[Note "Ab" translates in super communicate as "nothing", "not" or < VERY

BAD >. Initially therefore Ab Ra M is "Not of Ra". I need to be careful for Abraham may not be a "real" figure but rather in Super communicate terms a "type of person"; that is, one who make himself "acceptable to God".

That in essence is the message the Christ was trying to get through. It is NOT important to be acceptable to humanity, to accept mans' s values, but to be acceptable in the sight of those who sit in Heaven, and of God in particular.

Now if Earth is the foot stool, where is heaven? The Truth is obvious. It must be in space beside the stars!

The boat of Millions of years brought Ra to Earth, and took him away again. He is quite capable of travelling here, but we are not capable of travelling to him, unless he first sends transport.

The pictures and the hieroglyphs were trying to say that, and to give the locations in the sky of the various planets, but if the importance is not appreciated by those who are writing the text, it is likely that much will be lost.

Thus the "star pictures" of the Egyptian tombs do not look like our understanding of the sky, because they did not have a complete grasp of it. Or at the very lest were not prepared to let it be seen as obvious. But in certain respects they stated clearly that they understood.

So too with the Mayans of America. The accuracy of the calendar should tell something. Where did they get that accuracy from? Did they just "discover" it, or was that the "message" which they hid for a more discerning, peaceful and technologically advanced society to discover? The only problem is that when that more advanced society did "discover it", it discounted much of it as being fictitious nonsense because it could not interpret it.

If the base of the perimeter of the pyramid at Giza does in fact give an accurate measurement to scale of the circumference of the Earth, it should be blindingly obvious that that did not happen by "accident" but was part of a specific design. Equally to suggest that the pyramids might be part of "heavens mirror" if only a time shift was involved is also to ask a question. It is a question which may be made more difficult if the pyramids are judged to have been built AFTER the date which ties in with the "mirror in heaven". But that might be explained by an attempt to work backwards, to leave a memory of a past event; of a specific time because that was important. Did it tell of a visit by some "star people" and did they leave something, to be found at a future date?

Equally, although viewed as a burial chamber, they might in fact not be that, but may simply be containers, specifically designated, containing some small artefact. How about a small crystal "ankh"?

And what of the nearby sphinx. Traces that the Sphinx was once painted red hold a clue. A red cat . Now who would the Egyptians be thinking of?

The "goddess" Sekhmet was usually shown in red. And according to a book I have on Egypt[Geddes & Grosset- Ancient Egypt Myth and History ISBN 1-85534-333-3], she was an individual to be placated. And Wallis Budge in his work makes as similar comment about the red colour and Sekhmet.

Without mentioning her by name the description; "the Angel of death" would be appropriate. Was it the "red cats" who were summoned to attack at the event now called the "Passover"? It is part of this hypothesis that it was.

Here again a kind of super communicate is at play. The letters H K and T, are descriptive of a place and to be included as part of her name would suggest that she was from that place. It is part of this hypothesis that the name of the place is a large DRAS CITY on a < FOOTSTOOL > in this Galaxy [Specific name removed for personal reasons] of LARGE red cats, like BI PEDAL TYGERS, city number three of four.

But it unlikely the statue of the Sphinx would be to Sekhmet. Perhaps it is the memorial to another star figure. There is another who would cause a problem. Again a red cat, and usually referred to by the short form of his name as head [TAN] of [SARDURON] [Dras Military commander!]

It is part of this hypothesis that the long or formal name is "Tan Sard Ur On," and that I will use in the future to designate him.

Now immediately I use that name I note a problem. "Ur" is included. However it may simply mean that in the city of "ur" it was Tansarduron that the people worshiped, [human

21

blood sacrifice again] and that would NOT be acceptable to The I AM. Thus if Abraham did indeed reject the Tansarduron, he would make himself potentially acceptable to The I am.

As I have said, this is part of a hypothesis. Whether it is "right" depends on whether the evidence is there to support it . The evidence is not to be made to fit, but must be used correctly. That is a requirement of truth.

As part of this hypothesis there are two more red cats. They are not so obvious.

Tay Ha TY is another red cat, but I say that only because of the super communicate aspect of the name. For as "Thoth" he is hidden in the representation as a baboon or as the ibis bird but, correctly understood, it is his ability to "shape shift" which is disclosed. What about a fourth. The Apis bull gives a clue, but it is with the description of "Mithras" that a super communicate aspect is seen. This time it is MY Y DRAS, and that ties in nicely with the Mayan of the Americas. Yet again a LARGE RED BI PEDAL TYGER STYLE INDIVIDUAL, but this time hidden behind a Minataur appearance. Note; I might, in super communicate terms refer to the "My Y Dras" as " My K El" or "Michael", which is to designate him as the "The Principal or Head of the "Red Cat" society! He is way above the Tansarduron, and like Tay Ha Ty, is a friend to RA.

There are other "space" figures, like the Gorgons. Much to be feared, as would a serpent.

Many in the "Seti" programme, in the various secret United States government projects in particular may be dismissive of Extra Terrestrials. Again there is a suggestion, born of conspiracy theories, that the United States have links with Extra terrestrials. But if that is the case, <u>and I would doubt it</u>, it is not with the "Tay HA TY or the MY Y Dras" .

Communication with such as the My Y Dras and the Tay Ha Ty is going to be difficult. These individuals have access to "Boats of millions of years" and are able to travel super light. Their planet is not just around the corner. I put it at 15,000 light years distant!

I am well aware that to the physicists and others it is not possible to travel faster than light. I would submit that it is obvious that it is possible to do that, simply because the galaxies exist, particularly the spiral galaxies such as this.

What is it that holds the galaxy together? Is it gravity or is it something else? What is it that keeps the respective stars at a particular distance one from another? What is it that causes the Earth and other planets to spin, and what is the relevance of the spin direction? I am not able nor willing to offer answers in this work. That I ask them is sufficient to highlight matters which need appropriate answers.

In terms of this hypothesis, why no communication from those in space?

The answer is really quite simple. Who here would wish to speak to the Ta Ha TY, to the My y Dras or to Ra himself? And what would Ra have to say to this his creation?

Not a lot to say.

All over the world there are various faiths all vying for followers. Some do it peacefully, some not so.

Most have no interest in RA. In terms of this hypothesis that is what he wanted, because he GAVE all authority to his SON, the Krystyesus!

4
Communication

"I do not need to speak at length, to communicate brief words are best"

This work is not intended as a difficult read. I hope that it is designed to be an easy read, and to be enjoyable.

This hypothesis depends on the "Aliens" being real, and to have visited this planet at time in the past. As I have said, for convenience in this text I am using the figure of "RA" since he is depicted as having a "Boat of millions of years" and of traveling in it. I take that description to be of what I would call his "Chariot of Fire". I use that description because that "super communicates" to me, whereas "spacecraft" and "flying saucer" and "UFO" do not super communicate.

Current received wisdom, certainly as taught to me in school, does not admit of super light travel. Yet it is my view that the "Boat of millions of years" is just such a description of a craft which is able to travel faster than light-thus the reference to millions of years.

Now it is possible that the translation from the hieroglyph which gives that description is not correct, but I do not think that to be the case. Indeed that description is important.

If I take the hieroglyph of the winged disc of RA, and take it as it appears, there is in that description, the "Chariot of Fire". The fire bird of Phoenix may be a similar term and if I use "PY ON NY KS", that may indeed describe something which takes its occupant back to an < ON > ; the word < ON > meaning a city on a distant footstool".

If again I take the "star in the night sky" as appeared to the shepherds over Bethlehem at the time of Christ, I again have the Chariot of Fire, and that the wise men should also be tracking a star, brings in again the Chariot of Fire.

However the communication "appears" to be remiss. In fact I would submit it is far from that. Indeed it is up close and very personal! Perhaps too personal!

Allow for a moment to consider Christ as "stepping down" from the Chariot of Fire". He does that in the sense that he is "made human" but, as previously indicated, if I am talking of creatures who can "shape shift", while he appears as human he retains his "heavenly memory". As he grows he is able to react with individuals on the planet in a manner which would not be thought to be threatening. However, with an understanding which is vastly superior to that of the local inhabitants, he is ultimately considered a threat, and as is reported, it is arranged to have him judicially murdered; for a murder it was.

Given that this is a hypothesis, I can allow myself the luxury of the individual on the Chariot of Fire who observes this crucifixion. For convenience I shall call him RA, but in the sense that he was the father of Christ, the description of YH2UH could also be applied Whether it is his son, genetically, or by adoption, in either case, the judicial murder is going to anger that individual. What it also demonstrates is that if the purpose of the exercise was to create a people who turned away from human blood sacrifice, it has spectacularly failed.

That is the view from the Chariot of Fire. That is likely to be the comment that Tansarduron would have made to THE I AM THE.

At this point it should be borne in mind that the occupant watching this judicial murder has the capability to travel millions of light years in a very short time. The power that such a craft requires is massive, and its firepower is considerable. The ability to vaporize a city, is but a microscopic part of its power and armoury. However to vaporise a city does not demonstrate power, other than of the capacity to murder.

So what that occupant does is to do something much more spectacular. He takes the mutilated body of Christ, and he restores it to life. In addition, as if to make the point he gives him "all authority in Heaven and on Earth." Thereafter he has Christ removed, and as is given in this hypothesis, is renamed as The Lord the Krystyesus.

Ra then retreats from the planet, possibly to consider his position after yet a further bruising impact with the local inhabitants, to watch, if he desires, from a distance, and over a number of years.

It is a fundamental part of this hypothesis that, with the ability to travel "millions of years" I am talking of a very powerful civilisation. If I compare the meeting of Cortez with Atahualpa, Ra can watch the interaction of the two, but from his Chariot of Fire, he can AT THAT TIME travel from Madrid to the high Andes in a split second! Like the blink of an eye as they use their matter transfer equipment. And he can do that with Atahualpa ! That puts Cortez into Pilate's shoes, and with a judicial murder over money; this time for gold, which immediately becomes polluted!

And if there is any doubt of the matter transfer equipment, close inspection of Acts 8, at verse 39 where it says "The spirit of the Lord took Philip away.......he found himself in Ashdod", actually shows it in operation!

It is a passage again which demonstrates the power of instantly removing an individual. Philip was not hurt by that removal, nor did he record any special feeling about it.

That passage in the Good News has been available for over 2000 years. It may have been subject to various interpretations, and all I am trying to do is to give it a different interpretation. MY position is that my interpretation is open to criticism, but equally should be carefully considered as a real possibility.

In talking of the "Boat of Millions of years " as a real craft, I must view its occupant as particularly powerful. Equally I think that I have to accept that he is not alone, but is probably conform to his title as THE KING OF HEAVEN the head of a vast and very powerful civilisation.

How many planets? How many Galaxies? It is part of this hypothesis that HE is over ALL galaxies. How do I then view him as the small individual as MaTT?

The answer to that is with much difficulty. The concept of "God with us" as is taught in Christian teaching is easy to say, but I would submit, not nearly so easy in a strict understanding.

As a small individual, I am left with an individual who knows how everything works, and who for reasons best known to himself, likes interacting with humanity. But as should be obvious with this hypothesis, he does not just react with this people. He reacts with others within what is his universe.

As far as this planet was concerned, in giving ALL authority to the Lord the Krystyesus, RA then arranged for the temples to Ra to be overturned. That was partly of necessity, since if the hieroglyphs were translated there was a real possibility that a more advanced and understanding civilisation might realise his connection. By virtue of this hypothesis I have now made that connection, and again in terms of this hypothesis before it goes anywhere, Ra will check whether he will allow it to be published. I may be allowed to finish it, to check that I correctly understand, as in an examination question or thesis, but publication may be stopped.

It is part of this hypothesis that Ra has already relented in part, because he has allowed a certain piece of stone to be left with hieratic, Greek and hieroglyphs to be discovered, and has allowed a translation. Indeed it was he who had allowed both the creation of that stone, and its finding, and I have no doubt will take an interest in its location!

The pyramids were and are in ruins, but the knowledge with which they had been built remained. To remove that would require that the pyramids were taken down stone by stone, and all memory of them erased. He had allowed the opening of the grave of Tutankhamun, with all its splendours and had watched as much of the treasure in the hieroglyphs was ignored because it did not fit in with the then current wisdom on the planet. Still there was a prospect that at a future date that would be seen.

Still there was no cause for him to visit. The destruction of the cities of Hiroshima and Nagasaki, did alter the perspective of those on this planet, but would not be cause for Ra to visit. Quite the reverse, for while it may have appeared "necessary" it simply confirms to Ra, what he already knows, that the people of this planet still love human blood sacrifice. On that basis there was, and is no need to communicate.

It is an essential part of this hypothesis that this civilization of RA hate human blood sacrifice, which is in technical terms the "abomination of desolation". That is my understanding, and that is what, for thousands of years that civilisation in space have been trying to say to the people here.

And still with their weapons of mass destruction, that is what the people of the planet are not willing to give up.

That is what the Prophets of the I AM were trying to convey.

There is no point in communication with Heaven, while the planet is covered with blood, and all the messages sent out by Seti will simply be ignored. What will not be ignored is what those in Heaven can see for themselves. There will come a time when they will take action and that despite their distaste for Human blood sacrifice. In certain respects, by turning away, Heaven's protection is removed.

All the mass of radio transmissions from the planet can be picked up and accessed by RA. He is able to watch everyone. Not only from our own transmissions, but also from those of his own equipment; far more sophisticated than anything yet devised here!

In terms of this hypothesis it is not little green men. Instead it is of powerful beings who are able to walk among humanity and to look just like them, while at the same time having the capacity to relay the messages super light into Heaven, and to work to Heaven's instructions.

Revelation is probably where the references are to be found. When it talks in terms of "messengers "and allots to them a number that ties in nicely with the position adopted in this Hypothesis as RA sending "messengers"

In many respects much of Revelation is in super communicate terms, but equally it is possibly the case that John was given a "vision", which is to say a pictorial view of <<< SY ON >>> and his writings are an attempt to describe that part of it which he was allowed to see!

I say "allowed" for I am concerned especially with the super communicate aspect, that I do not tread on "heavenly toes".

In essence the <<< SY ON >>> of this hypothesis is indeed a very large city, probably akin to New York in the style of its buildings and taking in an area the size of Los Angeles! No small city that, but a dwarf by comparison to its nearby neighbours, where the red cats stay! For the purposes of this hypothesis there are 4 major red cat cities, each with a population of 500 million Red cats!

I have no proof of that. I cannot see to the distance of 15,000 light years. I put RA currently in Andromeda galaxy [M31]at 2.2 million light years distant. Certainly while he is in M 31 Galaxy it is unlikely that anything major will happen here at Earth. And if I am correct with this hypothesis, he has no need to return.

However it may be that those in <<< SY ON >>> would wish him to return. What would make him return? If those in <<< SY ON >>> represented to him that something on Earth was to his liking, he might............send one of his messengers as a preliminary to making contact.

What is he looking for? It is part of this hypothesis that Ra protects Earth. It is one of his planets and there can be no ET intervention without his permission. That does not mean to say that there is no intervention, just that those who do it, need sanction.

Given that the authority now rests with the Lord the Krystyesus it is up to him. After all although <<< SY ON >>> may be at 15,000 light years distant, with a Chariot of Fire it would take a mere 5 days to travel from <<< SY ON >>> to here.

But then what?

5
Contact

I have watched several Science fiction films which deal with "first Contact" with aliens. Some of them have tried to do it carefully, but most lack the vision of a "reality" of intelligent creatures in space. Pictures of "grey" aliens [unless intended to represent the grey cats] do not mean anything to me. Show me a red cat or a grey or black cat and I would immediately take interest. The difficulty with that is that it would tend to "prove" this hypothesis. And for the purpose of this hypothesis, the various cats, [which I call <<< TYGER >>>] and RA know that. The Lord the Krystyesus knows that.

But it is much more than that. It is the proof that ALL the miracles are real, and they are but a fraction of the power available. Technology thousands of years distant in the future available now. And that is only to them "existing " technology.

But by virtue of the radio transmissions and the television transmissions, we have been making contact with RA and the others, except that we did not appreciate that! It is THEY who can watch and assess the level of development and whether "contact" is appropriate.

Currently the contact is at a "monitoring " level. It is watching by Ra and the others of his civilisation while not interacting with it; or interacting with it in very limited ways. In many respect the stories of contact with aliens are the ones they are most likely to consider as representing the attitudes of the people of the planet. Thus while the poor of the planet might wish for the "contact" the rich, and in particular the rich countries would only wish the contact for what they could "exploit".

As the Red cat Tansarduron would say, "It has not changed."

In essence it is for RA to take an assessment. Which is where the contact comes in. They have demonstrated that they have the capacity to inter act if they so choose, in a way which is virtually invisible. Take away the "miracles" and one of their officials can be made to look just like an ordinary individual. But there is in that a problem. For although the individual looks the same, he or she still has his connection with the civilisation in space.

That "space connection" would, according to certain interpretations of how the military would react, mean that VISITING officers of the GALACTIC CIVILISATION would be under attack here. Even the story of "Star gate" causes concern because of its treatment of RA. Of that film and indeed the subsequent television serious, the question for the Galactic Civilisation is then; how accurate is that portrayal of such contact?

The "Star gate" is an interesting concept. I had dismissed it in part because it just does not seem to fit. However on inspection it fits much closer than I expected. I have to remember that in terms of this hypothesis what any film producer is allowed to produce is ultimately monitored by the Galactic Civilisation and will only be produced and printed if they consider it appropriate. While it may all seem to simply be about money, they are capable of using just about anything which is produced and making it work to their ends.

Manipulative? Not really. It is simply a checking process.

With the plethora of "Star Trek, Star Wars, Star gate to name but a few there is a desire for space exploration. It is difficult. Much more difficult than was World exploration at the time of Columbus, or of Vasca da Gama. And the risks for failure are equally great. The Apollo missions brought tragedy and the Space Shuttle has brought it failures. Light speed travel is still the realm of science fiction, super light speed travel virtually ruled out. Unless that is.... Is it possible to bend space? Which is where the star gate comes in. Is it the mechanism for doing that? The trouble is the technology is dangerous. Exceptionally dangerous. And before allowing access to such it is necessary to check out those people who would intend to access it. It is not equipment to be "stolen" or "borrowed". In essence that was Ra's test of Osyris and Isis, a test which they failed. The test was given again with Lord the Krystyesus and again it was failed. What would happen on a third occasion when they made contact? It would not be the same as before, but it would still be contact. The passage in Matthew 24, vs 29 to 44 and again Mark 13, vs 24 to 37 do both indicate a problem in space which might be typical of a large "stargate" being opened in the proximity of this planet. These passages would tend to suggest that the Lord the Krystyesus(as Christ) had some very clear idea of the tremendous forces which could be applied to the planet; and with potentially devastating consequences.

If he is "God" then he should know exactly what the forces are and how they are created. However if he was as he said, The Son of the Most High, then he might not know because much of that information would remain with his father.

Matthew 24, vs 40 demonstrates use of matter transfer equipment.

As I said this is a very powerful civilisation. VERY VERY POWERFUL. It has to be to "drive the powers in space from their courses." For a long time, it has been communicating, and in a manner which can be understood. Part of the problem may be that we, the people of the planet, do not want to understand and are hiding the information from ourselves.

[While the biblical texts do disclose an understanding, they also disclose an understanding that is VERY limited and NOT accurate. Thus a lecturer in Applied Metaphysics at Hermarut using that text about "driving the powers in space from their courses" would expect his students, mainly in the 20 to 25 year age to know exactly what is being talked about. Essentially it is the slow adjustment of the < Footstool > and the local star in particular as the mechanism is set up to allow, or when previously closed, to re open, what is the super light travel connection to and from different and distant inhabited footstools. The <HIGHLY TECHNICAL APPLIED METAPHYSICS POINT > is that travel is ONLY ALLOWED between COMPATIBLE FOOTSTOOLS. It is not a matter of "trekking about the galaxy". That might make enjoyable science fiction, but it is NOT the reality in Scientific terms.

While the Seti programme may be searching for Alien signals, these GALACTIC civilisations in space only use such LOCALLY; within about 100 light years. They use super light transmissions so Seti is not going to find anything. Additionally with the GALAXY STYLES, particularly the BARRED SPIRALS, there are enormous security protocols in place. That does not mean to say that it those in space cannot communicate with Seti, rather that they choose not to do so because they have no need. First they will need to see some indication that the many messages which they have left *are being collected* and seriously considered in proper and CORRECT SCIENTIFIC TERMS.

The various texts which have been left by them, currently viewed as "religious texts", are available, but the "interpretation" of such has been restricted and while that continues to be restricted by the various religious authorities, the enlightened galactic civilization will NOT PERMIT contact, except on a strictly limited basis . Indeed given that I have said that this is suitable for use in < Applied Metaphysics > how this text is used will be examined by those Galactic Civilisations!

In this connection it is the various Christian Churches and their civilisations which have to be careful. How are they currently treating their religious texts? Are they working with them correctly, or are they simply worshipping the "word" and not applying the "spirit correctly". This is NOT a fictitious exercise, it is a <u>VERY REAL ONE</u> .

The Conveyancing document which runs "in the Name of God Amen" is, in terms of this hypothesis likely to find favour with Galactic Civilisations because it talks of the "correct understanding". But when it is make mechanical and electronic as with Automated Land Registration systems, it is immediately apparent that the local population do not have the same science as those in the vast Galactic Civilisations.

The same can be said for financial transactions. While "credit cards" are indeed something which a Galactic Civilisation would use, the use of "numbers" as in a PIN over a signature is a serious ERROR in dealing with the HIGHLY ADVANCED GALACTIC CIVILISATIONS. This is because of < TECHNICAL POINTS > which MUST be appreciated BEFORE any meaningful contact can take place. It can take place with "advanced" civilizations able to travel super light, but of PARTICULAR GROUPS there are certain FUNDAMENTAL STANDARDS which must first be met.

This is particularly so for INTER GALACTIC contact and travel.

While many scientists and Churches and indeed religions might dispute that, what has to be considered is how they would view the return of the Lord the Krystyesus as a REAL and living individual. That applies particularly to the Christian communities, who would doubtless find that the view adopted by the Lord Krystyesus was, conform to his position as the time of his visit to Jerusalem some 2000 years ago, much more liberal than the strict interpretation of what he said. And worse, those powerful civilisations would be able to provide the video recordings so beloved of the television channels to remove from the Good News in particular the element of uncertainty (faith) and replace it with historical fact!

Is contact with such a powerful civilisations wanted? My view, and it is an entirely personal one, is that most Governments would NOT want contact with such civilisations, would view them as a major threat, and consequently such Governments would be regarded as hostile by that space civilisation. They are likely to instruct NO contact, BUT they can also overturn Governments who are seriously < AGAINST THEIR PROTOCOLS >.

Realistically most Governments do not wish alien contact. The Sub light science as taught in Schools and Universities is a political necessity. The best scientists, certainly in respect of the larger and most powerful governments have huge scientific institutions, all of which are trying to push the boundaries of understanding to the limits ;usually with a military pay off.

Again of all this is watched by these powerful galactic civilisations, both from a distance and at close quarters. But it is not just the technology which is watched. It is also the type of society. Most modern societies have very extensive rules and regulations without which much of modern society would not function. Some of it is very material, but others are not. Things which deal with public safety are important. But things which set out to defend a purely dogmatic position are not. However it all tells that space society what the inhabitants are like.

The inhabitants of Earth, in certain quarters, may regard themselves as tolerant. However the view from space is of the planet as a whole. This if large chunks are NOT tolerant, those space civilisations cannot communicate with "tolerant" parts for fear that the technology they possesses may somehow fall into hands which would use it as a weapon. In that regard the story of the siege of Troy and the wooden horse is but one example, which while tactically expedient, shows a danger which will not be missed on those civilisations in space. They may be thousands and millions of light years away, but by admitting even part of this society to theirs, except where they exercise total control, it could put them at risk from contamination. And that they will not permit.

Look at what happened to the people after the incident between Ra and Isis. It told Ra, what he already knew, that the people could not be trusted. And he was not pleased. It is recorded that he relented from a total destruction of humanity.

In the Bible that story is dressed differently as Noah and the flood. That story tells how Noah escaped, and with a number of animals.

If I revert to my super communicate, it is perhaps trying to tell me that Isis did escape and that she and Osyris set up camp elsewhere. They were not alone, and other civilisations developed which ultimately came into conflict with each other. But with each trying to hide from the reality of what had happened, some more than others, it should not be a surprise that the various religions set out the same message differently. And yet THE TRUTH is there. If it is looked for with all understanding, it will be seen that it always was there, although not immediately seen.

And so for thousands and thousands of years RA has watched. And he still watches. From a distance? Yes, and perhaps not.

If there is a real risk it is that RA makes an expedition. That is not altogether unexpected, for he is the very individual who would qualify as being "like a thief in the night". He cannot steal anything because as a technicality, it is all his in the first place. What is it that he wants to check? In my view it is only one thing. The Justice System. That is his particular interest. And the one that is most at risk from his attentions is the one which HE considers to be the "best" on the planet. That was HIS test for the Romans, and it is seen in the trial of Christ before Pilate. That same test is seen again with the judicial murder of Atahulpa! And again the villain is Rome!

Which system would he pick today, and what would his assessment be? Given the prior tests, it would be likely to be before a "Christian" justice system and accordingly, in terms of this hypothesis, the best of these is at greatest risk from his attentions! Scotland, in particular, with its Roman system and that aspect may pose a very serious risk to the Scottish System and Rome, which was missed by James I and 6 and his "Star Chamber".

And current legal teaching that "ignorance of the law, is no excuse" could be used "mirror fashion" by RA to devastating effect. Can the people of the planet claim to be in ignorance of the message of the Lord Krystyesus. Some might try, given that the political rulers have made it difficult for them to hear the message. But the message is clear. "All authority is GIVEN to the Lord the Krystyeus."

It is entirely a factual matter as to what the position is on the planet at any point in time. And if the warnings in Revelation are not clear or are misunderstood or misinterpreted, before any serious action is taken, the Galactic Civilisation will make the position quite clear!

Watch the earthquakes and volcanic eruptions. They might simply be required to activate the < Footstool > mechanism and to <REPOSITION THE FOOTSTOOL > . Thus the comment, not necessarily correctly understood, that all these things will have to come to pass. [Note here. My use of < footstool > and the chevrons indicates that this text is a revision from that originally written in 2004 and the adjustment is made to more accurately reflect the Scientific content in the New Hypothesis. There is a MATERIAL difference between a < FOOTSTOOL > and a planet. And in an ordinary context when a "stool" or particularly a "footstool" is < THROWN > that has a specific and scientific meaning; likely to mean an actual shift of the footstool position. Once that is understood, it can be seen that the London Fire of 1666 is involved in the

< FOOTSTOOL REPOSITION >. Note here that I have not used the word "Great". That is because if I am talking < FOOTSTOOLS > and < REPOSITION > I have to be careful since I am aware of the underlying science.]

6
Technology

"The theory may be brilliant, but if it is of no use in practice, it is a useless theory"

This hypothesis proceeds on the basis that large and powerful "friendly" alien civilisations exist. They have visited in the past, have endeavoured to assist humanity, in the past, are doing so now, and will do so in the future.

They do not want to create puppets, but equally they have certain defined standards which they wish to achieve for those civilisations which ARE MEMBERS of their "Union" and those who wish to join it. In essence it is a <STAR UNION> of various STARS and THEIR FOOTSTOOLS. Thus "Star Wars" is not a joking matter. As Science Fiction it is quite acceptable BUT such fiction underscores the "Reality".

My original calculations was that the GALACTIC CIVILISATION had tried twice to make contact, and to progress this "civilisation." The first, which was a failure, was with Osirys and Isis(Adam and Eve). And the second was with the Lord the Krystyesus, which was a "qualified" success. It has not been a complete success, for large tracts of the planet do not currently give due deference to the Lord the Krystyesus.

What of a third attempt?

That now looks to have been with Atahualpa ;and that was a bigger failure than with Christ. And what is worse would almost certainly have been drawn to the attention of Christ! Small wonder that Christ said to Peter that he had prayed for him! Watch here that Christ's words are "super communicate". They are more likely to be directed not at Peter himself, but at his successors in office. Thus the real and serious problem with Atahualpa, and the Inca. Indeed even Isaiah and the words used of the Egyptian priests might be leveled at those who murdered Atahualpa. The desire of those in the Galactic Civilisation was that Human blood sacrifice is BROUGHT TO AN END. For that cause Columbus is PERMITTED to CROSS the ATLANTIC OCEAN.

In Heyerdahl's case his successful crossing of the ATLANTIC OCEAN had a FAR, FAR, FAR greater significance than he appreciated. For in ESSENCE he was TALKING to and BEING GUIDED by that GALACTIC CIVILISATION.

In 2009 I call it the <<< HIGH, IMPERIAL and UNION GALAXIES >>>, which is in <<< STYLE >>> a <<< BARRED SPIRAL + SYFERT + SCULPTOR COMBINATION >>>.

Put simply it is mind boggling enormous!

As I use that <<< STYLE >>> correctly I would now view it that such Galactic contact is "available" but, and it is a big but, it may involve a substantial retuning of thousands of millions of individuals. And most importantly it has to be something which the people of this planet wish AND that the galactic Civilizations are ALSO willing to let their individuals be seen. And if the people of this time do not wish contact, there will be none and the Galactic Civilisations might simply withdraw at this stage, and leave the inhabitants to their own devices. They may view it that our level of understanding is not sufficiently advanced, and we lack interest. Our efforts to understand a "Bible Code" have been restricted to just certain partial texts and have been restricted to pure mathematics and fortune telling which, although they may provide some amusement to those vast and powerful civilisations, do not lead them into a contact situation.

Those civilisations have interests of their own. The project which was set up at the beginning with Osyris and Isis, and which failed, has now borne fruit with the creation of the "Christian" people.

All is not well there. There are large divisions between different "factions" such that communication between such groups is not unified. They operate their own rules with regard to Communion in particular, even to the extent of shutting out the Spirit if it does not conform to a particular dogma!

That attitude does not find favour with those Galactic civilisations. Equally they are aware of the occasions, usually in the past, where the Christian Church has indulged in human blood sacrifice; usually dressed up as "heresy".

It has attacked thinkers who did not conform to the required dogma, and has murdered such! It is in that area that they check. While society indulges in judicial murder it is NOT acceptable to those Civilisations and they will not make contact.

What was the position in AD 2003?

There are two views. One from this planet, one from the civilisations in space.

The view from here is to struggle. Various probes have been sent by the United States, Russia and by the Europeans. But it is simply scratching at the surface. In real terms it hardly stretches into space, is vastly expensive and is not producing a real prospect of travel to distant planets. But then again some people would not wish that. And that brings in the problems for those galactic Civilisations. Do the people here really want contact ? Do they wish to know the reality?

I that connection I have to answer in the negative. It is perhaps disappointing, but that is the view I take. I take its principal <<< ATLANTYON >>> city in this Galaxy to be <<< SY ON >>>, and I put it at a distance of 15,000 light years! It could be further. It most certainly is not local! And the < ATLANTYONS > have cities on other < FOOTSTOOLS > in many galaxies!

Viewed by that Atlantyon Civilisation in particular, many here do not wish to go to "SY ON" . Many have their own idea of Sy On, and it most certainly would not fit with their requirements! What can be said, and indeed what was said, "There are many rooms in my fathers house, and I am going to prepare a place for you. I would not tell you this if it were not so" John 14, vs 2.

GNB 137

There is a vast universe with many planets in it.

Who is to go to SY ON? And that has to be viewed from a particular angle. That of RA.

For it is part of this hypothesis that following on the Crucifixion, RA departed from this planet, in his "Boat of millions of years " and headed out to.................lets say the Andromeda Star systems [M31], and found himself at on an island offshore from the principal city of < Tyem >.

Now for the purposes of this hypothesis that island is not dissimilar to Tenerife, nestling about 100 miles off shore from a large continent. It inhabitants are Grey Cats, and their system is a restricted system. That means that all of M 31 is off limits except to the grey cats, and their respective species; including the < Atlantyons >. However on that island Ra stays with an <Atlantyon> population ; those who have been and are pleasing to him.

At 2.2 million light years distant M 31 is far from prying Earth eyes. There can be no hope of reaching it in "millions of years". Yet from what I have said, Ra went there "after" the crucifixion of Christ and is currently there. It would take him but one earth year to travel here! I will let the physicists work out the power required to do so; according to their theories. [There is another technical point here, which on revision I have to add. It is of the < VISIBLE INVISIBLES >. I will leave that for the New Hypothesis .]

Now it is very easy to say that I am quite wrong with this hypothesis. That it is full of more holes than anything else (hopefully not black holes!) That I have to accept. With the physics I have been taught it all seems impossible. And yet, if as I say, the Truth is obvious, then I suspect that some very obvious things have been overlooked. [Black holes is an incorrect description of what are Black Stars].

I turn my attention to the hieroglyphs, and the texts of the old Egyptians. Allow for them to be trying to hide from Ra's power and anger, some things have been marked and changed, but others will not have been. There may have been an attempt to disguise, but some may not have been disguised because they were so fanciful.

"A Boat of Millions of Years" seems strange. But take a hydrogen filled balloon large enough in size, like an Airship and it will float through the sky. We can do that bit quite easily with our technology. So far so good. What I now need is the "star gate" mechanism; that which the physicists feel can bend space and time. Now I disagree with Einstein. If you travel faster than light, you do not go back in time. That is an "appearance" event rather than a "real" event.

M31 exists in a set form at this time. This galaxy, which for convenience I call Dras, [A Barred Spiral] similarly exists in a set form. Both are spinning and both are relative to one another. The distance may be vast but can be plotted, and consequently covered.

Take a particular ring mechanism. One at this end, one at the other end. Like the star gate. Activate a field so that a < DOUBLE HEADED SERPENT > is created from one ring to the other. Compress the distance (shrink time), and it is possible to cross that distance, if not instantaneously, then in a very short space of time.

Which brings me to the hieroglyph of RA. When starting this text I had assumed that the Chariots of fire (Ra's fire disc) actually flew over the star and moved from star to star using the gravitational field of the distant star, magnified, as a pulling mechanism. What I had not spotted was another possibility, that of a massive star gate which itself was "airborne" and through which the craft was flown. Thus in contrast to the current Science fiction series, the star gate is not an "attachment to the earth" but a type of vehicle; part of the AIRFRAME.

With the forces generated, particularly if it is desired to cross from here to M 31 placing the "star gate" on the planet would be very dangerous and is of the WRONG STYLE.

Whilst when I originally wrote in this text, I thought it would likely upset the magnetic field of the planet with possible serious consequences and might cause a partial earth crust displacement, I now understand that it is the < UNDERSTANDING of the CORRECT SCIENCE > which is important.

Thus much of the science fiction, while being good "hokum" is seriously in error on style matters at a science level. [It is very much as the new Hypothesis will hopefully make clear about the STYLE of BOAT. Thus with Ra 2 and Heyerdahl, there was MUCH more SCIENCE in the second Ra boat; it was built to the correct style.

The story of Icarus is thus also relevant. Did someone in times past try to activate the star gate but with equipment which was not correct, the gate, therefore, unable to activate, and did the earth's gravitational field then pull the craft back down to the planet causing massive disruption and leaving the occupants of that "Boat of Millions of years" either marooned here or very dead?

Allowing the story of Ra and Isis, and the attack by Isis on Ra for his secret name, was Isis trying to gain access to the password of Ra to allow her entry to the Chariot of Fire and to the Star travel; the Double headed serpent? And if she succeeded in that (and text would indicate that she learnt the "secret name ",was she then unable to control it, causing it to crash, leaving Ra stranded and without his "equipment" including the regeneration and matter transfer equipment? After all in human from his body is only "temporary".

Care has to be taken because, in terms of this hypothesis he is a "Trinity" individual and it is the Spirit which is important.

However for the purpose of this hypothesis, despite releasing to Isis his secret name, I view it that Ra returned to his Chariot of Fire. He was very angry at what had been done. Thus the story of his anger, and of his daughter who was sent out to destroy humanity, before Ra relented.

What really angered Ra was his appreciation of the massive destruction which could have been caused by the "misuse" of his chariot of Fire and the inappropriate use of the < Double headed serpent >. [The wormhole of science fiction and the sub space both point to this understanding. I use the Double headed serpent both from the SIZE point of view, but also to illustrate the difficulty and danger with this Highly advanced technology].

7
The Contradiction in Terms

In an effort to understand more about the old Egyptian system of gods, I acquired two "Text Books". E.A. Wallis Budge, "The Gods of the Egyptians". Immediately I notice that the "spellings" have changed from those in usage in other English language texts. Spelling is not my strong suit, but that is perhaps because of the importance I attach to the super communicate.

I regard these texts by Wallis Budge as pretty extensive and his commentary on much of the written hieroglyphs, particularly within the Egyptian tombs, authoritative. My interest in them is to ascertain, with reference to this hypothesis, if there is any link to those galactic civilizations.

The first link is the "Cats". That is those "gods" who are represented in Cat shape. On page one of the second volume, referring to Amen and Amen RA, there is a reference to twin Lion Gods, Shu and Tefnut,...........and with Temt, the female counterpart of Tem"

Now given my interest in super communicate, I look at the actual words. In English Roman text they do not mean much. "Shu" I have difficulty translating until I recall that in super communicate it is a short form for the smallest particle of matter (possibly to physicists here a particle yet to be discovered). [Shu sy shota] That would translate possibly as "the place at which for the purposes of maintaining peace, matter is created or changed to energy". Rather a lot of English words to express the word "Shusyshota".

The reference to Lion Gods is to refer to the Cats, and in that context I note the use of the double "T" in Temt, and also and particularly "TEM". My first reaction to that is to add a "Y" to "Tem" to give it "Tyem" which would have a similar sound to Tem. Thus it would depend on how the sound is recorded as to whether it is appreciated that it has "Y" in it or not. But the double "T" is another reference in super communicate to "The King of Heaven". So in essence the text is sitting there telling for thousands of years about the "King of Heaven" while appearing on the surface to say something else.

In the context of this hypothesis, < Tyem > would be a reference to the Grey cats, rulers of the M 31 (Andromeda) star system. At 2.2 million light years distant they are not just around the corner. Frequent visits by them to this Galaxy and this location are not likely. Thus if they visited say 15,000 years ago, it is very likely that any record of their visit may have been lost. A full description of their names would equally likely to be lost. But, again for the purposes of this hypothesis, the name structure used for names is to designate them by reference to a "City". Thus, as one might say a "Londoner" so they would say they were of Tyem and as to who they were, it would be necessary to know the other part of the name. [eg. TYEM Am Amayton].

The next individual to catch my attention is Tayfnut. Here again using the super communicate I come out with < TY FAN UR YS > [An important official of the city of < Fan >].

He, however, is NOT a Cat but rather a humanoid creature, with a skin not dissimilar to that of a shark, and having a mouth with similar type renewable teeth, and grey in colour. In short, he is not the sort of individual to meet on a "dark night". He is in charge of the galaxy known as Pykas, and I would describe him as a "Pykan" .In some respect the name "Ty Fan" is interesting.

On page 90 of Volume 1 of Budges work, he lists various "grey cats". It reads to me as a list of individuals from different parts of Tyem. [Am Amnu; Am Antchet; Am het Sequet k hetepet; Am neter het; Am Hetch paar; Am sah; Am teh; Am het ur Ra; Am Unnu resu; Am Unnu meht!]

Coincidence? In terms of this hypothesis there is no such thing as "coincidence".

Here in this text, hidden away, but yet obvious is what appears to be a simple list. And it is. Of districts of Tyem, or of officials! Visitors at an earlier time. First contact with aliens, not now a future event, but a historical "fact". And this is the first record of such in an identifiable form, that is if super communicate is understood! Which brings me back to the Cats.

For the purposes of this hypothesis, RA wanted a people who looked like him. The suggestion by Budge that the Egyptians saw RA at one stage like a Cat I discount. [But I have to be careful because I have to accept that it is possible!] I am discounting his "cat " appearance because that does not tie in with the Biblical suggestion that man was created in the image of God. And I am fairly certain that the Biblical texts, AND the old Egyptian texts are there for the same purpose. To PROTECT the species! And they are also to allow humanity to develop in such a way that they might one day join directly with the "Company of Angels" [Those that sit in heaven],and be allowed the "Star Travel" to which they currently aspire, as evidenced by the space programmes of various governments.

Space is the province of the King of Heaven, and to travel in it, it is necessary to observe certain rules; which are for the protection of the species and of the materials with which the Universe is built.

The contradiction in terms is that while the biblical references to Egypt are somewhat derogatory it is from Egypt and its ancient tradition that much of our current understanding has come. However in certain respects Egypt got it very wrong, and it was necessary to put in place a new teaching so that the defects could be removed. As I read through the work by Budge on the "Gods of the Egyptians" even I am forced to the view that they simply had TOO many "gods" and most of them were the creation of Man!

However some of them were "real" individuals in their own right and very powerful individuals. As this hypothesis asserts one of them in particular was not of Egyptian origin, and predated all of them. I am referring of course to the YH2UH, who in this text is associated with RA.

Rather curiously Budge used the term "Amen" of RA, which would mean that on each occasion within Christian tradition when the word "Amen" is used, and it frequently is, reference is indeed made to "RA". As I have said it is part of this hypothesis that RA and YH2UH are one and the same, so there is not any conflict. Add further to that, that it would be part of this hypothesis that it was YH2UH who removed the Lord the

Krystyesus at the time of the Crucifixion to SYON, there is in essence no conflict at all.

Moses, as a prince in Egypt and who wrote Genesis, ought to have been familiar with the traditions of RA.

If I take from page 2 of volume 2 of Budge's work that not only is the god himself said to be "hidden" but his name is also "hidden" and his form or similitude is said to be "unknown" then I have in essence a very close description of YH2UH!

Give him the human form, which he has as "Amen Ra" with the strict adherence to "Maat" as "Truth" and I have an individual who, while having created the whole universe can appear as just a little man. And for good measure, if I allow that he can take a Cat shape (which Budge suggested) an individual who can "shape shift."

Into the "mater transfer" put a human in, and then a cat figure out. Human in, Pykan out, and so on.

Is small wonder that the evil spirits were afraid of the Lord the Krystyesus if he had power to put evil spirits from humans into animals such as pigs! Yet again evidence of the power of those who possess the matter transfer equipment.

Today all the science fiction stories are just "fiction". What in terms of this hypothesis these very ancient texts say is that the individuals who can do that are REAL, have been here in the past and have every likelihood of returning; indeed have the capacity to watch even as I type or even as this text is read!

I have to accept that they are very frightening, and probably few more so that the Red cats, Sekhmet and Tefnut. [If that is changed to Tay Fa Nut, I have a red cat from the city of Taydaranakushton]. Both of these names super communicate. In the case of Sekhmet the super communicate aspect is with the "HKT" in the name. Unlike the other where the name of the city is taken from the first three letters, Sekhmet's city is incorporated into the name in letter form. The head of that city is a "tan" as opposed to a "Ty" and I would call the city, for the purposes of this hypothesis, "H̲eyK̲eyT̲retSalOn", the "On" ending designating it as a city. The other "Tan" and in red cat shape is "Tan Sard Ur on", and he is better known by his short form "satan"!

It should be noted that what is currently called the "sard" system may simply, by association with its name, be one of < DRAS > associated systems.

Now the problem and real danger with the Red cats is they have telepathic abilities, and it is that which causes the problem for a contact with humanity. Which brings me to a biblical passage where Moses is allowed to see the back of the head of God, because as it says, if he saw the face, he would surely die.

I am not comfortable with that passage. But there may be another explanation which I will come to shortly.

Note also Exodus, Chapter 19, vs 21,and of the warning not to let the people look at God for if they do so "many of them will die".

With their telepathic abilities the Red cats are able to see into the minds of humans. Without "adequate shielding" they can find the weak spot, and use that to snap the minds. The result is death. Now certain of the Red Cats may be able to shield their minds so that the damage is not caused. That grouping are called "Ty". But the "tan" have no desire to do that. In any meeting with a Red cat it is necessary to know with which individuals any contact is made.

It would be part of this hypothesis that on the night of the Passover it was the Red Cats who put in their appearance. It is they who would be able to assess who were "firstborn" and to "frighten them" accordingly. With no protection against the Red cats the result was fatal. And being space creatures, they did indeed "pass over" the houses of those who were under the protection of RA. Thus on that night the people of RA were born. [I had adopted this style relating to the Passover on the basis of current teaching. However the < CORRECT TECHNICAL point is < REPROGRAMMING of the DNA > While I use "dna" in this text, that is not the correct name. It is < STAR SEQUENCED MATERIAL > and so cloning and general tinkering with and storage of dna should NOT be attempted. That includes in particular cloning and stem cell research. It is simply WRONG SCIENCE! It is also very bad science when that is used in a science or fiction context since that immediately discloses a very incorrect understanding. The same applies to evolution. There is an "improvement" in style but it is a STYLE matter; most certainly not a battle zone!]

The heading to this chapter is the "contradiction in terms is essential to certainty." What is meant by that? It means that if the fact is not a "contradiction" it is probably not accurate. It is a bit like Newton and his laws of physics about and "equal" and "opposite force". But the forces and MATTER this hypothesis is dealing with are massive.

It is part of this hypothesis that to create matter what is necessary is to lock in tremendous forces or energy. And when these forces are released, particularly if it is done in a particular way, the result causes rather a large bang! However what is important, and where the real power is, is NOT to create the big bang, but rather to contain or maintain the force, or alternatively convert it to energy in such a way that its structural integrity is SAFELY maintained .[In mater transfer equipment it must be monitored carefully to preserve the "life force" of an individual. In certain terminology their "soul" or "Spirit", the term "spirit" being preferred because of its "trinity" association.]

[The New Hypothesis will cover the correct technical point of < HOSTING >]. Want to matter transfer an individual? How much hydrogen does he or she contain? Rather a lot. And what of the mental process. How is that preserved? Needs a very large, and very quick "computer". And it needs something else. It needs equipment which can "maintain" the physical entity and especially the spirit.

Take the physical body as a "computer disc". Each "blank" disc looks the same as another. Some might have blue coatings, others red coatings, but each computer disc is to do the same. It is to store information.

Now a Computer Disc and a DVD look very similar but one can hold much more information that the other. One human is MUCH more intelligent than the other. One is a "DVD" version while another is simply a "computer Disc"!

Were it just so simple! But it is not. And a human being is vastly more complicated than a computer disc!

Take one piece of a lock of hair. Put that in the matter transfer equipment and it is possible to "rebuild" the whole individual. Yes it is a type of cloning, but a very special type of cloning. It is done by those who created humanity in the first place. Now take that hair, recode it for a Red Cat, and the finished product, although starting off as human, becomes a Red Cat!

As I have said; cloning is WRONG science.

These exceptionally powerful galactic civilisations DESIGN and USE MATTER TRANSFER. It is that equipment which is used to perform the miracles. So when many of the Christian tradition have already discounted the miracles, such will NOT impress the large and powerful galactic civilizations for whom its operation is relatively routine.

They will spot that the miracles are an unwelcome distraction to the "business " of running a major world religion. That is the VERY POINT noted with Jesus Christ.

Watch also how Christ is viewed. Is it as good guy, son of God, or God or as something else? It is NOT a matter of personal preference, even if it can't be proved. It is FACTUAL. To say, just take it on "faith", and leave your money in the box as a donation to a glass window, a pew or if particularly wealthy, an endowment to a particular college, will not be acceptable to those Galactic Civilisations. They will NOT be pleased, especially with the gap of 2000 years, or in their case in excess of 5000 years! They will note that the miracles are bad for business; except to the extent that they can be manipulated for financial gain. They will spot how the drug companies would suffer if the miracles were provided. Of course there would be an interest in the "patent" for such "miracle machines" or "miracle cures", with the Government presumably taking that away for security purposes and monetary gain.

It is a very angry RA who sees such deception! The desire for money above anything else. A choice is given. Miracles and justice, or money and injustice? And what is picked? It is given up to Pilate, to the "best" justice system of its day. But it is not just for Pilate. It is for Rome and for Millions over the millennia to come. They chose injustice and money. For thirty pieces of silver they sold out the miracle man, and his connection with the people of space.

Now, nearly 2000 years later I am trying to show to those who sit in Heaven that I have tried to understand. I have not used weapons. I have used the word as I was given. From Genesis to Revelation. I have looked for the Truth. I have fought for Justice. I have looked for it. I have weighted myself in the balance, and..................I have been found wanting. I have tried again. But I have failed. The justice system has failed me.

It still suffers from the same problems. It is not interested in truth. That concern is an "irrelevance". In the confrontational style, which is justice in the United Kingdom, Truth has been destroyed before even the first pretence is made with the taking of the "Oath"or the "Affirmation".

And as for the money. Chances are that the largest wallet, the deepest pocket financially, will win! And in certain cases the deepest pocket in the United Kingdom comes courtesy of the State and its Agencies! If they approve the backing, the opponent, may be forced to concede defeat. Litigants with no funds, can exhaust the legal process to obtain their " human rights" and in the course of that cause "injustice".

It is all a contradiction, but in essence the Truth is there. I have called this society "a society built on injustice, which loves injustice, a society which has sold out justice for money and which has introduced human blood sacrifice by the back door."

Many in this society will disregard and disagree with such comments. But they are not directed at the United Kingdom. They are directed at those in Heaven.

Christ said, "Beware he who comes like a thief in the night." In certain respects it is not clear what he meant. But what I take him to mean is watch out for "MaTT". That is, watch out for the Lord of Heaven who comes to check out the Justice system. He is not talking theoretically but factually of an individual! The concept is easy for me to say, much harder to see. It is the Concept of RA physically present. And if not RA, it may be one of his officials. The SEVEN angels of Revelation. RA asks his "numbered" officials to check the planet to see if it meets his requirements, to see if it has changed, to see if it has learnt. The seventh Angel is the one to watch. And what does he report to RA?

"They have learnt to perfect murder. They have the mass murder of nuclear weapons, or of other weapons of mass destruction. They have dictators who abuse and murder their own people, who load suffering onto the backs of their own people, while living in palaces themselves and exempting themselves from the rules they load onto the back of others. [Matthew 23, vs 4] Indeed a society built on injustice which loves injustice!"

The speed limit is 50. There is bus lane, and it is empty while the rest of the motorway is jammed. There is a politician in a car . He is in a hurry . He can use the car on the bus lane and drive at 70 because it is necessary for his safety and he is important. Indeed he may even be first among equals!

Heaven's Official is not going to regard this as a "SY" society. It is not a society which works for peace. Look at the daily newspapers. What is preferred. The Truth or Lies? It is simply factual.

Any attempt to "gloss over " inconsistencies, attacks "SY". And if there is first one lie and it may appear minor, except with the greatest of care and a desire not to do that in future, there will be larger and more serious lies to follow.

I do not need to provide a list. Tansarduron is keeper of such lists. He also has spotted much more besides.

Pilate asks, "What is the truth," and does not wait the answer. I have given the answer in this text and it is not possible to change it. But what is important to me, is to ask the question carefully and using the understanding of that to try and grasp the Truth and work to create a greater and more lasting Peace.

So what then, I ask, happened on Mount Sy NY. To whom did Moses speak?

Firstly, Let me assume that it was NOT Ra, but was red cat. Who was it? Was it the Ta HA TY, or the MY Y DRAS trying to help humanity, or was it the Tan Hekt, or indeed Tansarduron, out to mislead an already lost people?

Secondly .Was it the I AM himself, the < PLASMA INDIVIDUAL > YH2UH, who had given to Moses the sum total of the wisdom necessary for his chosen people "Israel" to make progress?.

Or, thirdly, was it Akhenaten, or one of his followers, who having desecrated the sanctuary of Hathor at Dendra, [daughter of RA,{as Ha TY R}] and her Temple in Sinai by setting it on fire, then had to make up some story for the people watching from below, not appreciating also that he had destroyed the then last remaining "telephone" link with SYON. From stone "HEAD DECORATION" of "TWO TABLETS ON A FIRE DISC" and with < ATLANTYON > text they could not read, the people back engineered a language and text. The only "flaw" in that and the back engineering necessary, was that they required individuals to tell them what was on the text and they had to resort to murder to try and obtain the decipherment. As for the "stellar charts", which had been there in their highly stylised form. Burnt as graven images. As for the Glass plasma screens with their decadent and obscene images; Smashed.

The "star charts" if properly understood and decoded will give what even the most massive telescopes cannot. A chart, like an Atlas, of the inhabited and uninhabited planets in various galaxies, of safe areas and of dangerous areas. The "original" stone tablet may be lost, but the star charts have always been "safely stored". They are The GALACTIC CIVILISATIONS Property and they can replace them or not as they deem appropriate .

In many respects Heyerdahl set out to FIND EGYPT'S SECRET and SACRED GOLD. Gold, as advanced technology, more valuable than "Egypt's" obvious gold treasures!

Current Christian teaching has it that the second option is the correct one. Still for the purposes of this hypothesis, indeed for the purposes of the Second Option, I have to look at One and Three. And although I am taking option 2, I am taking it WITH the star chart of option 3.

8
Options & Super Communicate

At the close of the last chapter I wished to consider three options concerning the incident at SY NY,(the spelling I use in this text), when Moses was given the Ten Commandments. I use SY NY because it super communicates very nicely. Being brought up in the Christian tradition I am most comfortable with the second option, but I have to consider the other two. Indeed even if the second option is correct, that option requires the consideration of the other two.

Before attempting this text today, I read from Wallis Budge, this time about Osiris. I would change the spelling to O SY R US, to designate him as the "Son of RA". That I take from the "R" in the name, but also from "SY" which is present. The "us" I have not entirely discounted, since it is present in the name of the Lord The Krystyesus . Given that Christ is the "son of God" the implication is that "US" simply means " son". My understanding of the super communicate that "SU" at the end of a word designates the feminine gender; by adding the "S", "SUS" becomes the masculine. When it occurs at the beginning it is reversed, so that SU is feminine and TSU masculine! In particular the word combination "Ty RA Tsu " or similar ("tsu" ending) may designate the individual in super communicate terms as "daughter of" literally "Mighty Ra daughter"! That would mean that the name "Hathor" is not appropriate and a corruption, since it does not super communicate but an individual who could be said to be "Ty Ra Tsu" would more likely fit the position.

The goddess "Amateratsu" of NY PP ON might therefore fall to be regarded in that capacity, albeit that the spellings are different! Nippon, itself also beautifully super communicates, with the letters PP indicating a very special link to the "ankh" .The Ankh in that connection is the "ankh" as shown on the pictures of the Egyptian gods, the only difference being that it is a real item made of a very special kind of crystal. Carbon in the form of diamond comes to mind!

People who can make diamond in "shapes" are powerful! My understanding of super communicate is limited. I do not regard it as something I made up, rather something to which I have access, which is released to me from time to time and which I must use carefully. I am frightened to use it as a spoken language because I did so once and it gave me quite a fright! However I have come some way since then and I am now reasonably comfortable with such parts as I have allowed to be seen here. Like the comment in Acts, some who read this, if it is published, may regard it as nonsense. I am satisfied that it is not.

Given that I cannot speak it actively with someone who understands it fully, I am restricted in what I can glean. Sometimes it takes a long time, examining a word from different angles to make it "fit" super communicatively. I am conscious also that as I try to make it fit I may distort from what was intended. To a certain extent that is irrelevant because the super communicate is real and it will correct itself.

As I have said, I consider the name of "Hathor" to be a corruption. Given my position as a western European, the description of "Ha Thor" could be said to super communicate to RA, by virtue of the Nordic connection to "Thor". In essence I have been brought to all of this text by a Nordic Route. It was of course Heyerdahl and his "Ra Expeditions", the book about his journey in a papyrus boat over the Western Horizon to America!

As I have been working with the super communicate of this script and the revisions, I am now of the view that "Tayfnut" is indeed of the city "Tay" and that the proper super communicate for Hathor is "Ha TY R" and with "Tsu" designating her as daughter. Ha Ty R is of "human" design, but Tay Fa Nu T is of Red Cat design.

Super communicate would have TSU as masculine, particularly where it starts a word. Thus Tsunami is "masculine" but written in "Roman" script "TSU Na MY" comes out as a "negative=dangerous TSU in a number 5 (tone control element actually being spoken.) Given that the wall of water is very dangerous, the "NA" is quite appropriate.

I have been meticulous in stating that the RA of this hypothesis is totally opposed to human blood sacrifice. That sits in very neatly with the instruction; "Thou shalt not kill". That fits in neatly also with the figure of Christ writing in the sand, rather than to lift a stone to kill the woman caught in adultery.

BUT I MUST NOT FORGET, Ra does have very powerful weapons! The ability to move the Earth crust to cause a massive flood is just one .Fortunately it appears he is slow, very slow to anger. However I am aware that in terms of this hypothesis there is a very delicate mechanism which he can employ and which can lead to catastrophic results, and where he is not directly involved; simply that he "removes" his protection. And I MUST watch Revelation. Yet another weapon is the RED CATs like Sekhmet, who might be sent forth at a Future "Passover"; albeit with specific instruction not to touch those who have the symbol of the living God in their forehead; meaning in that sense, those who have been baptised in the Name of the Trinity!

Is that what happened at Nagasaki? At Dresden? It was firebombed, when it was in certain quarters not regarded as a military target! In terms of this hypothesis Dresden was "protected", but that protection was "withdrawn" because of just one incident of human blood sacrifice. Of the millions who died in the Concentration camps did ONE matter? But ONE DID . He did not look like one of RA's individuals, but none the less he still was. Now he will sit in that island off Tyem and with the name Tsuragy Hyran.

Have I gone a little off beam? No, it is relevant to what happened at SY NY. I take Sinai to be SY NY and super communicatively I take that to be "The voice of Peace". But it is a particular voice of PEACE. It is equivalent to the Voice of God! Thus the implication for me is that the word given to Moses at Sinai was just that; The word of God. That was my starting point with all this text.

But how far did it stretch? If I take the understanding to be that "to communicate, brief words are best", then it was simply the Ten Commandments. It was not and is NOT all the detailed rules of Leviticus. In fact as soon as Leviticus allows "human blood sacrifice" it is most certainly NOT the word of God!

So what happened?

Taking from the Third option the "star chart" the suspicion is that there is another "super super communicate" within the Leviticus text. And that is the star chart. Since "human blood sacrifice" is NOT allowed, where it is mentioned, it is likely the star chart tells of very dangerous hazards- which may be fatal. Thus to be avoided. The "back engineering" has allowed the accuracy of the "star chart " to be maintained. Again it is possible that the text has to be "cut" each time "human blood sacrifice is mentioned".

What has happened is that the REALITY of what was seern and done has been CAPTURED and set down in stylized form in the Biblical text. It is thus EXPERTLY HIDDEN and requires to be DECODED and READ. But unless you know that you are looking for it, it is a SEALED BOOK! As a star chart it is a detailed chart like a marine chart, but highly "stylized" because of the destruction of the actual star charts.

The various books of the Old Testament (it may only be some of them), relate to various galaxies. Genesis I would take to be this Galaxy.

The chart is read as follows: The galaxy is divided into planes. Along the middle plane a letter will be used to designate it. Thus :

A G H G B K Y H I O T C C G H T L P
G H K K L P C D H K L T W G B T N
K W C T H D S K N C S Y O B C H N D

Given an alphabet in which 24 letters are used, C is here taken to be the galactic plane. Depending on the order in the "alphabet", letters before "C" are below it in the Galactic plane, letter after C are above it. The C C in the top line, the C in the middle line and the C C and C in the third line are all in the same "galactic plane". Since this is an example, I can use the Current Alphabet and order. Thus "d" coming after c is one level above, so it is the plane up, whereas K is "seven up" [Not 8 because I have left out J as that letter is not used in super communicate] .

It should be apparent that although quite simple in concept, as a detailed chart, a large computer is needed to accurately decipher it. And if I am taking of the particular text of say Genesis, I might need to use the "Hebrew" alphabet.

However, as the star chart is super communicate it is not Hebrew, which is to be used. It is the super communicate alphabet. And I am not sure of the order of that. Each letter has a number allocated to it. [This was my Hypothesis as I wrote it in 2003. Sounded good, and in line with the mathematical theories. However the actual information is much more subtle. In many respects the important parts are the < STAR NAMES > many of which are unpronounceable. Thus many of the strange Biblical names and the shibboleth].

My route to this text has been with much emphasis on the Good News. Thus the story of Adam an Eve has been looked at, and as I have said, I take that to be of Osyris and Isis. Why the names were changed is not entirely clear, except that Isis by her conduct in setting the trap for RA, had greatly upset him and he had reacted very violently to the inhabitants of this planet.[It also neatly and conveniently hides the Egyptian source material].

I originally thought that in super communicate, Osyrys was the son of RA. However that did not fit in comfortably with the English [Romanised usage.] The cartouche of Osiris as romanised was as Us AR. Now immediately I see that if I drop the "a" from AR, I am left with "Us R", which very nicely translates as super communicate. It appears from page 113, that Budge comments that of the Ancient Egyptians; "the significance of the name in the minds of those who invented it cannot be said." He might not be able to say it, the Ancient Egyptians might not be able to say it, but super communicatively it is coming through loud and clear. With the eye of Ra, and the Throne Above, it is of the individual who was given by RA the whole planet as his kingdom but who through the actions of his "wife" was thrown out of the "Garden of Eden", and Eden, as it was put into the freeze, with RA departing for ....some far Distant Galaxy.

Given the absence of RA, who then gave the "Ten Commandments to "Moses".

Let me take option one. Let me assume that it was NOT Ra but was a Red Cat. As I said earlier, which one? Ta HA TY, the MY Y DRAS trying to help humanity, or was it the Tan

Hekt, or indeed Tansarduron, out to mislead an already lost people?

SY NY I would contend holds the clue. It would be unwise for either the Tanhekt or the Tansarduron to pick SY NY as a location for the transfer of misinformation. To do so would incur the wrath of RA, because they would have transgressed one of the things which he regards as most sacred to him, namely that which is HIS PEACE. The "word" out of which he created the whole universe, and that which rules the whole universe. It is not a fictional concept or word, but a word of tremendous power.

Ah! but the physicists of this time would say; 'the Universe is Chaos'. 'Not so', I would reply. If you look to the stars in the night sky there is clear order in the placing of the stars. Look even at the large galaxies and there is clear order. Indeed in the layout of those vast spinning spiral galaxies such as this one in which this planet exists, there is much to be learnt simply from the design!

So that leaves me, if I take option one, with one of Two Red cats. Either of them is in a position to have RA physically present because they are both friendly to him.

Both the Tay Ha TY or the My Y Dras would have sought RA's permission BEFORE interacting with the people of this planet.

Moses had come to Sinai by way of a passage through the red sea, when the walls of water were seen to separate to allow the Israelites to pass.

That is NO problem to those in charge of a Chariot of Fire. With their massive shield generators used to create the "wormhole", they can easily separate the water such as the "Red Sea" to allow the people to pass. And is there a super communicate significance in the "Red Sea"? Is that designed to draw attention to the "red cats"? It is factual in that it is "there" but the specific designation may be relevant, especially where super communicate is concerned. Note also that the shield does not harm those who walk through it. That is typical of the use of the power. It is tremendous but is used carefully.

I allow then that the first set of tablets is indeed given by Ra. Here I take the opportunity to give him his "new" name as

YH2UH, but quite specifically it is quoted to Moses by him that his name as "I AM WHO I AM".

Now I could write that as super communicate but I decline to do so. I can comfortably use a straight "English" translation as "THE I AM THE" because I have written that on a number of occasions and I have been quite comfortable with it. However in super communicate the "am" part is an altered word. It is a bit like the "you" and "thou" in English or the "usted" in Spanish.

Having given the text to Moses, "The I AM The" departed. But Moses has not gone far before he sees the people with the golden calf, a symbol I take of Hathor (despite any contrary suggestion that it may be said to represent Ra) and is most displeased. The tablets are broken before the people. [Note if they were looked for now it may be possible to find the actual "broken tablets" since in the dry desert they would last reasonably well.]

In due course it is necessary to go up the mountain to receive a second text. At this point it is part of the hypothesis that The I AM has long gone, leaving one of the two Red Cats still watching the individuals. It now falls probably to the Tay Ha Ty to "replace" the damaged tablets and that is done. The same short detail is imparted on the tablets. Moses goes on his way. However it is possible that Moses, got a little more by way of background information from the Tay Ha Ty which allowed him to write Genesis with its background. If that is the case it is possible that with Genesis one, the Tay Ha Ty inserted material which would really only be relevant to Ra about matters at the time of creation! The gap in time between Genesis one and two not being appreciated by Moses who recorded it. Again since it was important to divert information away from Osyrys and Isis it is very convenient for certain detail of the time scale to be left out!

As I have said, it is brief words which would tend to suggest that they have been given by THE I AM, not the detailed lists of Leviticus or the list of generations in other old Biblical texts.

Where text attempts to justify human blood sacrifice, for the purpose of this hypothesis, I am going to discard it as simply not being the word of God. With due deference to my Lord the Krystyesus, I would consider that he took a very similar view; a view to which the Christian Church has failed to adhere. I have only to look to the mass of "executions" and "burnings at the stake" carried out by one Christian tradition or another to see that, in terms of this hypothesis, the so called Christian Churches have missed the point IN ITS ENTIRETY. And it is not just that I am talking of the Christian Churches of hundreds of years ago. Current Christian Churches could equally be said to have lost to the plot and to be charting a course not dissimilar to the Pharisees about whom Jesus spoke!

Given the power I am ascribing to THE I AM THE or to RA, the names here being interchangeable in this text, Ra can easily deal with the people . As I have said the mechanism may be difficult to see, or to appreciate, especially if he simply TURNS HIS FACE AWAY, thereby removing the protection which he has offered to certain places and to individuals. They are "protected" in the strict sense and come under his "wing". That I suspect is what a number of the Prophets were trying to get across to the People of Israel, but with little success.

While to Ra the mechanism may be understood, I am not entirely clear about its operation. That is out with the scope of this text. Christ said to "fear God" but in the sense of this hypothesis, God is a loving creature. He does NOT indulge in Human blood sacrifice. However, if a massive abomination is caused, if his sacred name is desecrated (and that is for HIM to determine, NOT for man) then he can take action. As the text says, "revenge is his."

Probably the easiest route is to hand individuals over to Tansarduron, and he can deal with them. He, as the telepathic red cat, can easily see into the mind of individuals and see their fears. He can maximise the "punishment". That punishment, while it may be dealt out in part to the living, is primarily for the "dead".

Thus murders, and idolaters, etc, are EXCLUDED from the presence of The I AM, and may not be admitted to the holy city "SY ON"

The passage is quite specific in Isaiah.

SY On in that sense super communicatively translates as the "Peace City". It is part of this hypothesis that if Governments in particular do not protect their own people, and ask them to cause a human blood sacrifice, it is likely that Ra will remove any protection which may have been provided by him to that civilisation.

Thus in the case of Hiroshima and Nagasaki, they may have been quite safe until two Japanese had been "killed" in exercise of the "divine wind". At that point Ra (and I use that deliberately here, rather than YH2UH), would have removed his protection. The cities were then doomed.

As I have said earlier, Dresden for its part fell into a similar category. YH2UH can act in some strange and mysterious ways.

Many might complain. Where was God? Why did he allow that to happen? The problem here is that because of ISIS and the incident with the serpent, RA has left the region!

I am trying, by virtue of this text, to show that I have fought to understand, not by using violence, but simply by using the understanding and the word as it was given by Moses and others. I am asking for RA to return because I "would like" the use of the matter transfer equipment to "repair" the damage which has been caused to some poor souls, who through no fault of their own, have suffered greatly. I am asking the King of Miracles to allow the miracles to take place, but a to a far greater extent and with far larger numbers than was done at the time when Christ was present on the planet. For that I need Ra with his Chariots of Fire.

If I put Ra at 2.2 million light years away in Andromeda star system, he is not nearby, and it is easy for him to turn his face away. Yet again an illustration of what is done. It is not the violence which he does, but rather what man does to man.

Who burnt the "heretics" at the stake? In Western Europe it was the Christian Church, and the local rulers, be it Kings, Princes or Others, who usually did so for their own material gain! They abused their power. The murders were NOT done by GOD!

That is part of the problem with the "secret name". It MUST NOT be abused. With an "unspecified" deity, there is no risk of the secret name of God being compromised. Indeed in this secular society many have taken comfort in the atheist tradition. But that does not work where God is real even if he is at a distance of 2.2 million light years!

Indeed I could put him further away to a place I call Llycot Lleydran, which is a particular galaxy where on one side there are stars, and on the other side nothing, for that part of the Universe remains to be built! And I sometimes say of YH2UH; "Infinity plus one = The I AM THE".

Let me now turn to the third option

This is easier. It starts with the historical time of Akhenaten. Originally Amen HO PY IS 4. Now while Amen Ho PY Is might be translated super communicatively and peacefully, Akhenaten does not so nicely super communicate. Indeed I spot the letters HKT. Did he meet one of the Red cats? Did one of them impart to him some of the knowledge which had been hidden?

As Pharaoh he had access to the state secrets and that would include the secrets of the priesthood. If the "aten" cult was part of RA, then it does leave open just exactly what was said to him.

In certain respects it is correct to say that the power for this local planet comes from the sun. In simple terms the Earth and its local Star is a gigantic distillation plant! It is not making alcohol-except in so far as the grapes and other products are processed to do so, but rather it purifies daily vast quantities of water, which it moves about the planet and deposits in areas where it may be of benefit. In areas of drought it is possible, with much knowledge to build desalination plants, but none is as efficient as the mighty fire disk in the sky.

"Go build you city in the desert Akhenaten. It can be supplied with pure drinking water." After all there is none purer than that which has just been distilled! There is a suggestion made by some that Akhenaten was Moses. I am doubtful of that. But it is more likely that it was one of his "sons". Not Tutankhamun but possibly another, even one as suggested who was made a son by "adoption".

I am comfortable within the suggestion by Messod & Sabbah that Israel which left Egypt was indeed the people of the "aten " religion. But the question has to be, who gave the instructions? And did they make up more than was real?

All the text in the Good News can in terms of this hypothesis be done. It is within the technical capabilities of the vast powerful civilisations in space. But equally those civilisations could allow the "atenists" to follow their own path. They do not want puppets but they are looking for a particular kind of creature; independent and intelligent ;fearless and yet still kind.

For the third option I am going to allow that Akhenaten was made privy to certain state secrets and he took note of these. The first was that most of the Egyptian gods were not that. Most were creations of man statutes who were moved by priests working them from behind. But one- the Almighty was real. So he asks for a name. He is told the name is "secret" to which he says simply, "Amen RA". At that point he is told that it is not Amen Ra exactly!

The large fire disk in the sky is indeed Ra's property, but he can travel in the heavens, and there are other creatures out there. At this point it is possible that the Red Cats make their appearance, probably as an indication that they are real. Sekhmet and Tefnut (possibly Ha Ty R) but possibly also "TaY Fa Nut " in super communicate" where "fa" is an indication of colour, possibly red! [Ta Fa Ma Ra is the super communicate word for colour].

He is not convinced but the priests tell him that he will find certain more powerful equipment in the temple of Ha Ty R at Dendra, and at another temple in remote Sinai. He does not believe them but on a future date he attends at Dendra and he is shown the equipment. To our eyes it would appear as computer equipment, but to him it is entirely fantastic. What he is not aware of is how far advanced this equipment is. He is told not to touch, for there are delicate an dangerous parts. He may have been shown at that time the anti gravity unit and the shield generator and as a party trick may have seen them operated. Once that had been done he left, but the scene and the display of power had left an impression on him.

It was but a small step to go to overthrow the "gods" in favour of the "aten" "Religion" realising that it was the power of

RA,and even his daughter had to submit to him. And the secret name was important. In many respects it may have suited the civilisations in space to see him operating in this way, and it may have provided RA with what he saw as an opportunity to create a new people, the People of Ra ["Is" being the super communicate for People.]

But all was not well. The people unaware of the special connection were not receptive to having their local and friendly gods replaced with a remote god of horrendous power. The scene was set for the departure and that then came to pass, in the exodus of the Aten people of RA.

I rather liked Messod's suggestion that the next Pharaoh after Tutankhamun, Ay facilitated the Exodus and even that as Palestine was then Egyptian territory he was simply giving to the people the land he promised to them, the "Promised Land" but where super communicate is concerned it is not so simple.

That takes me not to Dendra but to Sinai where Ha TY R had a small temple and in that temple are stored keys to the secret equipment. That, when the Atenists reach it is then smashed, set on fire and the whole as viewed from below is like the mountain on fire. Given the powerful nature of the equipment, I have no doubt there were huge explosions. What had been "rescued and hidden" by the Atenist leader was the Shield generator. A piece of equipment the Atenist leader used to allow the water of the Red Sea to separate. But what he needed were the keys to operate it, and judging by events, he did not get the keys. Or at any rate if he did get them he did not find out how to operate it, other than to do the party trick that had been shown to Akhenaten. Indeed it may be that the 40 years in the desert was spent simply trying to work out how to operate the equipment. Did the Atenists as Israel as they might be called appreciate how very powerful it really was? And if this hypothesis is correct it is probably just as well that the Israelites did not find the controls!

In the end of the day it was boxed it up in a "golden ark", declaring, as was quite correct, that it had tremendous power and it was ultimately "lost".

In essence it was a fearful weapon. It was a piece of equipment they had to lose. It was also a piece of equipment that Egypt wanted back! Did they get it back?

When the Temple at Jerusalem was sacked, was it taken back or was it taken much later in Roman times? Was it part of the device used by Christ to walk on the waters and to calm the water?. It could certainly do that, but preferably while controlled by a Chariot of Fire. Had a small replica been made of a shield generator, sufficient to operate locally and to allow Christ, like Moses, to use it for "party tricks"? But it could not be allowed to fall into Roman hands. And yet my suggestion is that it might have done. Did it come into the possession of one of the later Roman emperors, after Christ, and was it finally sent to the furthest borders of the Empire to be "hidden" because someone appreciated that it was dangerous! Those who knew how to operate it properly had long since died and in essence it was useless.

But you cannot hide a shield generator, especially from those in space. It will, even when in an inactive state, tend to create energy fields. In proximity to a series of high tension lines it could be "masked" but there would be a risk that it could draw power from the high tension lines, so that although apparently inactive, it could become "active". However if it had been switched off using its "key" it would not suddenly become active.

To whom does it belong? Well if it had been "stolen" it would not belong to those who had removed it. Its key is personal to the owner. As the last residue of the "lost" civilization, which was the pre cursor of ancient Egypt and all other civilisations on this planet, it could belong to the Tansarduron or to Osyrys. But if it had been removed from the Chariot of Fire it would not operate properly.

It may be the property of Ra. Did the snake bite go too far? Was Ra murdered? Is the desire even now to murder RA!

The poisonous snakes are frightened of RA and well they should be. As the Lord of Light, Lord of Hydrogen fusion, as the Lord of the Power Laser, they are at considerable risk. They are put at greater risk because of the text in Genesis!

The eye of Ra is an interesting description. It allows that RA sees much more than others and to a certain extent it is not possible to hide from RA.

The problem with option 3 is that if it is real, it gives a major problem with Genesis and Exodus. Basically it means that much of what has been said, much on which the current civilisation is built, is built on a false premise. That does not necessarily cause a problem, for it might simply be running a "hypothesis".

There is a different problem if it is true!

While considering options one and three, I am going to take option two as accurate, but restrict its accuracy to the Ten Commandments. SyNy is in essence, super communicatively translated as "Great words of Peace". Thus the Ten Commandments fit nicely into that, but the subsequent text, particularly when it deals with human blood sacrifice does not. Like much of modern day legislation, it is part of this hypothesis that it was made by made by man for man's use and mostly as a tool to preserve in power those who held positions of power and to murder, albeit with the legitimacy of "due legal process AND the word of God" those who disagreed.

It is part of this hypothesis that to use the "Word of God" as a justification for murder, is indeed to break the sacred commandment that name of the Lord of Light, the King of Heaven, YH2UH, RA, is NOT, absolutely NOT, to be taken in vain! [Note while I have left this text mainly as originally drafted I have made a few adjustments. There are some technical points omitted and they are glaring].

The Golden calf is OFFENSIVE because Moses has spent some telling the people of the individual involved and what is the CORRECT name. Thus amun or amon are NOT CORRECT. It MUST BE <<< AMEN >>>. Note Again here that I use the Three chevrons. There is a VERY IMPORTANT APPLIED METAPHYSICAL point here that must be understood. Those who have read The New Hypothesis first should hopefully appreciate that.

The words of "super communicate" are in many respects < ATLANTYON >. That is a language which, like English, Spanish, Russian and Chinese, has to be learnt. Thus as I am not very good with languages, my understanding of it is very limited. But I am aware that much of this text is itself super communicate, so that it will not lend itself to translations to particular languages.

The Threns language and the Atlantyon are BOTH to be found in the hieroglyph AND in modern usage. That is how the super communicate works. It is NOT a fiction. It is controlled by the < FIRE DISCS >.

9
Through the Mists

While I will turn my attention to the prophets of the Old Testament shortly and to Isaiah and to Daniel in particular I am taking a break from my "job" to consider Job. One of the aspects which is immediately apparent from "Job" is of the conversation between The I AM and satan(who in this work is usually referred to as Tansarduron). It is that aspect which lead me to the figure of Tansarduron, not as one who is out with the presence of The I AM but one who has access to it!

That does not mean to say that Tansarduron and The I AM share the same space but it does mean they can "communicate". In essence in this work, RA not wishing to be directly involved in dealing with the difficult elements of some of his creations, can arrange for them to be handed over to Tansarduron to be dealt with. And it is not so much that he cannot deal with them himself, but rather that RA allows the lesser of option of handing over to Tansarduron, rather than being dealt with by him! Equally as highlighted in Job, it is Tansarduron who is only too happy to bring to RA defaults in humanity.

If the story of Genesis is taken at face value (and in many respects that is difficult) then it is the Tansarduron who refused to bow down to the new design of "human" creatures which are made in the image of GOD (RA) but who though looking similar lack the power of RA. In many respects they are second rate and a powerful creature such as the red cat is not disposed to bow to them. This annoys RA most particularly when the design team, including the My Y Dras and the Tay Ha TY, indicate that they are pleased with the design! Difficulties with choice of design have been accommodated and three distinct design types have been made; dark brown skinned/black, pale white skins and yellow skins. The basic metabolism and genetic design is the same so that inter breeding to form new styles is entirely possible. Still they lack the telepathic abilities of the Red Cats, the physical power of the

Red Cats and as such are viewed as second rate by the Tansarduron. But the upshot of that refusal to bow, was that that Tansarduron was ejected from Heaven, probably sent to Earth, or at least journeyed there, and it was that Tansarduron who caused the friction with Isis, and the resultant incident with the serpent(when it bit RA on the foot) as opposed to the incident of Adam and Eve as narrated in Genesis.

From whom did Moses get the Story? If I take option 1 of the first three options in the chapter (8) it was Tay Ha Ty who provided Moses with more of an explanation than the simple Ten Commandments, and enabled him to write, albeit in coded terms, the Genesis story. All reference to Osyrys and Isis is carefully hidden as "Adam and Eve", as also is RA and the incident with the "serpent" in the "Garden of Eden". It is not shown as the particular incident with RA, which if it had been repeated in that style would have immediately drawn attention to RA. But that was probably well understood by the early priests, who had been priests of "Aten".

Given the Genesis story, and the insistence to Moses that the I AM THE was the designation he wished, the desire was to put some distance between the RA of the old Egyptian myths and the YH2UH of the new "faith".

One thing the Genesis story does say is that if Adam and Eve ate of the fruit of the tree of knowledge they would be "like us". That is doubtless the reference to the ability of those who sit in Heaven to use a version of the matter transfer equipment to regenerate their bodies, so effectively to live much longer, possibly without limit of time!

That humanity, and Isis in particular, only had a shortened form of life, was the poison injected into that society by that Tansarduron, and its consequences after the incident with the serpent, meant that Isis and Osyrys were expelled from the garden of Eden (the continent which is now Antarctica). That was done and by means of a gravitational shift, it was placed in cold storage, any of its monuments and equipment being buried under miles of ice! A very inhospitable place to find a link with SY ON!

Isis and Osyrys were sent out to find new homes and to make their way in the world, and that without the benefit of the SY ON link and without access to its technology.

In their case they went to Egypt. Others from that civilisation went elsewhere, and most of them taking with them the clear message of the trouble that had been caused by the attack on RA. It was something to be avoided in the future!

The time scale is so vast, and the concerns of those fleeing so great about the anger of RA, that much of what they had understood was lost. They were expected to start at the beginning. Not necessarily at the complete beginning, but at a very early stage.

Given their privileged status, with access to technology now denied to them, it was necessary for them to have others do much of the work for them. That was not necessarily the best way to proceed, but given the attitude as demonstrated with the incident with RA, it was an "expedient solution".

Osyris (or properly "US R") was not alone on the planet. He had been given authority over the peoples who had been put there. That was in his name. He had been made king over the people by the authority of RA[The symbols of the throne over the eye (of RA)]. So it seemed appropriate that he and his party could make use of the "others" who did not have the elevated learning that he had.

Systems of writing, particularly the ancient super communicate script was hidden. The language of the Middle Kingdom [China] may be said to contain large elements of the super communicate in its wordage but a different style was adopted from the "letter form" typical of the Super communicate script and of Greek, Latin, and today English and most of the western European languages. Indeed development of a language different was required so that it could be seen to be entirely different from that which had gone before.

That is difficult. While it may be difficult to learn a language it is equally, and probably more so, difficult to obliterate it. Ultimately the new form of writing was devised, which we now know as hieroglyphs and came into usage and was ascribed to as devised by the Tay Ha Ty. That assertion may or may not be correct.

Why did RA restrict the life span of humanity? Genetically it must be possible to extend it substantially. It is part of this hypothesis that the short duration gave RA the opportunity of selecting those designs he wished to have "admitted" to SY ON. In essence, with the arrival of the Lord the Krystyesus that "option" is now available to all. However many do not wish that option, while as yet others may be unaware that such an opportunity is available because they have been restricted from hearing the Christian story!

Now while thus far I have treated US R as Adam, and as a failure as a result of his wife's conduct towards RA, with the interpretation I have given to the Genesis story and the perception by some that in Christ as the second Adam, the difficulty of the first Adam was resolved, there is another aspect which I have to consider. And that comes in the main from the Egyptian texts to US R.

I am still using the super communicate aspect, but this time I have to consider US R, not simply as the "Son of RA" but the personification of RA himself, in human form ;in the form as MaTT. And this time it is not the story of the serpent which is relevant, but rather the story of US R being imprisoned in a coffin!

Given that Isis was responsible for collecting the broken parts of US R after he had been ripped apart by Typhon [and care must be taken here because of the super communicate aspect with "TY FAN" there is altogether a very different aspect to that Story of US R.]

The prayers as recorded by Budge as given up to US R, indicate that those seeking favour had tried to lead "good Lives". That such should be done makes little sense if, as I have suggested, US R was in fact not wholly good himself. And even if he was, he allowed his wife to take advantage of RA.

But by introducing the character of TY FAN, it causes me to question the whole story. Is perhaps that story and the whole panoply of the Gods of Egypt simply a distraction from another and REAL event?

I regard the Pykans, whose city is FAN, to be in accord with RA and work towards peace. I regard them as being physically like "sharks". As such they could easily tear a fragile

"RA" to pieces. Again that aspect is alluded to in the other version of the RA story, where he is said to grow old and feeble. How can a God who is the same yesterday, today and tomorrow "grow old"? It is in the aspect of the contradiction in terms that this has to be watched. So as to appear "one" with his people he will "appear" to grow old. After all Christ did not remain as a Child but "appeared" to grow older!

Having arranged for the creation of Humanity, it may be the case that RA wished to become as part of his creation. He may have had wonderful plans for his new creation, and to his friends he invited them to his island home. But some of his friends (the Gods in the sky) had turned against him and were setting out to trap him. In this weak human form he "appeared" vulnerable, and so a scheme was devised to attack him. Whether it was, as is otherwise said, with the assistance of Isis or without, it does not really matter. What happened is that RA was trapped.

Allow it to be a "gold" coffin of the type which was found in Tutankhamun's tomb, the gold might have restricted the "calls" which RA could have made for assistance. And as a gold coffin it would be seen as valuable commodity, and one which could be allowed to sink to the bottom of the ocean! Murder, most foul!

I pause in my typing. Surely such thoughts would have been considered in times past? But there is more. RA has arrived from heaven in his "Boat of Millions of years", as have the other star "gods." They then remove themselves from the island they have left and with their capability hide RA and the Continent under a sheet of ice and remove his Chariot of Fire. He is effectively trapped in his Gold coffin, beneath the sea, under ice and light years from "friendly" galactic civilisations.

In one of the versions of the US R stories it is reported that Isis finds most of the bits (except that part which can be used to generate new life) and puts US R back together so that she can have a son, the son Horus who goes on to avenge his father. However that story may be a virtual fake, for if it was a fake it would still leave US R in the south Atlantic Ocean around Antarctica in his gold coffin!

Given that it was a Gold coffin, the effects of erosion on it by the water would be negligible. However it would be likely to be in the sediment and not easily located .

That second story of US R started out as cover, but in terms of this hypothesis is now seen as that. It has perhaps only taken 25,000 years, or possibly longer. I now see it as a "possibility" so the possible "murder of RA" is now under investigation!.

"What is truth?" asks Pilate. That is a dangerous question.

I have assumed here that it is easy to pilot the Chariot of Fire if its occupant is not there. That I now do not consider to be correct. It needs a key to operate, and that key is shown in the hands of "most" Egyptian gods. I might call it, "Ta Ankh K". I might translate that as a "director's key" the particular director being an "official" within the government of SY ON, one of the 24 Directors who are spoken about in Revelation!

Indeed in the first story we have Isis trying to murder RA by setting a poisonous snake on him. Does that not qualify as attempted murder?

It is reported by Moses himself, who wrote the version of Genesis and Exodus, that he "killed and Egyptian". Some have suggested that that may mean that he killed a Pharaoh, and in that connection the likely candidate is Akhenaten, or possibly, in accordance with factual evidence, Tutankhamun!

Given what I regard as the abhorrence of Ra by human blood sacrifice, there is an immediate concern with the Exodus version, and particularly of the human blood sacrifice rules of Leviticus.

The desire of Moses was to move away from the "many gods" of Egypt. They were to be overturned, as is quoted by YH2UH. But if as I suspect that YH2UH is in fact RA, the individual who wished to overturn the old Egyptian gods was one of those implicated in the murder of RA ; of Us R. As a murder it became very messy!

It does not stop there. It carries on from that. In due course when The Christ comes on the scene it is spotted again that there is potential trouble if the link is made to the ancient history. It is reported that Christ was taken into Egypt for protection from Herod, but it is possible he was taken there simply to visit relatives, and those relatives may have been those in possession of the old knowledge about RA; at that stage much diluted and much lost!

On his return to Israel, Christ took issue with the religious authorities on human blood sacrifice. It is reported he could work "miracles" so it is likely in my view that those in space friendly to RA assisted him, since he was doing what Ra had taught.

But if this aspect is correct, why did they not look for RA? If you are told a falsehood, and it is presented as fact, it can be difficult to disprove.

"RA was disappointed with humanity...." The story of the incident with Isis and the snake is reported. The Earth crust displacement is something he has done, and he then leaves for a distant galaxy! Say Andromeda. It is far away. While he certainly has the capacity to go there, and to return, there is no need for he is quite safe there.

I have assumed earlier that it was the Red Cats who assisted with the miracles, but it is possible that it was also the grey cats from Andromeda themselves. And it may have been reported to them that RA had left for another location, such as Galalvery Alvo or Llycot Lleydran which are so far away as to be not worth the chase!

However it is unlikely the grey cats in particular would, have been placated by that "statement" and may have been looking around for answers.

Given the assertion of this hypothesis that YH2UH and RA are one and the same, the Trial before Pilate could have been presented to them as an opportunity to test. It may even have been put forward by the Tansarduron himself and since it would be a test of the type RA would do, the grey cats may have pushed too much for clarification. But would they have missed the story of US R? Even if spotted it could still be said simply to be a "version" which was not "real" and had just been put in place by RA himself so that he could remove all opposition save that in his special form as YH2UH.

I am sure that the grey Cats would have listened carefully and watched. They may even have allowed to operate certain of the "miracles" in the hands of Christ, as much to test out those who were putting that version forward as to see how the local population reacted. When he was judicially murdered, that could then have been used by the conspirators to prove that "IS RA EL" has not learnt the lessons which Ra had set for them.

Suggestions that the grey Cats returned to their "own" galaxy would have been subdued for fear of making them suspicious. They are more telepathic than the Red cats, and have shielding telepathy, and a suspicion was probably in their minds. It could have been allowed that the new "IS" (people) would be allowed to develop and they could return some 1000's of years later. As for Christ. He was to travel to SY ON of course where he would be "safe".

I have no doubt the grey cats would have offered Christ a place in their galaxy. They may even have called it by name, but in that respect, with Christ being simply a man, (although assisted by those in heaven,) he may not have been aware of the significance. He may have opted to go to SY ON! After all many on the planet today would seek to go to SY ON. Busy place!

The text of the Christian religion was yet to be devised. Four texts were offered and noted by the grey cats. Certain passages required to be adjusted AND INCLUDED because certain of the miracles where THEIRS. They had arranged them; they had caused them to be performed. Take away all the miracles done by (for example) the red cats, and their miracles would remain. Remove reference to their miracles, and they would instantly known there was a problem!

They doubtless insisted that their text remain and given the importance of MaTT, I would suspect that "Matthew" contains their miracles. The others have a problem. The Grey cats were instrumental, with Ra in the creation of humanity. If the others muck it up too much, serious questions may be raised which could lead to serious galactic conflict, and that despite the reluctance of Ra to allow such.

Given the distance of Andromeda, all that is required is to persuade the grey cats to return to Andromeda, and not to pay too much attention to Earth, which in any event is within Red cat territory(this galaxy).

With all authority given to the Lord the Krystyesus, (by RA) as reported, the grey Cats have no problem and leave. The matter is doubtless reported on their return to the principal of the Grey cats, who will be none too impressed. But she is far away and she has her own Galaxy to consider.

Christianity evolves. It is not pure because it had a divided heritage. Much bloodshed is caused, much hurt. It continues to the present day. The old conspirators are satisfied. While notionally on text ALL authority is given to the Lord the Krystyesus, in practice that has not happened. Conveniently they can leave large chunks untouched because after all RA MA is a personification of RA. The insistence by others of the Omnipotence of YH2UH leaves RA in that persona unassailable. All the while the gold coffin remains in Antarctica.

In the system of the Grey cats alarm is raised. Huge mushroom clouds have been reported and with super communicate hundreds of thousands are reported killed. Where is RA? What is going on?

It is part of this hypothesis that the grey cars can be here in a year from the Andromeda Galaxy. The red cats can be here in 5 days! It will be 1946 before the grey cats appear to find out what has been going on. An ambush could be set up. Not to attack the Grey Cats craft. That would be too obvious, but rather to attack them as they operate the matter transfer equipment. That is done by allowing them to think that they have deposited their own people, while in reality capturing them. That might require the assistance of an "earthly power" Now which earthly power would align itself with the red cats?

At the same time as sending their own people to the planet(to appear in human shape) the grey cats, fearing that all is not well, allow certain of their information to be stored by "humans". In certain instances that has disastrous consequences, but in a few instances they are able to use the information gleaned to ascertain whether it is earthly or heavenly forces which are causing the problem. They can see clearly that large chunks are not giving authority to the Lord the Krystyesus and that in many respects the planet is a mess. They are not pleased . They are inquisitive to the presence of the Lord the Krystyeus . The answer is given that he has decided it is not yet time to return. All the while the grey cats are becoming more and more concerned about what has been going on. Ultimately they dispatch one of RA's guardians, whose job it is to check out the position and to report back. The report is delayed for some time [Revelation 10 vs 6] but when it comes it is not the bearer of good news.

There is not an immediate reaction. After all it is merely a "hypothesis". It would be unfair to attack the Red Cats or the Pykans simply on a "hypothesis". So they watch. Not from a distance, but from relatively close quarters and in a shielded chariot of fire. And this time, not with a few, but with many. And of particular concern are acts of human blood sacrifice, for that would determine most accurately, whether the people are for Peace and RA in his persona as YH2UH, or whether they have in fact attacked him.

And why, they ask, has the temple to the most high not been rebuilt? Is it too costly? There is a silence on that point. That it cannot be rebuilt because it might offend the sensitivities of others is going to be exceedingly offensive to the grey cats! The best that can be offered is that, with the Christian Churches being in positions of power and showing that all authority is with the Lord the Krystyesus, there is no need.

But that is not going to go down well either. For it was "agreed" that he would have that power. It was said RA had given it to HIM. If that was the case, why is it not self evident. The truth is, after all, obvious. What is made manifest is that large quarters DO not given authority to the Lord the Krystyesus and DAILY perform Human Blood sacrifice." This is merely a hypothesis and that part proceeds on the basis that US R was murdered by powers in space because they were jealous of him.

The third option, if preferred as that given in Exodus makes it easy; that YH2UH is different from RA, and that he "attacked" RA. That causes concern, unless it is that YH2UH wants and loves human blood sacrifice! In terms of this hypothesis that is most certainly NOT what RA as YH2UH wants! [NOTE : Much of this chapter as originally written looks plausible, but like the boat Ra 1 is fundamentally flawed as to design. Originally I had drawn this together from texts as written and available to me. But as I understood with the New Hypothesis, the information has to <u>COME FROM M 31</u> and from the THRENS and ATLANTYONS and in particular the Visible Invisibles.

In many respects this text is like an exam paper and on the work written before this note the Professor of Applied Metaphysics would mark as ZERO because the fundamental scientific point is about the correct technology <u>being sent from M31 and similar and other Galaxies</u>. That is FUNDAMENTAL and MATERIAL. The Professor would also be concerned at the use of the YH2UH rather than the form AMEN, especially when the wrong pronunciations as "amon" and "amun" have been pointed out. "E", "Y" and "I" are in many respects inter changeable. The language in question is < ATLANTYON > and it is a < REAL > language with its own syntax rules and has to be learnt.

10
YH2UH

"I am who I am, that is my name" (GNB 61 Exodus 3, vs 14). Note also the emphasis put in the roman script in blocks. It is emphatic.

I have taken a great deal of trouble with this script. I have worked with it for over 20 years possibly slightly longer. It has not been easy to write, and this is one of the most difficult parts. For the purposes of this hypothesis RA and YH2UH are taken as one and the same. Why take the variation YH2 UH instead of YHWH? It is not really easy to determine. In essence I put it down to the super communicate. What the passage in Exodus is saying is "super communicate." It is not strictly a "flat" language like English; in the sense that English is written linearly from left to right. In essence it may require to be read top to bottom, like Chinese! But within the words there is a spirit.

I regard them as "the words of power". It would be correct to say that they require to be spoken in a particular way to give them effect. That does not mean that they require to be said forcefully or indeed very loudly. Indeed they are appropriately called, "the still small voice of Peace". The word of "The I AM The" The real question is what, super communicatively happened at Sy NY. (Sinai, in its usual spelling)

Super communicate immediately begins to deteriorate as soon as human blood sacrifice is involved. Why then all the instructions to the people not to go near the mountain? If the forces which are applied to the mountain are massive, then it would be dangerous for the people to go there. It would be correct to say they would "die". It would not be correct to say they must be killed.

While initially having reservations about the fusion of YH2UH and RA, in the sense of the description as "the Lord of Light" or "the Lord of Hydrogen Fusion" I am satisfied that the description is appropriate. But what it does tell me is that the concept is MUCH larger than I had contemplated at the start.

The start of this hypothesis was the position of the Lord the Krystyesus, who from a Christian viewpoint is the personification of "God with us", Immanuel in that sense. That runs off the tongue in the Christian tradition, especially at Christmas time, and it is entirely appropriate. What this hypothesis is doing is to put the "who" into context, and with a particular reference to "Truth".

It is with regard to the "Truth" aspect that consideration has to be given to the incident at SY NY and later on to the life of the Lord the Krystyesus as described in the gospels.

In what is in essence a secular society in the western World, there is increasingly little space for the real "The Lord the Krystyesus". Certainly in the sense of this hypothesis that he is a real figure, alive today, aged around 2000 years old, and looking like a man of 21! How is it possible? It is possible with an understanding of the complete physiology of the body, and an understanding of the mind with the ability to manipulate the body.

The brief look given by John in Revelation of SYON does not adequately do it justice. But how could it. It is a view similar to that taken by a peasant who had never flown, travelling in a hypersonic plane, being put down in modern New York for a few minutes, and then returning again to the place from which they had been taken. How do they describe it?

As I said earlier, I had three options of what happened at Mount Sinai. If I take the second option, that is that YH2UH is not the same as RA, and it is RA who is the real individual, I have tripped up. Equally if I take one or three as the real options, and YH2UH is real, I have tripped up. On that basis I lose regardless of which is picked. If I accept as accurate a version which is NOT accurate then regardless of whether it is RA or YH2UH, my understanding is not correct.

Normally with a hypothesis it would not matter. But in this case it does matter, because of the importance of Truth. [Here I spot MaTT] in the English word. The real question is what is TRUE!

During the course of my Law Studies, it was said that theories were for "arts" students, lawyers dealt with certainty. It was either right or it was not!

Thus my statement that "right and wrong are relatives and not absolutes, and that in a world of relatives the absolutes are easy to understand but the relatives are not" would not seem to be appropriate. It takes me back to the phrase about the "contradiction in terms being essential to certainty."

And so I am uncertain about what happened at SY NY. Moses may have said one thing, my Christian tradition may have told me to stick to that, but it is required that the options are considered. Indeed there may be more options! It could be for example that at SYNY Moses handed over technology which he had taken out of Egypt, and that these are not "lost". He may have returned them to their "owners" and been duly thanked for so doing, being allowed thereafter to lead his people onwards!

In this the year 2003AD, it does seem strange that if the word actually came from "God" there was not more of a concrete input into it. "Thou shalt not Kill" and with an explanation given for it. Perhaps I am looking at it with 21 century eyes and that it was necessary at that time to say it as it was said. The "Thou shalt not kill" accords with no human blood sacrifice.

What about the first commandment?

As I wade my way thought the commentary on the Egyptian Gods I am struck by the huge number of them and the way they were "fluid". If the particular name did not fit for a particular district, change it. In consequence the "same" god could appear in another area as a different individual, but was in fact the same individual!

The general impression is that they were "man made", and that certainly applied to most of their names. As I have considered earlier, some were not and in particular I do not consider that RA fell into that category.

If I consider simply a text such as that on the "Metternich Stele" it is RA who is ABOVE all the other Gods, and is shown in his capacity with the "jets of fire around his head" [I add this note here. The jets of fire particularly as THREE HORIZONTAL LINES around the head SYMBOLISE a < BARRED SPIRAL GALAXY > They may be found in certain Stained Glass windows, particularly in a Church setting with Jesus in front of them.]

It does not matter that the stele is much more modern than the time of Moses, for it is its texts, as translated, that indicate again the story of RA, and of the story of Isis to stop the Boat of Millions of years. Rather interestingly on P272 of Budges second volume the text is a commentary to the effect that the first composition is called the "Chapter of the incantation of the Cat".

I have considered that at SY NY, it was RA who was present and who allowed the meeting. I have allowed also that it was the Red cats, but with that Stele drawing may attention again to the cats, I must also consider the possibility that it was the "grey cats " from M 31, Andromeda.

They are at such a galactic distance that, from a purely practical point of view, if they travelled here with their technology, they might have to cordon off a large chunk of the mountain beneath their craft because it could be affected by their equipment. Equally their presence as seen, as Grey Cats, might have caused a problem for the local population such as Moses, particularly if he was expecting "Red Cats".

It can be difficult within certain sections of the human population to deal effectively and comfortably with white red, yellow and black skinned individuals, let alone to have to deal with other very powerful and intelligent creatures who resemble in part animals we simply treat as pets! While efforts are currently made on "race relations" relations with the "animal world" are none too good. How then would these mighty inhabitants of space be viewed? Most probably as a "real and present danger". How much more would those who accompanied Moses have been terrified? As I have said there is a risk with the Red Cats that they can kill simply by looking at a human!

The figure of Moses also causes me difficulty because he is reported having "killed". In the sense of this hypothesis that is NOT acceptable, and he and his people MUST be kept at a distance. In essence that is what was done.

The text in Isaiah, Chapter 65, Verse 25. "……….on SYON my sacred hill, there will be nothing harmful or evil".

Quite specific that and if I take SY NY to be similarly "sacred" by reason of is "SY" connotation what was Moses doing there? Certainly given the Christian tradition there is the matter of "Forgiveness for Sins." I should at this point say that from super communicate point of view Sin is merely a form of "Sy Na". In that sense "Na" should not be used with "Sy" It may be allowed in that usage, since "SY" is pre eminent in the first position. That makes it No1, Sy which makes it "Great". Little Sy, with any other number would simply be indicative of a "calm", but is entirely a different matter. In English usage, when I am referring to No 1 SY, or No 1 Peace, I usually write it with a "capital P" to designate it as different.

As is my custom I leaf through the pages of the Good News, and am checking Exodus. In essence what I am trying to do is to use the "SY" element of super communicate to Check out the text. That "SY " element is vital. I turn to Exodus chapter 32, which relates to the smashing of the first set of tablets, of the golden calf, and then to my horror is story of the "Levites" the priests of THE I AM THE, killing 3000 men! I am, in the capacity of one dealing with SY appalled! This is not "SY". This is murder, human blood sacrifice.

In the intervening texts, 26 I have the description of the tent of the Lords presence, 27, the Alter, 28 garments for the priests,29 instructions for the priests. I pause. I am not comfortable with this in the essence of "SY". I am not comfortable with it in respect of YH2UH the < LIVING PLASMA >.

The < LIVING PLASMA > does not require the services of human assassins. The Lord of Light does not require the assistance of human murderers.

Why are the snakes frightened of the lord of Light? Because of the heat. It is more than that. As the Lord of the < FIRE DISC >, and in the capacity of the Lord of Light, the "lightening bolts", are deadly and vaporise in a split second.

The Ten Commandments as given in Exodus 20 start with the comment that "God Spoke". That is to be compared with Isaiah and other places where the name used is "Sovereign Lord". Now I accept that I am not familiar with the original text as written, but my understanding of super communicate tells me there is a MUCH different emphasis.

In essence where passages use " The Sovereign Lord", it is with feeling of an individual who is real and who is IRRITATED with the dull learning of his protégés!

This passage in Exodus is a little like the small statues (idols) of the old Gods which were made to move by the operation of the priests, rather than by the power of the Lord of Light! "I AM..................worship no God but me" verse 2 and 3. It may be slightly embellished in the text, but the words I AM are clearly there.

Verse 4 is the instruction NOT to bow to any idol.............I tolerate no rivals. "Zero Tolerance" a phrase of political correctness, does not mean in "SY" terms what it purports to say. It means "we are intolerant". Some might say of that, we have justification, but that does not fit with "SY"

[Note there is a technical point about POSITION and STYLE and NAME. That takes me back to <<< AMEN >>>]

Again the figure of YH2UH as the lord of the < FIRE DISCS > does not require to be intolerant. He is so powerful that such comment is farcical. It demonstrates a lack of understanding! What this passage does demonstrate, from a "SY" point of view, is that someone had told Moses, who is credited with writing this, that to "communicate effectively with God" there was a way to do it, and that required a particular approach!

Given that I was brought up in the Christian tradition, while that appears easy for me to say, I am now aware that it is VERY TECHNICAL. I may POSITION myself on a beach, on a street, in a health club, in a church or even in my bed, but in all of that I have to consider the POSITION and APPROACH. In essence what I am trying to do is make my self ACCEPTABLE to the SPIRIT which is for PEACE. Essentially it is a PHYSICAL EXERCISE done to certain STYLISED RULES and it is these STYLISED RULES which are "encapsulated" in the TEN COMMANDMENTS .

While I have my own style others will have their own style, but certain aspects are MATERIAL and MUST BE CORRECTLY UNDERSTOOD. It is an attempt to understand/operate the words of power!

The fundamental is that GOD is REAL and WILLING to listen. That HAS to be the Starting point.

The Lords prayer is a good starting point as is the use of the words of "The Peace", which is essence is the Peace which flows from God in the first place. For emphasis, as much as for comfort, the words, "Almighty, eternal and living God, hear my prayer that this day I pray before you, saying Our father which art in heaven. ...." This is done so that it may be seen to give all authority to the Lord the Krystyesus. At the end the word "Amen" is used. I am now conscious of Amen being a short form for Amen RA, which ties it together nicely.

The instruction is not to bow down to any idol, so it is not necessary to bow in any particular direction. Indeed that is the first test of the understanding of "SY". Yes an individual HAS to be in a particular position, but that is determined by the SPIRIT . Thus it will FREQUENTLY CHANGE both as to location and as to TIME. To insist on a particular position or in a particular place is likely to mean that an "idol" has been introduced. In that sense, and in the pure sense what may be regarded as a "special prayer" is lost. Yes, it may be an "ordinary prayer" but not a special one .

The exercise which is a < STAR > one does have specific rules and is part of < ATLANTYON GALACTIC PHYSICS >< SPORTING >.

I am reminded of Buddha, but I am not of the Buddhist tradition. Again I have to be careful to preserve the purity of the prayer if I am to preserve "SY". That means that I have to accept the Buddhists and their tradition, but first I must respect THE I AM THE. I can accept in "SY" terms that the "da ma pa da" may be a path of enlightenment (and it super communicates) but in the real sense of the instruction of this first commandment, I have to be careful!

Progress with "SY" and effective super communicate, in the sense of a prayer, can be difficult. But it can also be easy.

I may step into a church, and being casually dressed short trousers instead of long, for I am simply a visitor, and in another denomination even, can offer a silent prayer. I do not make any show, do not kneel. Indeed in all respects as viewed I may be criticised for my appearance and my bearing. But the thoughts in my head at that point are of "SY" and it is a request first to be "acceptable" to the King of Heaven.

"Accept thou my prayer, MIGHTY King of Heaven"

Even though I do not feel I have made the contact in prayer, often sometime later I will realise that my prayer was heard. Again it easiest when such prayers are for others!

Such thoughts and prayer are at conflict with a society which instructs its priests to Murder. Viewed in those terms where that is done, the God being worshiped is most certainly NOT the "GREAT I AM", and it would not be appropriate for me to enter such areas.

Note the use of the word, "Great". Again in super communicate, it is like "SY" AND should not be placed with certain individuals. A "great" horror would be entirely inappropriate because horror implies fear and "SY" is entirely different. In that sense the words "awful horror" would be appropriate.

The feeling of SY is a < HOSTING > exercise done by the < LOCAL STAR > and other < SEQUENCED STARS >

Fundamentally NO hosting, NO galactic travel.

Hosting is essentially a feeling of enormous beauty and power so wonderful that while apparently fleeting, is so beautiful that the desire is to make it last. But it tends to be fleeting. At the same time there is a realisation of its power, which explains why it has to be so fleeting. To a certain extent I could describe it thus.

Take a crystal glass. Pour water in. No problem. Take a similar crystal glass pour boiling water into it and it shatters. If not immediately, then in a few seconds. Now what "SY" means is that it is necessary to make the "vessel" [the human] into a "new Vessel" that is like unto a special glass, so that when the boiling water is poured into it [The Spirit of Peace] it does not shatter. In an instant it is done.

As the Disciples of Jesus wait in the upper room, petrified at what is to happen, they are, by means of the Spirit, changed. The Spirit is at first poured into them so gently with no feeling of pain rather of joy that it is almost unnoticed. Then gradually it is powered up so that it is as though on their heads is a tongue of fire and they are able to speak in "particular" kind of super communicate and the story of Acts is made real. But the knowledge of how it is done comes from far away Galaxies, and from a very great civilisation!

The I AM THE is whom they worship, and while they may have been slow to check out the text of Exodus, certainly would spot that it is not fully "SY". The texts of Matthew, Mark, Luke and John can be said to contain "SY" as also can part of Acts, but the mighty civilisations of these hypotheses in space watch the whole texts.

Bible code! They know what is THEIR code and will instantly know if it is accessed. As to other "Bible Codes", they will listen to what is said, but will note that it does not grasp the message they left. They left star charts and an understanding, which if properly understood would persuade them to communicate at a more "immediate" level once again!

Leaving aside the remainder of verses 4, 5 and 6 of Exodus, 20 I look at verse 7. The instruction is clear. "Do not use my name for evil...........for I, the Lord your God will punish anyone who misuses my name."

Now that is very close to the "secret name of RA". It also goes a long way to explain the tart reply, "I AM WHO I AM". It goes some way to explaining why it was written YHWH, and I have explained thus far why I have changed it now to YH2UH. [The computer reminds me of a potential typing error of YH"UH]

I am taking great care with this chapter. I am giving ALL deference to THE I AM, and I am relatively comfortable that I am not disclosing at this stage anything which I am not supposed to .

I do not use "jehovah" because super communicate does not use a "J". I have considered how that sound would be written, probably as "geah". The lack of it in super communicate does not cause a problem because in essence it is the same point that is being made. As soon as the "J" is put there then the individual concerned is NOT, YH2UH. Do anything using that name, and it is not the GREAT I AM, in the strict sense.

The Spirit which is "SY" does not like strict rules, so as I move about all these different permutations of names, the one aspect which I have to be careful with is the name, described in

Revelation, 19 at verse 12; "He has a name written on him but no one except himself knows what it is." The passage then goes on to say, "His name is the Word of God."

In essence what is said in that "Super communicate Script" is of a written name and the suggestion of this hypothesis is that it is the secret name of RA; in the script of super communicate with which HE is familiar.

However, as I have said, great care has been taken by me with this, and it is part of this hypothesis that that secret name, like a password, is very important for it might also give access to the "Boat of Millions of years" the star ship, the real galactic star ship.

In essence what this chapter is saying is that in this material world if the wrong approach is made to God, it is not that God does not exist, but simply that he has not been spoken to in way he can be expected to hear or to respond.

There is among many in this "material" world no desire for a real "god" entity in the first place. So by such, he is regarded as a complete irrelevance, and the importance of the "10 commandments" and the science in them easily overlooked. Indeed that is done even by those who profess to know better, and who like the Pharisees in the time of Christ, give instruction!

Regretfully where it is ignored, that is done at peril. For the purposes of this hypothesis I have amalgamated YH2UH with RA, since both of these individuals in their different ways have lead me to this hypothesis, and I am comfortable with that in "SY" terms.

For thousands of years any suggestion that there might be a link has been ignored, glossed over or accidentally or deliberately obscured. I have been led to this conclusion by the texts in Isaiah. I will come to that later. However misplaced, I may be I am now drawing attention to it in much the same way as The Lord the Krystyesus did. I am seeking after The Truth, and that in the sure knowledge, as he said, that it "would set you free."

By using the title as "the Lord of Light" in respect of YH 2 UH, and linking that with what is the obvious local < FIRE DISC > in the sky, I am allowing for a "Lord of Might and Power". In the small seated figure of MaTT or in the seated figure of Amen Ra, I am allowing for an individual who can control it. The pilot of a plane does not "own" the air, nor the vacuum which causes the lift and allows the plane to fly. But by understanding the physics it is possible to build a plane and to make it fly. I may be a reluctant passenger on a plane but I have to admire the power of those engines, of the design team which built it, and of the pilot who flies it. Thus it is with the figure of RA. He travels in the Heavens using the power of the stars. He is able to compress space and time so as to have the ability to travel in space. He does not want to touch the engines (as you would not want to touch the engines of a plane in flight).

In the case of YH2UH, I have an individual who knows exactly how the "hydrogen" is created, exactly how to form the wormholes which allow the space travel, because in the very beginning, he CREATED everything. Where the miracle is at its greatest, is that HE is a real person! And the personification of that may be either as "RA" or as "the Lord the Krystyeus" or as "another individual of his choosing!"

The TRINITY concept is very important, and I would regard it as no minor matter that the use of water is the symbol of baptism, for it emphasises the "Trinity aspect of The ONE God." As the Hymn says,

"Guide me oh thou Great Jehovah" It may have a "J" in it, but as sung, it is to the Glory of God. It is THE I AM THE, The Lord of Light who is being praised. And I do mean praised.

How sweet it sounds!

<<< Amen >>>

11
Contradictions

I have just considered YH2 UH in the sense as RA. It is now appropriate that I consider the "daughters" of RA. I have briefly considered Sekhmet, as also Tay FA Nut but these I regard as red cats or grey cats; not as humans!.

For a "human" figure the figure of "HA TY R" or Isis would be more appropriate. Now in earlier parts of this hypothesis Isis has been given a very bad press. The attempted Murder of RA is the starting point. And if that was her father, then it is very nasty indeed.

In essence I would probably prefer the figure given the name Ny K, because that super communicates. However super communicate of NY K and HA TY R is very similar. Simplicity in super communicate tends to suggest importance. "To communicate brief words are best".

The super communicate aspect is covered by the hieroglyphics of the name of Isis, particularly in the written form, "Ast", possibly as UST, simply to mean "daughter of." In this sense the hieroglyph of a half sun and throne might tend to suggest that she was the "daughter of RA". It is part of this hypothesis that RA had two daughters. So what is going on?

I have earlier said that "the contradiction in teams is essential to certainty." So where am I with this hypothesis? I have two different versions of the Isis story. In one; she is the murderess, in the other the victim, the widow of her dead husband UsR.

Now if I try to super communicate the whole idea, she cannot have been at the same time the two opposites. For my purposes here I am going to take her in the form of the widow of US R. Now in this regard there is an interesting concept. Given that the society in which I live (and some more so than this,) is male dominated and women have a very much subjugated role, the assumption is that in this version Us R, which is Osiris, is in right of the ruling part, rather than his wife. This is assisted by the "Adam and Eve" story, where again the woman is the villain. Is someone deliberately trying to damage the character of Isis? If that is the case, potentially there is trouble, especially if she is HA TY R; daughter of RA. It raises again who gave what to Moses at SY NY, and the fact that it was given at SY NY should not deflect from the fact that that may have been used as a "cover", much like the "divine wind" was improperly used and caused human blood sacrifice.

The SU ending is feminine, while the SUS ending is masculine. "AmateraTSU" contains the masculine TSU element and dividing it into super communicate elements, and altering the pronunciation slightly, I have "A MA TY RA TSU" which would then be rendered properly as the " Elder (Number 1) daughter of the Sun God(masculine)". MA=1, TY = MIGHTY, RA= YH2UH and TSU the individual. The daughter is the "A", as the abbreviated gender specific FIRST SOUND, where the male would simply have started with MA or has TSU put in front. As in TSU MA .(Son First) (Mo = second) RA MA is thus the "One and only". Compare with "RA MA SES" and "MO SES" as the First and Second "SES" If "Ses" should in fact be "SUS" the two names mean the First and the Second Sons!

This is not to take away from YH2UH that he is entirely "self created", but allows that he has two daughters. That immediately gives a problem with Osiris, and then with Krystyesus but in the case of Krystyesus that problem can be solved simply if RA has a son "by adoption". [There are of course other possibilities which I will consider when considering the Lord the Krystyesus.]

The people of A MA TY RA TSU are still very much alive on the planet today.

Why should I decide to adopt the second version of the Isis story rather than the first and the incident with the serpent? I have not done that entirely, but there is a passage on Page 21 of the second volume by Wallis Budge on Isis which I have to consider. This concerns the incident when her son" HO R US" to use a super communicate spelling, has been poisoned.

"O Isis, pray thou to heaven so that the sailors of RA may cease rowing, so that the boat of RA may not depart from the place where the child Horus is. Then Isis set forth a cry to heaven and addressed her prayer to the Boat of Millions of years;

and the disc stood still, and moved not from the place he was . And then Thoth (Tay HA TY) came.......... No evil shall come upon the child Horus, because his protection comes from the Boat of RA."

Now on reading that I am immediately struck with the similarity to the interpretation that this hypothesis has put on the "miracles" that they are the operation of the matter transfer equipment of the Chariot of Fire! And here, thousands of years old is the word from stone! Not in tablets yet to be found, but on actual ancient Egyptian monuments or on other funeral writings from which this story was taken!

[I have to be careful, for in essence with what is in effect a little book which contains these writings, I am effectively opening a little book, hidden and sealed for Thousands of years. That can be taken to DA NY EL or to Revelation at Chapter 10!]

That the "disc" is said to stay still is curious. Does that mean that the sun stopped its travel over the sky? That is what the text is suggesting, but is that "factual"?

Given the physics taught here on Earth, that is "dubious", although in terms of this hypothesis I am aware that there are tremendously powerful forces involved. Is there an explanation?

The Chariots of Fire are massively powerful. I describe them "as of fire." It is therefore possible that it could be made to lower its shield (or to power up its shield), in response to the "Words of Power", (a transmission to it) and to appear as another fire disc in the sky! If the writers of that passage had said a "second sun was born from the sun", then such might have been appreciated. However if the shield was powered up this side of the sun (that is between the planet and the sun) then a little like an eclipse the shield of the Chariot of Fire would "hide" the real sun. If the position of it was sufficiently close to the planet, then it could blot out the movement of the sun, so that the sun would appear to "stand still." Again if its brilliance is brought close to the planet, then within limits, it could appear to make the sun go backwards. [There is a passage in The Bible when the sun is said to be made to go backwards]. If it is positioned by the side of the sun, it could make the sun appear temporarily "oval", like the shape of an eye "of RA". The passage to heaven is then "through the Sun" (eye of Ra) except that it is not. It is into the chariot of fire, by means of the matter transfer equipment.

Compare the wording with chapter 35 of Isaiah. Verses 5 and 6 talk in terms of the blind being able to see, the deaf to hear and the lame to walk. All of these things are possible with a Chariot of Fire and its matter transfer equipment. Verse 8 which deals with the "Road of Holiness" might be said to describe that route through the eye of RA to SY ON. Although Jerusalem has been used in the actual text, it is HOLY and distant SY ON which is really being talked about. I will come to a more detailed consideration of Isaiah shortly.

This then is the line taken in this hypothesis. That the Chariot of Fire is able to power up to such an extent, that the brilliance of the sun can "appear" hidden. That still leaves all the physics of this planet intact, BUT, and it is a huge but, it means the Chariots of Fire are exceptionally powerful. Think of the power! Again that is stating the obvious if they can travel the 2.2 million light years to Andromeda system in a year!

The name as a "Boat of millions of years" again says that it is able to travel that distance.

If Isis is the daughter of RA, then in the strict sense, for the purposes of this hypothesis, she would have access to a boat of millions of years. She might have no need of it, while quite comfortable on the planet, but if like her father she tired of the planet, then likewise she may have departed.

I feel that I am stretching the point to make the text fit. If Isis, or Ny K or Ha TY R has access to the Chariot of Fire, why is she not able to use that to locate Osiris? Again the point may be that the "gold" renders the search mechanism inoperative shielding the life signs. Equally it may be that it was Osiris who was the problem, because he did not look after Isis properly! [I imagine that quite a few wives of this date feel that their husbands do not look after them properly].

If I use the term "Ny K" for Isis and super communicate it, it will be seen that she has the "Ny" which means voice and might properly be translated as words of power. In the strict sense of the picture representation of Isis she holds in her hand the staff and the "ankh" in her hand. That staff is akin to the letter "N" as written in what I regard as super communicate. It has to be contrasted with "AN", which as "ananan" would signify a present tense. The closest symbol in hieroglyphs to the "N" symbol would be the "flag", and its repetitive nature would suggest a Continuum. "Ananan" is somewhat like 22 over 7, which is Py. Py again has super communicate connotations, especially as PP.

I am not fully conversant with "super communicate". I could not ask for "a loaf of bread" using super communicate, and I am not sure that what I use in letter form is "pure super communicate" but rather what may be an underlying pattern or code which is useful to "check out" information ;particularly where disinformation has been spread over a long period of time! [In this instance I am talking probably at least 15,000 years. I could perhaps add an extra zero to the end!]

Current received wisdom has "evolution" as the route for development, but that has a problem. How did basic species evolve to a "higher level" and how after the "destruction" of the dinosaurs, were they able to be rebuilt? The same applies to humanity. Despite our current technology we cannot build a human from single piece of hair, let alone atoms of hydrogen, carbon etc. In essence much of what we regard as evolution is simply a process or programme for the "improvement of a basic species". That requires a programmer!

There are one or two aspects which need much closer inspection. It is all one to say there were dinosaurs here, because of the fossilised records, but that information, when dealing with powers such as the local < FIRE DISC >, may not be altogether correct!

Yes there may have been dinosaurs, and yes they may have died out millions of years ago. And yes the planet may have been hit by a meteor, but that does not mean that "humanity" evolved from a "soup of bacteria". It is part of this hypothesis that there was a major design input!

It is part of this hypothesis that RA, or YH2UH made himself, and that concept has to be treated carefully. Given the Genesis text, and I would suggest the old Egyptian texts, humanity is made in the image of God, and it is not something which just grew from a bacterial soup!. If it was from a bacterial soup, it should be possible to "grow" humanity from such a soup now.

If the resistance to that is because of a design element in evolution terms of "millions of years" care has to be taken since the "Boat of Millions of years" may have the capacity to do just that, but in a much shorter time scale! Does it take its name from that? Still an essential element I would submit is the ability to "inject life" into the body. A little like loading the computer programme to a disc!

It does look as though the mind set of most of the individuals on this <FOOTSTOOL> is stuck in the days of old; possibly some 5,000 years ago! They are not currently the enlightened galactic individuals required for Galactic travel.

As NY K, Isis has a presence today. It may not be seen as that but it is there. I understand that it is her figure on top of the Brandenburg Gate with four horses in front.

If you want four horsemen of the "Apocalypse" then those four horse would do nicely! As the daughter of the sun god, and with access to his technology, she can crack a mighty whip!

All is not well in that connection for, as I have alluded to above, the Japanese may have in their goddess, one of the daughters of RA and with the correct super communicate name. While it might be HA TY R, it might be her sister. And two of their cities suffered mightily recently. Where then was MA TY RA TSU?

Given the terms of this hypothesis when human blood sacrifice is NOT to be permitted, what is going on? That brings me back again to the figure of YH2 UH.

With such resistance, as far as this text is concerned to human blood sacrifice, what happened to Nippon, and why ?

I have found that question among the most difficult in this hypothesis. I have to consider again "the contradiction in terms."

In many respects the sun is beautiful, but up close it is very dangerous. Long before reaching its surface, any human would have melted and been reduced to single atoms. To get near to it "safely" it is necessary to be completely shielded, which is partly where the shields of the Chariot of Fire are used. With the ability to shield from the sun close to it, separating the waters of the red sea is a minor detail, and very easy.

The figure of YH2UH or RA of this hypothesis is unquestionably powerful, but it is the <u>ability to control that power</u> which makes him "powerful". It is the creativity aspect which is important. He is the Lord of Creation.

It is easy to perform the "abomination of desolation" but to rebuild, that is real power; especially where the rebuilding is done from a quality and durability point of view.

Any text which supports human blood sacrifice, is in terms of this hypothesis, and in terms of the "SY" aspect, to be scrutinised carefully. Where blood sacrifice is sought, it is almost certainly a "sin" (SY Na). While in certain circumstances there may appear to be extenuating circumstances, murder is murder, whether it is done judicially or not.

Equally it is human blood sacrifice to refuse a blood transfusion, when it is known that to restrict that would cause a human blood sacrifice. Care has to be taken with such matters as abortion. It would be the view taken in this hypothesis that when perfectly simple and effective contraception is available in the form of sheaths or pills, it is quite wrong [and SY NA] to use abortion as contraception, because it is not such. And in any event abortion is really playing with genetics, since it will restrict the future population<u>. More importantly</u> it is likely to leave serious mental scars on those involved. Watch however that the accusation of "murder" could be pointed at those who make abortion more difficult, particularly if that leads to physical harm for the mother and the doctors.

Again suicide in terms of this hypothesis, should not take place. It is murder of the individual by the individual.

In considering this point, I am aware that individuals have deliberately put themselves in positions likely to be fatal, for the benefit of others. Such conduct was commended by the Lord the Krystyesus, but even that text causes concerns, because it could so easily lead to unnecessary human blood sacrifice.

That said, I have to accept that the words used to describe the valiant efforts of the British fighter pilots in the Battle of Britain; "Never was so much owed by so many to so few," do relate to sacrifice. [While there was a small chance of their survival, they were not deliberately sent to their deaths by the Government. That has to be contrasted with the kamikaze pilots who were! It is because of the mistreatmet of their OWN pilots that the Japanese lost the two cities. Human Blood sacrifice is NOT ACCEPTABLE, especially as promoted by Government or their military . It is a FUNDAMENTAL. [Tansarduron is DRAS military and he will NOT put his troops at risk!]

I require, as part of this hypothesis to be concerned for those who have sacrificed much; particularly when it is viewed with the wording, in the sure and certain hope of the resurrection unto eternal life.

I am with this hypothesis, not trying to take that away, but I do not doubt that it is one of the weapons in the hands of YH2UH and of RA, to refuse admission to SY ON of those who could be construed as a threat to the Spirit which is for Peace; and an individual who has killed falls into that category.

Tansarduron is Dras Military and is given orders by the DRAS < VISIBLE INVISIBLES >. He is NOT one of them. THE I AM THE is a < VISIBLE INVISIBLE > and that individual is a GALACTIC INDIVIDUAL; often the HEAD of a GALAXY or GALAXIES! That < INDIVIDUAL > is a difficult one to explain and that is reserved for another work . A Galactic Director, who is able to control the "stars" as the individual RA or YH2UH is not one to upset!

Slow he may be to anger but I have to accept that he does get angry, and like any angry individual will take appropriate defensive measures.

It is part of this hypothesis that for very good reasons human blood sacrifice is NOT to be done, and that that is MATERIAL. I could use legal speak and say that it is an "essential condition" and pre requisite for admission to the SY ON of YH2UH and of RA.

It is now time to consider the prophets of the Old Testament, before going on to consider the position of the Lord the Krystyesus.

12
Visions and Reality – More Contradictions

Before moving to Isaiah and then to Daniel, I must consider briefly the text of Genesis and Exodus. Allowing for it to be written by Pharaoh, it does not cease to be the word of God, but the context in which it is written has been changed. In essence it is a Hypothesis, NOT a reality. Various figures did not exist, and they can be moved [as Messod and Sabbah have done in their book] to real individuals who had entirely different names from the Biblical ones. But certain of the physical aspects of the Genesis story, and the Exodus story are important.

The flood is real, but as an Earth Crust Displacement or something similar which involves the whole planet spinning to a new location, it is much more massive than spoken of in Biblical terms. The paradise was lost and the names of the main players and LOCATIONS have been changed. And the secret name of God? That is to be protected at all costs. That to a certain extent is done with the name "Jehovah" which does not "super communicate." However, the letters YHWH do super communicate.

Initially I could not understand what YHWH meant as super communicate. It is part of this hypothesis that it relates also to RA and is the mask for the secret name. That being the case what is it? All power of all creation, of the local star and of the King of heaven. Y(A) H(A) UU H(A) was my attempt to super communicate the word, or the letters. And then I changed it YA HA 2 U HA. As soon as I inserted the number 2(because W is 2 U), I saw it. As was to be expected. I might also say that it is seen in the terms A HU RA MA Z DA, which is relevant to Daniel and his time.

What both forms are trying to say is "The Lord of Light", more particularly the "Lord of Creation"; the Lord who created and controls the "Stars" who is responsible for the movement of the whole galaxy and of the Universe itself.

Beautifully hidden in YHWH. I do not know what the "2U" actually stands for but since water is by definition

"H2O" the water is maintained in the YHWH. After all without water there would be no life and without hydrogen it would be a very different kind of light. "Neon" perhaps!

This is a simplification of the concept. The Lord of the Galaxies (as I might now call him) is a nice title, one of many for the King of Heaven; for it demonstrates the ability to maintain tremendous power, albeit that over a very long time scale as currently understood, it decays. The big LOCAL fire disc in the sky is an obvious example of the power of RA, and of the rays of light which come from it.

Tow away the local star, move it out or in by just a little bit, and it will make all talk of global warming seem meaningless! Move it out and all life will be sent to the freezer. How the star and the planet are tied together is vitally important. In essence this is the < MECHANICS > which is activated and operated by the < INDIVIDUAL > who is the <<< AMEN >>>.

The current world worries about "weapons of mass destruction" but such are puny by comparison to the powers which hold the planet and its local star at a comfortable and useful distance! The contrast is also marked that it is the power of "Creation" and not destruction which is important.

The instruction of the first commandment to have no other gods before THE I AM THE, as he called of himself to Moses is very important. It is the unseen presence of The I AM as Paul later wrote, of the unseen God .

I will take some time with Isaiah and Daniel

First Daniel. Now while that is out of sequence, I do so because of super communicate. DA NY EL. That is how it would be written in the super communicate. DA is "Imperial" and "Galactic" for "The". It is like the English THE, not being gender specific, but is ALL POWERFUL. It is thus of God. NY is simply a "Voice". SY NY being [Peace Voice] "The Voice of Peace."

EL as I said, I am taking as "The", but in an Earthly form. If there are 2 "The's" in the word and with the voice in it, I might translate it thus, "From heaven to earth, the VOICE." Word order is important, with the first word [Two letter combination] setting the degree of importance.

Daniel had visions. [And vision is super communicate VY SY ON- route to the Peace City]. He was allowed to see Heaven and to write of it. But even here there is a concern and he is told to seal up certain things until the time of the "End". Why? The probable problem is that if the picture is made too clear, those in positions of authority will see their position as threatened, [because God desires something different from what they have in mind]. Those of Earth, lacking a proper understanding of the ways of Heaven are probably not inclined to follow on a path which leads to SY ON, and instead move in a different direction, possibly with disastrous consequences.

In Daniel's time it was again time for a change. Yet again Israel had been found wanting. What was Israel doing to make it so annoying?

Here I can turn to Isaiah.[EY SY YA] He also was given visions. One of the curious things about that work as I began to read it was of the shifting nature of the texts, from passages which would have real meaning to those to whom Isaiah was speaking, and passages which were clearly visionary and telling of a future time. Isaiah is critical [Verses 8, 19] and 20 is highly critical of the practice of consulting mediums. But the person who is given as being most critical of that is GOD himself.

Much of the early text of Isaiah is in text which, in super communicate terms, is the word of God in actual spirit!

Isaiah 6, is of particular interest. Here Isaiah is given a vision of God. In the terms in which he writes it is difficult to glean just exactly what he sees. The winged creatures, with six wings. [Helicopters?] Very strange. And what of the burning coal which is used to touch his lips in verse 6. It is stated that "Isaiah's sins are forgiven, which was doubtless very nice for Isaiah. But more importantly what is done is that he has been allowed to touch that fiery coal from the "ALTYR IN HEAVEN" so that then, even if unseen, his words have particular authority. That authority is not clearly seen, for it is of GOD and it for him to determine what is said, how it is said and the time at which it may be used.

In certain respects as I read the first few chapters of Isaiah, I noted that it appeared repetitive. But then perhaps that was only to be expected as Isaiah tried to make his message heard. Certain aspects of what he said had NO relevance to his time. They related to a time far in his future, a time that may be now, in the recent or distant past to this time, or in the future yet to come, both near and distant. And if they are in the "future" time, it does not mean for a moment that the time is certain. It is as though there are many staging posts and the route may change depending on the choices taken.

In the text of Isaiah, the word for God there used is "Lord", and I may prefer to use that. The Lord is quite candid about his behaviour. In Isaiah 8 at verse 13 he is specific; "Remember that I the Lord Almighty, am Holy. I am the one you must fear. Because of my awesome holiness I am like a stone that people stumble over, I am like a trap..............."

The term "Awesome Holiness" is important. It does not say "Power". No it talks of Holiness. Chapter 6 at Verse 3 has the winged angels singing,

"Holy, Holy, Holy, The Lord Almighty is Holy. His Glory fills the world."

Statements of fact. And a question. What glory fills the World? In the obvious sense it is the light of the local star, of the sun! Here then is an indication that what is being talked about is *the power of the star*. But it goes far beyond that. I have used the term the Lord of Hydrogen fusion. The local star is a massive hydrogen fusion reactor (as current perceived wisdom would have it). And it is indeed greatly to be feared. But as a description of the Lord of the Galaxy it is of one who "controls" the local star. And it is not just that star. It is all stars in this galaxy.

It is here that the "big bang" theory of the universe collides with the spiritual and religious. It is in the NEED TO KNOW that progress is made. Yes it is all created, as we currently see it, as the ancients saw it, and our descendants will see it, but it exists as a reality now.

What does the term "awesome holiness" then mean? He who can control the star is "AWESOME". By controlling it, creatively, rather than destructively, he is demonstrating a particular kind of power. And that power is "HOLINESS". As a Galactic individual controlling stars in the Galaxy he is "AWESOME."

Holiness is the Power of creation. It is contrasted with that which destroys, but it is much more powerful for it is far harder to create than to destroy. It takes nine months for a child to be "created" but it can be destroyed in but a short space of time, even at the moment of delivery!

Isaiah 1 is interesting also. (In a manner not dissimilar from RA, complaining about the people he had created, before sending the flood,) so The Lord is seen at verse 2, being critical of his people, Israel. They have NOT done what he required. His criticism is quite profound.

Verse 3........ "They don't understand at all."

That is VERY revealing. If as this hypothesis suggests, RA and The Lord are one and the same, and that the people of Israel are in fact the "people of RA", then by the time of Isaiah, and as they would be defined today, Israel will have nothing to do with RA. They have a new Lord, the YHWH, and he in the sense of certain books of "THE LAW" has given them a meticulous set of rules.

Again a close inspection of Chapter 1 at verse 11, the Lord says; "Do you think that I want all these sacrifices you keep offering to me? I have had more than enough of the sheep you burn as sacrifices and of the fat of your fine animals.." And again at verse 12, a very telling comment, "Who asked you to bring me all this when you come to worship me... ..?"and He, THE LORD, goes on to criticise the new moon festivals, the Sabbaths. They are corrupted by "sin".

Isaiah is giving a picture of The Lord as very displeased and it is not a vision his listeners will have liked. His talk of them been taken into captivity they might understand, but this text, was possibly not strictly intended for them, but may be more applicable to this time!

"SIN" has taken root in this culture. Most of the religious authorities today delight in telling others that they are committing a "sin". Equally modern religions are as inclined, as was Israel at the time of Isaiah, to look to the rules such as are to be found in Leviticus, rather than to the Spirit as was intended. The explanation given is that The Lord "gave" the rules, but that does not tie in with this early part of Isaiah. It is perhaps because the rules of Leviticus were NOT given by the Lord at all, but were the creation of Man? If, as suggested by Sabbah and Messah in their work, and the Pharaohs wrote the Old Testament, it does put a serious question mark over the text of Leviticus and the other "rule" books of the Old Testament. That is compounded both by this text at Isaiah, and later by the "real" teaching of Christ.

It should be noted that Christ himself used text from Isaiah, and that is probably not surprising. There has been an attempt to suggest that the "Essenes", alive at the time of Christ were the successors to those who had come up out of Egypt, and that they had built an encampment on the same bearing as that ancient City of Akhenaten at Armana!

A relevant consideration at this point is the matter of "Sin". If I apply super communicate rules to the English word "Sin", I would take "sy" and then add to it "n(a)". That is something which super communicate says is NOT to be done. SY does not mix with NA. To translate it therefore, something which is a "Sin" is "NOT"= Na and "PEACE" for "SY". That contrasts with something which is "for peace" which is "good", and that which deliberately goes against Peace, which could be said to be "evil". [Compare with NA SY, where "na" precedes "Sy", which is grossly offensive!] I can use that test to examine ALL of the Old and New Testament and any other work written! I require to be careful because the fact that a work contains a "super communicate word or word" does not make it super communicate. If it conforms to the "Spirit" and is trying to assist to create peace, then it can be said to be "good" and it is likely the text is "super communicate".

The old test to which Abram was put was of the sacrifice of his son. That, as far as this text is concerned is an anathema. It is, to quote Daniel's terms, "the abomination of desolation". If murder is done, judicial or otherwise, and there is not the power to bring back to life or reinstate, it is the "abomination of desolation", which is performed. That applies also to the cutting off of hands and feet, of the gouging out of eyes. All of these things cause desolation and are an abomination. That expression "abomination of desolation" is "super communicate!

When the Lord says that Abram, was looking for a way to avoid sacrificing his son, it was the Lord who realised that in that individual he had found "an enlightened individual". The subsequent sacrifice of the "lamb" is NOT required and is unnecessary! Abram was given something in his name to show that "enlightenment." The word "HA" being super communicate of "light" was added to his name. The word "Ab" like "Na" indicates a danger. It is to be remembered that "Abram" was from "UR". That is part of TansardUR on's name, and consequently, he is with that pre nom "Ab" NOT for The I AM The. However once he has NOT sacrificed his son, he has "seen the light" and he is "enlightened". He is entitled to use of the sacred word "HA" in his name. Of his descendants, what it then means is not necessarily his physical descendants, but rather those who follow his lead, avoid human blood sacrifice, and can thus be said to be "enlightened". It is they who will be as numerous as the sand. Essentially only those who are enlightened are likely to survive!

Evil begets evil, and if it is desired to walk along the path of peace (" Da ma pa da" could be said to be a fair description of the path of enlightenment and peace), it is necessary NOT to perform the "abomination of desolation" which is the reference to "human blood sacrifice "; also a super communicate term.

The criticism The Lord makes in Isaiah that <u>he does not want the sacrifice of sheep, and that relates directly to that incident.</u>

What was most important for his new people, Israel, was that that they understood that there was to be no more HUMAN BLOOD SACRIFICE. And that is a matter which, in terms of this hypothesis, is regularly checked by those in Heaven!

Leviticus is full of human blood sacrifice. Exodus has some too. Christ was pushed on that point when he was asked to "cast a stone at the woman caught in adultery." TAKING THE VERY SAME TEST, he replied, "Let him who is without fault cast the first stone," and is reported as writing in the sand. Assuming that he was WITHOUT FAULT, which is one view of Christian theology, he did NOT lift stone. He has shown that he UNDERSTOOD, at least as far as The Lord, his FATHER in Heaven was concerned.

[I will revert to an aspect of this when I come later to consider the crucifixion of the Lord the Krystyesus]. So in terms of this Hypothesis, when RA took his people out of Egypt, he was intent on making a new people. He was aware of their lives in Egypt and of the punishment of death there used. For many years they wandered around in the desert, and the Lord "hoped" he would manage to get this message across.

However, it is possible that having removed his people, being reasonably satisfied with his efforts at that time, he left in his "boat of millions of years "leaving Moses in charge and left it up to Moses to make his own way and guide his NEW people. He would return for a re inspection visit later and check on progress. After all he did not want to "spoon feed them". They were not intended to be puppets, but a new thinking people!

But when the people asked for rules, Moses gave them rules! This again has to be contrasted with the suggestion that it was Pharaohs, rather than The Lord, who wrote the first five books of the Old Testament. Yes, the rules served to designate the people of "Israel" as such, but it did not necessarily make them "acceptable to The Lord". That is the point Isaiah is making. Or rather the point that God was trying to make through Isaiah to Israel. Indeed as it applied then, it may be said to apply now, although by this stage much aggravated by the Crucifixion of Christ!

It is likely that the text in Isaiah is MULTI LAYERED and super communicate *and* super super communicate. As I write it in super communicate EY SY YA, I am conscious that much of the text is about the REAL PEACE(that is Peace which comes from GOD), and that God is a real individual and also is a TRY NY TY concept. Thus the terms Kephra RA Amen does designate the Trinity concept, but it does not sufficiently hide the "secret name" which is much better hidden as YHWH. It still leaves me with a real individual. An Almighty and HOLY individual, who controls the stars!

[In the barred spiral context and the sequenced stars the GENERAL DIRECTORS of GALAXIES are VERY PARTICULAR about who they let on their FOOTSTOOLS .

The galaxy patterns are thus VERY RELEVANT, and this aspect is TECHNICAL SCIENCE].

The General Director of a Galaxy is thus like a pilot of an aircraft, or an operator of a machine and he is in a position to control that which HE MADE! This is after all the ATLANTIS hypothesis, named after the local STAR and as such it is part of this Hypothesis that AMEN RA (in the name that he uses upon his clothes- as indicated in Revelation) is THE REAL individual.

Moving on a little, I come to the text of Isaiah 9 and to the Lord The Krystyesus. Isaiah 11 also deals with the peaceful Kingdom. Note in particular, verse 9. "On SYON, God's sacred hill there will be nothing harmful or evil."

With reference to this text, SY ON means "The City of Peace" from the super communicate. Watch also that it is "God's!" That is the property of God. Its location is at the DETERMINATION OF THE LORD. (So while I may be out with the location I give in this text, the accuracy of the idea may be all that is required. Equally the information may have been supplied to me to write and it may be accurate!)

Watch, with particular reference to the present day, the return of Israel from far flung lands! That would indicate that that those passages MAY be directed at this time, NOT at ancient times. That is what I mean when I say that the text of Isaiah is multi layered. Verse 15 talks of drying up the Gulf of Suez, and being able to walk across the Euphrates. Bearing in mind that the Euphrates has bridges over it, it is now possible to walk over it! In contrast because of the Suez canal, there is a division between Egypt and Israel. At Chapter 14 it says that, at verse 2, "many nations will help the people of Israel to return to the land they were given."

Post the holocaust that was Europe in the 1939 to 1945 period, that is indeed factual. People may have eyes to see and ears to hear but are they still deaf, as indicated in Isaiah 6 at verse 9. These aspects are relevant to this hypothesis, for what is being suggested here is that RA is watching, and perhaps not from the far distance of space, but much closer. He may have sent his officers ahead to "check" out the planet and to provide him with a report. And in that connection the question may be, "Is it as bad as it appears from the television transmissions?"

This is not a flat work which simply relies on words. No, I am dealing with a very powerful individual and civilizations who have been powerful for THOUSANDS of years if not MILLIONS OF YEARS.

By Isaiah 18, The Lord is again flexing his muscles. Sudan is targeted. A clear warning is issued in verse 4, "I will look down from Heaven as quietly as the dew forms in the warm night of harvest time."

The text is not clear cut as to time. When the destruction of Egypt is talked about in Chapter 19, it might properly refer to Alexander and his successors the Ptolemys.[Ezekiel again comments on this]. Or it might refer to the destruction of Egypt by the Persians. But it probably refers to those who took Thebes; the religious capital!

Look at the criticism of the Egyptian advisors at verse 11. "How dare they (Egypt's wisest men......) tell the king that they are successors to the ancient scholars and kings."

In this text it is the Lord who is speaking. He is critical, because HE is well aware of the ancient history of Egypt and of the succession of the Pharaohs from before the time of Akhenaten (whose name was substantially expunged). Memphis is criticised by The Lord (verse 13) because instead of leading the people they have misled it. [That means that they were INTENDED to lead, but in fact have done the reverse, and that has "upset" THE LORD. What then was the cult of the Egyptians at Memphis? It was of Ptah. That again may be used as super communicate for "the Lord of Light, the King of creation "P T HA" [The Diamond Lord of Light]. Again at verses 18 and 19 of chapter 19 something curious appears. Again it is The Lord speaking and reference is made to "Hebrew" being spoken in 5 Egyptian cities. If, as has been suggested by Messod, that the land of Israel, was in the gift of Pharaoh, then the five Egyptian cities might well be 5 cities in current day Israel! If I use super communicate again HA FA, which is to do with light, is close to Haifa in phonetic sound!

Heliopolis, what was once called ON, is now modern Cairo. There they most certainly do not speak Hebrew! Not at this time.

But it is verses 19 and 20 which contain the surprise. As is well known the Ancient Egyptians built many monuments. What then is the stone pillar [Pylon] at the border of Egypt? Given the importance of the Nile it is likely to be on a pylon high up the Nile, possibly at the boundary with Sudan! But it might be adjacent to Libya. Siwa was once important. Or should I say "SY WA" And the word "WA" appears in the super communicate of "Chariot of Fire"

They have eyes to see and ears to hear, but they hear not nor see! Whose name is on the pylon? Is it RA's? But even were it not to be "Ra's" care has to be taken, because the whole text is super communicate and likely to be multi layered. And the "shifting nature" of the names of the gods of ancient Egypt make it entirely possible that it has been disguised with the name of some other individual, and that disguise would only be appreciated by the proper use of and understanding of the super communicate.

Rameses was prolific was his monuments, and put them at the boundaries of his Kingdom. Is it one of his statues? It is all difficult, but simply part of THIS Hypothesis .

I am going to leave Isaiah just now, for as I read more of it there is more of it to be seen. But what is quite clear is that The Lord is not pleased with what he sees, and with a people who have lost and ignored him.

Ra is certainly ignored in this the 21 century in the year of our Lord the Krystyesus. But Ra is not annoyed with that . After all, ALL authority in Heaven and Earth was given to the Lord the Krystyesus. It should therefore be NO surprise that the temples to RA are overturned. That is a prime requirement when ALL authority is given!

[Note here. The reference to the Temples being overturned highlights the CHANGE in style. The old style has gone and it is the NEW which is in place.]

13
The Overthrowing of Apep

This has taken me some time to decipher. However in the sense of the boat of millions of years, of star peoples, I now have a fair idea of exactly what is meant. Christ also referred to it as "the Truth will set you free". That is essence is what the overthrowing of Apep is about.

At present there remains a reliance on "lies" as an essential tool, especially in politics and in the diplomatic circles. To that extent it is a wrong understanding rather than "Apep", which is still in charge and that despite nearly 2000 years of Christian tradition!

Those who deny the Christian message, those who oppose it, those who say that there is no God anyway, are OPPOSED to the GALACTIC CIVILISATIONS, whether they accept that or not. Since in Christian teaching Christ made it clear that he was and is "The Way the Truth and the Life", if that is not accepted, then the individuals are properly called NA SY. And it is not possible to overcome "Apep" using lies. Tansarduron, who is DRAS military knows that! So it keeps the population on this "planet" and with an erroneous understanding.

Note here the use of the term Tansarduron for "satan" and "Apep" as something different, because it is part of this hypothesis that "satan" and "Apep" are not the same thing. Tansarduron, as I describe him, is the "full" name for "satan", IS a Red cat, dislikes humanity intensely, and will do all in his power to criticise and belittle humanity, especially to the I AM. Thus the passages in Job! Apep on the other hand is an entirely different concept. It is to do with the "heavens" and in this connection "apep" is a monster!

It is a huge "serpent" but it is not strictly speaking a serpent at all. Indeed the understanding of what "apep" is gives a new point of reference to the figure of the "serpent" on the crown of the Pharaoh. The trouble is that it is such a huge concept, that even now I have difficulty comprehending about what I am writing!

The key was provided in the drawing of figure of "Sekhet" or "Sekhmet". Now I am concerned with the different spellings of her name because of the super communicate in it. However as I have already said, I am satisfied that as an agent of RA she is the figure, with other red cats, who "flew over" on the night of the Passover". And I stand by that. Given the impending human blood sacrifice of Christ it gives a new insight into that particular "Passover" meal, when the new covenant of "communion" was instituted!

[In technical SCIENTIFIC terms the Passover is a < REPROGRAMMING > of the dna. Sekhmet is thus PRESENT because this is DRAS GALAXY. No reprogramming will be done without approval from Dras and the ATLANTYONS. This is added here to clarify having regard to the New Hypothesis] .

The drawing I am referring to is of the figure of Sekhet standing on a serpent, a big serpent, holding it in both hands, and with a SUN DISC on her head. She could easily be confused as a "daughter of RA". But she is a CAT, and as such not a daughter of RA, because his daughter, allowing for this hypothesis interpretation of Genesis, would be of " human form." [Atlantyon]. Thus A MA TY RA TSU, fills that position very neatly. I am however concerned that because of sensibilities, particularly in Nippon, I will not be able to fully say this. However I am not trying to be disrespectful. In many respects it is quite the contrary, for I have elevated her to the daughter of THE I AM THE, which would doubtless upset others!

Regretfully there are two very sad incidents which would tend to emphasise that she is the daughter of the Sun God, and what is more worrying I have identified that because the I AM was VERY upset about the misuse of his name, even though it is in his daughter's province, he made two cities < NOT RESERVED >; that is he removed his face and protection from them .

[Not wishing to be obtuse, Hiroshima and Nagasaki were the two involved. The third was Kobe]. Some code books have "cracked" since they did not have the correct science!

Who then is Sekhet? Her colour is red, according to Wallis Budge. Thus she is of the red cat type creatures. In terms of this hypothesis they are creatures created BEFORE the attempt was made with the individuals on this < FOOTSTOOL > and who assisted the Atlantyons in the development of the human species, and as such are creatures who live on and rule a different planet. I call it Dras, but the reference to Sard and that galaxy might be appropriate! I might regard any inclusion of the letters "Sard" to be a reference to them, in what ever order. I certainly look upon the "HKT" letters are referring to them or being connected to them.

Sekhet is standing on top of the serpent and with it in each hands. What she is saying is that she has "overcome apep". She is IN CONTROL of apep. If it was alive she has killed it!

Now the monster is "super light travel" by way of wormholes. The "apep" is the wormhole which allows travel to distant galaxies!

The text which talks of RA overcoming apep, tells also of the capacity of RA to do that. What is going on?

Recently travel into space has suffered a setback. First there was the "Challenger" and then the " Columbia" disaster. I regard both of these incidents as demonstrating that humanity does not properly understand about space, and worse is going along the wrong path in its space exploration! Rockets are fine for a payload such as a satellite, which can be replaced, even at massive cost, BUT where a human payload is involved, there is no room for errors. And there have been whoppers! Who has been covering up? Who has been economical with the Truth? A few inquiries, but as viewed by Sekhet and others in the heavens, a complete lack of understanding.

Essentially the problem is that exploration of space is being built on "Human Blood sacrifice." While certain pioneers in the United Kingdom may be trying to work it out on minuscule budgets, without Government support, most of the major players have built their rockets on "human blood sacrifice". That is the problem. Essentially it could be compared to trying to make a jumbo jet fly using human slaves. It simply will not work! [It may be possible to do it with the gimmickry of trick photography/video, but in a real sense, it does not work].

Currently certain Governments have at best been "careless " or "reckless" with the life of their astronauts. That is what "overcoming Apep" is all about. To understand the complexities of and to overcome the problems of "super light travel" the fundamental rule is NOT to KILL those who are involved. Some say accidents happen, but that will not do. It is fundamental.

Unlike the red cats, Humanity have yet to overcome "apep". Despite any alleged "enlightenment" in the Christian tradition, the words of the Lord the Krystyesus are often not appreciated for their "super communicate aspect." In certain respects that is hardly surprising for it is with this work that I am attempting to introduce super communicate. Until a proper understanding is demonstrated, the keys to super light travel will be "locked, barred and bolted." Essentially they have to be because the forces involved are massive!

If I ever wondered why the "biblical" texts seemed so obscure, now I know. Unleash the power by accident and a global catastrophe is the likely result. And in that connection a flood involving an earth crust displacement is minor!

Unlike Alexander, who cut through the Gordian "knot" to pass through, such an attitude will not work with these forces. They are "protected" both by their own power and by those who properly understand them, like the red cats, among others. And in Alexander's case, although he may have "cut through" the knot, and made himself ruler of a "world" including Egypt, it was a short lived triumph. If the biblical texts are examined, his rise to power was "foretold", but also was the undoing of it. With vast riches came failure and his empire came undone .

Travel through a wormhole, and not maintain its structural integrity, or cause it to destabilise, and the fall out would be likely to rip apart a good few planets, and possibly the odd star! It is not a plaything for children, and in many respects with its current attitudes, humanity is barely out of "nappies".

Now when it come to the overthrowing of "apep", apep does not have a definite article but overthrowing does!

Sekhet, by holding the serpent in both hands is saying that she has overcome "apep" and has control of it. In essence she and her fellow creatures can travel super light.! That is emphasised by the head at each end! Go in one end, come out the other. A "wormhole". And in this connection the "serpent" apep is a large "worm". There is a degree of super communicate in that "English" word.

What is wanted of humanity, is that it demonstrates that is has the capacity to fully understand and to "overcome apep". It also has to demonstrate the capacity to deal peaceful and <u>CORRECTLY</u> with enormously powerful galactic Civilisations.

The double headed serpent means that at BOTH < DEPARTING and RECEIVING FOOTSTOOLS > there MUST be PRIOR AGREEMENT to this type of travel.

This text may seem brief, and it is. I will return to some of its concepts later. For the present that is all I intend to write.

It may look easy, but I can assure any reader, that it has been very difficult. Very difficult indeed.

Thoughts of Alexander take me to Daniel and that I will consider next . And as someone rather unkindly put it in respect of Xerius, whom Alexander deposed, Xerius did not have much help from his God.

Where was "Ahura Mazda?"

14
The "One" God

In this text I am back with the super communicate again. What happened to "AhuraMazda"? Care has to be taken, for it will super communicate. "RA MA Z DA" which might be translated as "The One God".

The mention is of "RA" again, together with, from an English language point of view the "alpha" in the sense of the super communicate "Ma" for One, "Z" for "Omega" and "DA" which in super communicate terms is the "Imperial/Mighty, all powerful definite article." It is a bit like the English THE in blocks. It is not gender specific, as in masculine feminine and neuter. It is ABOVE all.

Now I am almost certain that Alexander's involvement was necessary. The suffix for "Alexander" is "The Great". In super communicate terms I may place "The Great" BEFORE, "THE I AM THE". That shows proper deference. In essence by putting "the Great" after his name "Alexander was not technically treading on the toes of "The I AM The", to put it somewhat politely.

I have been careful thus far to state that "NO human blood sacrifice" is a prime requirement. But I am conscious that there are times when "The I AM The" does allow a display of his power to be seen. Fortunately such displays are usually kept in reserve and usually used only when he has been seriously provoked.

Now it may seem a strange place to talk in terms of "A" to "Z" to begin at "Daniel", but in super communicate terms, it is more than appropriate. "DA NY EL" translated as "THE Voice"; in essence of THE I AM.

With the move into captivity in Persia, Daniel is brought to the Court of the king whose faith is of "Ahura Mazda". In essence what is being said is that now for the first time it is appreciated that "RA" and "Ahura Mazda" and "YH2UH" are all the same individual. That is quite a "Revelation" to use another biblical reference. Given that, it is not at all strange that the references in Revelation, mirror certain aspects of Daniel.

Both Revelation and Daniel are difficult, particularly with the imagery. By allowing Alexander to "conquer" Persia, [P R SY YA] the reality of what had been understood is again lost. It is as though those in charge in Heaven do not wish the material to be disclosed. AT least at that time. That after all is one of the closing instructions to Daniel, Chapter 12, verse 9, "These words are to be kept secret and hidden until the end comes....." Quite tricky that one. So also is the final verse 13.

It is all very curious. It is as though it has been carefully crafted by experts .A bible code? Yes, but in super communicate terms not nearly so obvious.

I read part of Daniel 11. It deals with the invasion of Egypt, when the king of Syria will take away, "Egypt's hidden treasures of gold and silver and its other prized possessions." That is of course what happened with the destruction of Thebes; modern day Luxor. Chapter 11 is interesting, for in verse 2, there is clear reference to the rise of Alexander, verse 3, that he will rule over a huge empire, and at the height of his power it will break up, and will be divided into four parts. Kings descended from him will rule.

Watch verse 5. In essence "Ptolemy" was a descendant from one of Alexander's generals. And it is from Ptolemy, and the "Rosetta" stone that much of the current understanding Egyptian theology is derived.

In many respects what I now understand is that the "biblical code" in super communicate terms is "packaged". That is to say, part of the texts are indeed super communicate, but they are surrounded by much "chaff and nonsense" so that the "code" element is hidden. The "cut" in the texts is probably where there is a reference to "human blood sacrifice", since in super communicate terms such an act is NOT appropriate.

Sir Isaac Newton, I now discover spent a great deal of his time trying to decipher the "code" in the bible. Modern day writers consider themselves to have "found" it in mathematical programmes. But pure mathematics is but a children's toy, at best, when compared to the Power of The I am The. As for my attempt at super communicate?

Since starting this I have learnt that I will be "allowed" to "reveal" (if that is the correct term) only as much as those in Heaven consider "desirable". I cannot fathom their intentions!

I may regard it sometimes as being necessary to see what the level of understanding is, particularly on matters relating to human blood sacrifice. In a culture which lives and loves, by Human blood sacrifice, there is no place for those who come from Heaven. Yet, if I understand correctly, they can and do use their power quire mercilessly.

The "Passover" is an example of that power being used. As I will say elsewhere, the individuals present I consider to be the Red Cats including Sekhmet. When I started out on this text, I simply used the "anglicised" spelling because I saw little need to change it. But working with this text and super communicate in particular, I noticed that the was a need to revert to the super communicate.

The Egyptian term "neter" for God I have changed to "NY TY R", which does NOT then mean God, but a "Messenger of God". Now in the case of "Sekhmet", if I change that to "SY K HA MaaT", I have an individual who is concerned with upholding the Justice of the "K Ha", "Lord of Light" and "his truth". In essence the figure is a "Justice Official" from Heaven.

The main difference with those in Heaven is that they have the power to "re create" using the matter transfer equipment. They can make new.

With the translation of the Hieroglyphs, it would now seem clear to me that only a "hazy image" was allowed to Champillon . With only a small clue as to the text, it had to be "back engineered". That is an acceptable modern tool in development of new technology, but such will not be as good as the understanding of those who originally wrote it.

Thus when I talk in "super communicate" I am talking about people who spoke "words of Power" BEFORE there was even the first Pharaoh on the throne of Egypt. That is why I say TA HA TY, rather than "Thoth", "Hermes" or "Mercury". And that is why I say he is of the "Red Cats".

So for that matter is "MY K EL" "The Principal RED CAT, and friend to RA, as also in the case of TA HA TY.

I now have a suspicion that while the hieroglyphs have been translated, because of the underlying power, those in charge have been careful to shield and to hide it. Yes, there is physics and astrophysics, electrons and atoms, and much power generated from the evolution but in terms of a "creator GOD" that has been shelved. Much of that has been caused by "his" priests, who have continued to load on to the backs of the poor a load they could not be reasonably expected to carry. Christ was critical of such in his time.

What is the problem with birth control? It is a medicine, and will help the poor. ALL Understanding will help the poor. That is why education is so vital, and why, when societies go down that route and to try to educate as many of their people as possible and to the highest level, they tend to make huge advances.

Medicine also is important. If a government is "reckless" with its population, not only does it not deserve to survive, it both weakens itself and like Nyppon in 1945 it angers the General Directors and their sequenced stars. If a society makes "unjust" or "unfair laws" the ordinary people will suffer, and will certainly not give of their best. They may be cut down in early years, and will not be able to make the contribution they would otherwise have been able to do.

It is my view that one of the most important things to those in Heaven and to the King of Heaven in particular is "Truth and Justice". It nicely sits within the word, "MaTT." It is the ONE thing which interests the King of Heaven, and it is the one thing for which he looks.

Where a society sets a high standard for its Justice system, he naturally takes an interest. In terms of this hypothesis The King of Heaven took a very close interest in the trial of Christ before Pilate. But it is much more complicated than that. And yet is not. As I have said elsewhere, the contradiction in terms is essential to certainty.

There is a clear warning in Daniel, Chapter 11, at 21. [Compare wording with King James Version, and chapter 12 and verse 11.] What is the "Awful horror" which is set up? Now as is said elsewhere, "Take care to understand what is being talked about."

In Roman times much "abuse" was made of the Temple in Jerusalem by the Romans and it mightily offended the local "Jewish Population", who saw it as an affront to the "I AM THE". However, what they did not grasp was that "THE I AM THE" is well able to take care of himself. That does not mean that like Christ, he can appear to be made the "sacrificial lamb". What it does mean is that VERY VERY GREAT care has to be taken when dealing with individuals, <u>particularly if there is any suggestion of a link to The I AM THE.</u>

Now today, if a Red Cat was present on the face of this planet many would attack it. Look what has happened to the Tyger population. Look what has happened to the Whale population. It is only a whale, some may say.

While to many it is an animal, and as such irrelevant (whaling interest for scientific purposes) it is NOT an irrelevance to THE I AM THE. Even the name "blue whale" in super communicate terms has to be watched, because it would suggest <u>a DIRECT link to the I AM THE</u>. [The colour of THE I AM THE, in the sense of RA, is "BLUE" and it is a "pale shade of blue." I might say it is of a similar colour to that used by certain airlines.

Unfortunately, some humans are particularly careless and reckless with the lives of others. That is not acceptable to and offends THE I AM THE, and is likely to lead to retribution. [Hiroshima, Nagasaki and Kobe]

In much the same way as the Tyger and the whales have been attacked, so also has humanity, with attacks on its airlines, with massive loss of life. Such atrocities are simply a "human blood sacrifice" and it is a massive one.

An attack on a Red Cat, of the "Seket" style would doubtless be seen by some as a "religious duty". Such who do that, forget or ignore that they also are creations of THE I AM THE. Such religions, in terms of this hypothesis, do not have anything to do with THE I AM THE. They are more likely to be the work of "NA SY" individuals. [In Revelation terms, of the "Anti Christ"]. Many would be quite happy with that. They may be atheists, or followers of another faith than Christianity or no faith at all. They might even be supporters of "THE I AM

THE" because after all there were to be "no other gods before him", as is said.

Daniel, Chapter 11 could be said at verses 33 to 35 simply to be telling of the foundations of the Christian religion, which came out of the faith of the Lord the Krystyesus. But the "Awful horror" is also mentioned in Revelation. What is going on? If I think of the city of Nagasaki on that August day, then I have another view of the "Awful Horror". That bomb was like a small part of the Sun, as thought a piece of "RA" had been brought down to the city. And in that context, it stood within the confines of the Christian Church at Nagasaki. [Note the Christian church there was essentially the Roman Church and the New Hypothesis makes comment about Location. Thus the attack on Nagasaki may have had much more to do with where Rome was NOT to go! A matter with which Hadrian was familiar! See the New Hypothesis].

It may therefore be that the "awful horror" is none other than the presence of "RA" in his destructive mode, which is in marked contrast to him as "the Little man of truth; that is Like Kryst" and "as the Holy Spirit."

Again if it is not appreciated what is going on it is possible for "RA" in the shape of a little man to "stand where he might not be expected to stand", [stand can be taken in the sense of "Stare" of Latin and of "Estar" in Spanish]. Watch the connection to the verb "to be" active in the sense of "ser -(s eR)" in Spanish. But he still is RA. Even with his power fully shielded, RA is still RA!

I see a reference in the pyramid texts to "Two Horizons". I suspect that is to do with the super light travel; from the "near Horizon" (Earth) to the "Far Horizon" (SY ON),with the wormhole "Apep" in between! And from the old Egyptian texts there is another problem. Like Daniel and Revelation it is hidden. [RE V(Y) EL A TY ON] There are the two stories of RA. In the first he is attacked by the serpent set by Isis, and in the second, he is intent on destroying his creation which is mankind, but relents. Again it is a "sekhet" [A red cat in terms of this hypothesis] who is sent to destroy humanity.

If I take the first incident to relate to the continent of Antarctica, when it was yet in a much warmer latitude, what then of the second text? Perhaps, like Revelation, it simply told of a "future time" which time is NOW history.

"Beware he who comes like a thief in the night"

In English terms that is a "simile". Does that Super communicate? "SY MY LE" "SY" = (Peace) MY=5 "LE" like EL" as "The". That would make "Sy with a number 5 tone control, which is not the same as "DA SY" which has a "one" tone control. But I have to ask; Do all words super communicate?

The answer to that is NO.

But there is a warning in that statement. Beware!

As I said earlier if a Red Cat was to come here, minus their Chariots of fire, he or she would be likely to be attacked by the powers here. By that I mean the governments. However it is possible that that attack would not be seen by the Governments. After all if they were simply attacking one of their own people, enforcing their own rules there would be no attack on the Red cats.

Not true. If the Red cat was within the body of a "human" and the attack meant that the body could not be "reconstituted" there would be a VERY REAL attack on that Red Cat in human form!

Allow that Red Cat to be living in say Lockerbie at a relevant date, then to use a super communicate sense, "without intending, yet causing" a red cat is killed.

Now if it was Tansarduron, there would doubtless be celebration here on Earth BUT it might be another Red Cat. Son or daughter of the MY K EL, or TAY HA TY. What would be the result?

Doubtless a request to RA by the Red Cats to withdraw from the planet. If necessary, a desire to remove their people immediately. How about a number. One, two? No, it might be much larger. Could it be 144,000! Needs a large force of Chariots of Fire to remove such!

Revelation 7, in this context is both interesting and cause for concern. Here is evidence of a "Second Passover". The twelve tribes in this connection may not be actual people, but rather creatures who are here as visitors. That could mean the "WHALES", the "TYGERS" and a number of others who have suffered terrible damage at the hands of humanity. And there is a danger to humanity if the creatures of Heaven request the removal of their beings which they have left here on Earth to ASSIST humanity! THAT it is a hidden danger is exemplified in the second story of RA. That is the story of how he is so upset with humanity that he departs from the planet! That is what, in terms of this hypothesis, is said he did after the Judicial Murder of the Lord the Krystyesus.

Suppose that I am only slightly wrong with this hypothesis. There was the third option, which I preferred not to take. That was not Kryst as the "son of God" in the physical sense but rather of an individual who was allowed access to "the Holy Spirit". Such an individual would in all respects be human, EXCEPT that they would possess the Understanding of Heaven. Upset that individual and he or she seeks to leave. The message is sent to those in HEAVEN to remove "THEIR" official. In this context their official IS the MANDATE OF HEAVEN.

If a Government says, "we cannot protect our own people"and among that people is "The Mandate of Heaven", such a Government is seen in Heaven's terms to be failing in its obligations to its own people to whom, in a legal sense, it owes a duty of care, in Heaven's terms.

That Government, which is NOT a "good Government" has to be contrasted with one which, fearing it cannot safely defend its own people, declares that "we will fight them (an evil regime which practices human blood sacrifice) on the beaches". The latter Government, though weak in a physical sense, is likely to receive a "gift" from Heaven!

Heaven has particular designs and requirements. And their requirements are not often those of the "local" Government. Revelation, Chapter 10, has to be watched. To describe him as is done, with a face "like the sun" is to make direct reference to RA. Does John mean, and is he warning of the IMMINENT arrival of RA, not immediately apparent with his power but just as a little man? The fire description is of an individual "burning with the Spirit" Again that Angel, is like Daniel, told to keep quiet. [It is a compass bearing as in POSITION – GALAXY-M51!] < WHITE CORDED SPORTING >.

Revelation, Chapter 15, again relating to the Seventh Angel has to be watched. I would say of the "Seventh Angel" that he is simply a "messenger". He is not NY TY R, but he could be, "AD ON NY", which would again fit for RA.

By the time I arrive at Revelation 15, it is more like the presence of RA himself. At verse 5, "The Temple in Heaven is open". If, as I have descried elsewhere, and if, as Isis prayed to ask the boat of RA to stop its travel in the sky, a Star Gate, adjacent to the nearby star was "opened" and several "Chariots of Fire appeared" then they might very well be descried by John as "The Tent of God's presence".

Revelation 16, 3 reminds me of a photograph, taken in Nippon of the dead dolphins surrounded by blood. They had been "killed" but the imagery fits nicely with that passage. Verse 7 again reminds of the importance of "MaTT".

Revelation 16, verse 15, "I AM coming like a thief." Given the I AM reference it is GOD himself, YH2UH or RA who is coming. And in essence he is NOT pleased! Verse 18 to 21 simply talks in terms of an Earth Crust displacement. Something RA has done before (the alternative version of the RA story) and something which regretfully MAY be in for the future.

I say MAY, and in blocks, for I am satisfied that it is NOT certain. That is not what Heaven wants. What is wants is to assist. But it cannot assist those who are unwilling to receive that assistance.

The Alpha and Omega part might simply be that there will be ONE attempt to communicate with humanity. It will not necessarily be by way of the SETI programme. It will be in terms as required by those in Heaven, and according to THEIR rules.

It may be up close and very personal, but not realised as such by the inhabitants of Earth. It may be an attempt by them to determine if they can "trust" humanity before they make contact. And if their assessment is that they cannot trust humanity, there may be no further contact ; and no obvious sign of contact. And worse they may designate this area of space as "dangerous" and to be avoided in the future; and prohibit the entry of humanity into their space!

No super light travel!

15
Misunderstandings

"What I understand others may not. They may not need my understanding and I must not force it upon them."

That phrase is to do with tolerance, and like the abhorrence of human blood sacrifice, which can properly be called the abomination of desolation, is important to progress.

So often intolerance and dogma will stifle truth and in consequence block the path to progress. That is still current even in the "enlightened democracies" of Western Europe. Religious "tolerance" may be taught, but that is difficult to apply where the "intolerant" seek to abuse and dominate the "tolerant". Fear creeps in slowly initially, but can be fuelled by a poor understanding and the results can be disastrous .Germany of the 1930/40s springs to mind.

While it might be thought that lessons would be learnt, that can take a very long time sometimes running to hundreds of years. In the scheme of thousands and millions of years it can seem almost insignificant, but many suffer through the desire of some to force "their understanding" on others; usually resorting to extreme force to make those not intending to comply, comply.

The old Egyptian "god" theology has gone, long overturned and I can comment on it. I am satisfied that many may not like my understanding of it, nor my interpretation of it, but what is important is that I can SAFELY make the comment, and within the confines of certain counties, to feel that my comment will be allowed a "fair hearing" and "freedom of speech". In essence I am trying to understand something which, while it might seem totally irrelevant to 21 Century Western Europe, nonetheless has in terms of this Hypothesis some important points to make.

I am comfortable with Mr. Budge's interpretation of the Egyptian "gods". One aspect that is particularly nice is that it appears to have been written before the First World War, and before the discovery of the treasures of "Tut ankh amen" and was an attempt to understand theology, long since gone, from a purely "scientific" point of view. Most of the magic spells are discounted(as I would be inclined to do today) but occasionally it is clear that some words were proving difficult to understand. Such comment of course attracts me to the super communicate.

Mr. Budge was giving some thought to the word "neter" for "god". I looked at it. At first sight it does not appear to super communicate. I look at the hieroglyph and I see the ½ sun; potentially a symbol of "RA".

Now I know that super communicate is concerned with phonetics. In a written form it needs a "tone" control, since the word, for example "neter1" does not mean the same as "neter 2" and there are 5 tones. In addition I have definite articles to consider, which I class as All powerful, Masculine, Feminine and two forms of neuter, one fairly "neutral" the other "dangerous".

If I refer briefly to "apep" as a serpent, I may have to pause a while to find the "super communicate". In that connection it is NOT apep, in that sense, but "ANA K ON DA". Da should not be present where a "snake " is concerned. An Anaconda is the biggest snake, but it is not poisonous. It is a "PY TH ON". It was also a species not know to the Egyptians, (unless they visited America, which Mr. Heyerdahl has shown they could have) but is a kind of snake which those in charge of the "matter transfer" equipment could easily remove from the "undiscovered" Americas to Egypt, to allow of Moses for his serpent to eat smaller serpents. Mr. Budge's comment that a huge serpent had been found in Egypt, if it had been carefully examined, may have turned out to be an "an a conda".

A figure like "Sekhet" seen standing on top of an anaconda and, with it in both hands, would be physically demonstrating again her dominance over apep, and again a very large apep! That it is not an actual "physical snake" I would contend is because it is shown with two heads, instead of a head and a tail [< FVRECKRAN > < VR RA KO THERA >, vulture K ON DA OR and snake VYPR]. In other words, <u>CORRECT NAMES</u> and <u>UNDERSTANDING</u> are <u>FUNDAMENTAL</u> for CONNECTIONS to the GALACTIC WORMHOLE TRAVEL and it is HIGHLY DANGEROUS if not correctly UNDERSTOOD. This is added here because of the Science of the New Hypothesis.]

Now I turn my attention to the word "god" and in the super communicate, for it is clear to me that from reading Mr Budge's text there is something here. What is it?

Vowels, A, E, I, O and U would be used in any attempt decipher a language. There is the possibility of the vowel not being written, so as to make "code breaking" more difficult. There is the concept of the "vowel" shift, so that where "A" is used the intention is to use "E", or "I" etc. In that situation "Apep" could become "Epap". Now with that in mind I turn again my attention to "Neter". Make the "E" into "eye" (which would tie in with the shape of the hieroglyph, with the sun over it) and I have "NeyeteyeRay" or shortened to "NY TY RA"

Now that has immediate super communicate connections. "Ny=voice" "Ty" equal to powerful" and "RA" being of course "RA, or YH2UH". So I translate that, of Sekhmet, as " The powerful voice of RA".

What it is really saying is that she is an important messenger from RA, Lord of Heaven. An angel of the Lord, in simple, easy to understand English!

As I have said earlier I regard her as being one of those who overflew on the night of the Passover, so in that connection, her description as an Angel of the Lord is immediately apparent.

If I turn my attention to that mightiest of Angels, Michael, and super communicate that, I am left with "MY K EL" In that connection MY is for the Red Cat city of that name, " K" is for the principal director of that city, and "EL" is as if to emphasis that. [I am aware of the Hebrew use of EL, and that does not cause a problem for it merely emphasizes "THE I AM THE"].

Now I am satisfied that that principal Red Cat director would help RA, and would be among the most powerful of his "messengers". As such he, with TAY HA TY keeps the other Red Cat, Tansarduron, who is military firmly in check. However, he is NOT likely to leave his planet.

If the word is indeed NY TY RA, what do the little flags at the beginning of that word mean as written in hieroglyph? From a super communicate point of view, I would use the words, "Kuraty1, kuraty1", so to that extent the word Ny TY R, NY TY R would be used in that style. It is done for Emphasis!

To confuse matters further, it would sometimes be used as a "Three" form word, thus "NY TY R, NY TY R, NY TY R", which would most closely correspond with the Christian "trinity" concept! That concept is to be found in "ME SY YA" which is simply translated as "3 Peace Masculine"! [The triple Flags represent the Triple Galaxy combination!]

In the word "Me Sy Ya" the tone control is seen with the number "3"(Me")and could be said to be "A man of Peace". However in terms of this Hypothesis to ask for "ME SY YA" is to ask for the "Trinity", that is "God with us". < FVRECKRAN HOSTING WHITE AU CORDED SPORTING >.

Now it is an essential element of this hypothesis that the Lord Krystyesus is alive and well and living in SY ON. What then happened in advance of the crucifixion, and why did the society is space withdraw? It did not withdraw entirely, because it resurrected him. What in essence they were saying is that, while he had not properly understood, they were satisfied that he had the ABILITY to understand AND had understood sufficiently so that he might be "taken up into Heaven".

Where was the problem? The religious leaders of the day had sought to trap Kryst and they were most upset by what they saw as blasphemy. What they did not grasp, [and what would probably still not be well understood today] is that the "misuse" of the sacred name is NOT for them to accuse, [that would be a Tansarduron approach] but for THE I AM THE. Thus in the end they did that VERY THING which they accused the Lord the Krystyesus of doing, and to a much more serious extent! They used the name of God to perform a human blood sacrifice. Matthew 25 "Let the punishment of his death fall on us and our children".

Now it is, in terms of this hypothesis, an absolute NO, NO to use the name of God for human blood sacrifice. And for the people of that time to say that Christ's blood was on their hands and that "of their children" is to negate that which

"Abraham" had done. You DO NOT harm your children because they are YOU and they are the next generation!

The comment of the people showed complete lack of wisdom and understanding. The consequences of that, and the judicial murder of Christ, are felt to this day. RA, (whom they did not regard by that name anyway) turned from them, ordered that His Temple in Jerusalem be overturned (which action was carried out years later by the Romans, when Jerusalem was sacked,) and following the resurrection of Christ which, it is the assertion of this Hypothesis that Ra or YH2UH arranged to have done, departed for M31 (Andromeda) Galaxy to turn his face resolutely from the planet!

Care has to be taken here with what is said. Effectively Ra simply "turned his face away" so that when the Jewish authorities caused an insurrection, which it was likely the Romans would crush, Ra was not available to help and protect them. Effectively "his wing" (in that sense the powerful Chariot of Fire) was not in the vicinity of the planet!

Christ is reported as saying that "if your eye offends you, pluck it out." For the purposes of this hypothesis, while that might have been pleasing to his listeners on Earth (particularly the religious ones with their love of Leviticus), his audience included not just the "human" population, but the KING of HEAVEN who was taking a very close interest in his progress. He DID regard him as his son, a new Adam, in that sense. However, that comment, is at complete variance with this hypothesis . [And is at VARIANCE with SPECIFIC REQUIREMENTS of certain VERY VERY VERY POWERFUL GALAXIES who supply material to this < FOOTSTOOL >] [< FVRECKRAN >, M 51, Whirlpool].

To that extent it is also, in terms of this hypothesis, at complete variance with those who sit in Heaven! If you pluck out your own eye you are involved in "self mutilation" (into which category circumcision could fall) and you perform the "abomination of desolation"). Circumcision is interesting, because it is an operation which can be "reversed" thereby demonstrating what his hypothesis is ALL about, namely that you do not cause human blood sacrifice unless you can reinstate! That makes Circumcision an extra special form of "super communicate" as does Paul's comment that "circumcision is NOT required." They are not mutually exclusive. They are telling the same thing. In essence Paul (who as Saul was "art and part" in the performance of human blood sacrifice as it is reported that he approved of the murder of Stephen) is saying that self mutilation does not serve any purpose. If those who are uncircumcised understand that self mutilation is NOT to be done there is no need to be circumcised.

Which brings me to the next point. Those that are circumcised, have to that extent succumbed to "human blood sacrifice" and thus it could be said they are therefor not acceptable in the sight of YH2UH. However if that was said, it would disclose a misunderstanding of what this hypothesis is all about. It also misses a DESIGN ELEMENT!

Circumcision having been done, at a particular time, in honour of YH2UH, and TECHNICALLY for health and DESIGN reasons, and with the understanding that you do not perform human blood sacrifice, because the operation can be reversed anyway, then there is NO "human blood sacrifice". Equally there is NO need to be made "uncircumcised" and indeed, if made "uncircumcised", it is again done in honour of YH2UH to the extent that it shows that "human blood sacrifice is NOT to be done" and is for DESIGN purposes.

While it may appear as a "circular " argument it is not. It is a very important "understanding". Thus if someone who had once been "circumcised" became "uncircumcised" there is no need for recriminations, and such individual would be likely to have a greater understanding than they would have had previously.

When Paul complained to God of the "thorn in his side," God said, famously and graciously; "My grace is sufficient for you." [Watch the use of the word "thorn"].

Where the "grace" of the Lord is upon an individual, that individual is truly blessed. This is to do with < HOSTING >. In terms of this hypothesis Paul was in difficulty for he was aware of his position with regard to Stephen. Having acquiesced in the murder of Stephen, he was in danger of not being acceptable to those in Heaven.

This is an IMPORTANT consideration. The words in Isaiah are quite clear. "Nothing which is harmful or hurtful will be admitted to SY ON". Essentially with the Trinity concept of YH2UH there is the "all powerful figure", amply illustrated by the huge fire disc which is the sun. In the strict and ordinary sense of that body, "Nothing attacks it......with impunity". However despite Amenhotep's IV view of it as the "aten", that discloses a quite incomplete understanding. The understanding is of the "MaTT" individual. And nothing which is hurtful or harmful must be allowed to come near to that "MaTT" Individual. It is HE who does not wish that. It is he who withdraws (as in the sense of removing himself to M31 in Andromeda) in terms of this hypothesis. It is that aspect which makes the position of God in Christ; and of the Judicial murder absolutely appalling. In doing that the people are actually saying, "We do not care if you were able to create the Whole Universe, are involved in its operation, we so HATE the concept of God being in a "little man", that we will show our utter contempt for God, simply by murdering the little man! We will make a good show of it though. Pilate washes his hands, and the Jews say they did not kill him, because it was done by the Romans.

While I may be comfortable with "certain" biblical texts because they super communicate, I must be on my guard to ensure that I am not misled by texts which appear to use a "super communicate word" to pretend that they are of "Heaven" and for "Peace", while in essence being entirely the product of man and NA SY in technical Galactic terms! Equally I have to be careful of super communicate texts which have been "adulterated" by the addition of impure texts, so as to make them appear quite impure.

I am beginning to suspect that Christ was indeed just a little man, but one into whom the "Spirit" had been poured. He was < HOSTING >. As <u>such he was "sensitive" equipment</u>, and would almost certainly not have been aware of exactly "how" the miracles were being performed. He would certainly have known if someone had "touched" him to ask for a miracle, but the exact timing of it, may have appeared strange.

At the same time, those in Heaven who were assisting with the miracles would have been concerned as soon as the comment was made about " plucking out of an eye, or the cutting off of a hand."

While the reinstatement can be done by those in Heaven, it is much more difficult to reinstate than to perform the "abomination of desolation". While I do not think the miracles would have "dried up" once the comment was made, there would almost certainly have been a reluctance to use them, particularly so by the inhabitants of Tyem. Those of MY and TAY may have continued there for a little while, but there would be no way that they would allow any to be performed before Herod or Pilate as "party tricks" to "prove" Christ's connection with them. That would also apply today to any demand for a miracle! Their equipment and their understanding is far to valuable to allow such. In the end of the day, their resurrection of Christ demonstrated their power, and it left it entirely to them as to when and HOW they returned, of what assessments they would make, and what judgments they would make. The authority which was given to Christ was given to him, and from their point of view, no one can stand "in persona Christi" save the Lord the Krystyesus HIMSELF.

Viewed from Tyem and from MY and TAY there would be amusement and disappointment at recent developments over the ordination of women "bishops". In their view there would be no problem because clearly despite the Church's position, the priests are Not "In Person Christi". It is simply NOT possible where there is a RISEN Christ. It shows to them a lack of understanding by that Church, somewhat akin to that of Christ concerning human blood sacrifice, and the plucking out of eyes. For the purpose of this hypothesis I have no doubt that such comment distressed and disappointed them, given that Christ had so clearly shown he was against human blood sacrifice when he refused to lift a stone to kill the woman caught in adultery. Accordingly for the purpose of this hypothesis, I am also required to " write in the sand" and to tear up Leviticus, because it actively promotes human blood sacrifice. Only one thing does Leviticus tell me, and that is that the Priests who made those rules, could have any clothes they liked, EXCEPT clothes like those worn by those in Heaven and the ATLANTYON's of SYON in particular. And in particular they would NOT be allowed to wear robes on which, in terms of Revelation, contained the "secret Name". Access to RA, to YH2UH, as the real individual, was to be denied them. As for the "Ark of the Covenant". Only those who are pure, who know not to use human blood sacrifice, may have access to it. What was it? I have said it was a Shield generator. But it may have been much more. It may be the "key" to the "Space time wormhole" As such, having seen their bloodlust, Ra would simply take his time to "remove" it from their "safe" custody, and put it where it was "available to him, if required", and in his terms, safe.

It is part of this hypothesis that those in Heaven[and in using that word I mean vast Galactic Civilisations] must despair as they watch and listen to the squabbles and bickering by those on Earth over matters of doctrine so far as relating to the Lord the Krystyesus. I might ask them to give me the Lord the Krystyesus to let him speak to the people directly, but their reply to me would be,

"Show to us that you properly understand."

"Am I not doing that," I would reply. "Are my words not faithful and true." Which of course brings me to Revelation!

"Not quite" they would say," What about those Egyptian texts you have been reading to assist with this hypothesis?"

"They do tend to suggest that just possibly, Heaven is real, but greatly misunderstood."

"Well, what have you spotted?"

I reply; "In Mr. Budge's work he talks of Tem and the minor "gods". These are not "gods of course, but rather "messengers". When on page 90 of volume 1, he gives a list of names of "minor" gods, referring to them by the pre name " AM", he is referring to the Grey cats of M 31 in Andromeda, who would be called, "Tyem AM ....Antachet........Tep........Het" for example. It is like a list of "minor" officials from different areas of "Tyem" who accompanied the "Lord Tyem" during an earlier "visit". It may be that the "hated" old Egyptian Texts have been storing valuable information for Thousands of years, and are still storing it. The texts are not "wrong" they are simply misunderstood. Thus the figure of Nut. My < POSITION > is noted.

I am conscious that the word "Nu" is described by Wallis Budge as being to the Egyptians "a boundless watery mass" out of which had come into being, the heavens and the earth, and everything that is in them." Vol 1 page 283. In essence, that is what the theory of "evolution" actually now says. It says it differently but it is the same. How much progress then in 7000 years? But in terms of this hypothesis it might be 21,000 years or even longer!

For the "<u>boundless watery mass</u>" would be a fair description of this < FOOTSTOOL > as it spins around the local star!

And what of those other strange primordial figures, masculine and feminine. Take as masculine, "Atoms" and feminine "Electrons" and there is an understanding, which while it may have seemed convoluted to the primitive peoples of Egypt, means something to those who caused it to be written, and to those who are genuinely seeking the Truth!

The main thrust of this hypothesis is that THE GOD, YH2UH and AMEN RA are one and the same; and MORE importantly HE IS A REAL INDIVIDUAL! That requires that everything which has been said has to be viewed carefully, and looking for The Truth. Revelation is probably simply warning of an impending visit from AMEN RA or other < VISIBLE INVISIBLE >. And here there is another problem. When many years ago I first thought of this, I wanted those in Heaven to come (in the future tense). It was only once I had made the comment that I appreciated that I could not ask for them to come (future) if they HAD come (past or present tense!)

If RA HAS or IS visiting, perhaps it is too late to do anything. If Revelation is that the "end" means simply that RA will leave, then there will be much gnashing of teeth when the Chariots of Fire appear to remove RA. However, perhaps all it tells is of a "future" event so there is yet time to prepare for that visit and hopefully not to be caught unawares. That may be more difficult than it appears. In terms of this Hypothesis, even and I have to say especially, the Tansarduron has bowed to the authority given to the Lord the Krystyesus. Yet on this planet millions do not do so. That is an assessment I make because it is quite obvious. How much easier for RA to make the same assessment!

There are difficulties with this hypothesis. Not least of these is the position of super communicate. If I change the "e" of the hieroglyphs, to the "Y" that makes " Seth" as "SY TH" or as extended "SY Tay Ha" In that shape it again tells of the Red Cats from Taydaranakushton, where the head of the city is "Tay HA TY" (Thoth). Has there been a fight in Taydaranakushton?

I have suggested elsewhere that there was a fight and "they were all jealous of RA and the world he had created so they set out to destroy it."

In many respects with the spread of disease the world is under attack. It needs the "new Discoveries" to make its people safe. It also needs protection from those who are seeking to destroy it.

There may be no way for those who sit in Heaven to "avoid" taking action of the kind described in Revelation. It may be necessary to have a visit from the red and Grey Cats and to have a "Further Passover";which is a reprogramming exercise and repositioning of the < Footstool > . Such would require to be authorised by RA, and such would almost certainly require a visit, if not by RA, then by one of the officials of his "justice department". It would be my submission, and part of the hypothesis that the "seventh Angel" of Revelation is indeed that "Justice official" of a particular department, number 7.

Equally I am satisfied that much of the old Egyptian theology was not even understood by those who practised it for thousands of years. It is much older. Their understanding of the "Tuat", which is now regarded as "hell", I would suspect simply described "The Heavens". That is partly because of the TT in the word. [Territory of the King of Heaven] [Even the expression "King of the Bottomless Pit", may in fact mean the "King of Heaven" if the Universe itself is regarded as a kind of bottomless pit!] If the contradiction in terms is correct what the people in ancient times feared was "individuals who came from the darkness" that is "from the NIGHT SKY". That is still a very relevant fear!

For all the power of the mighty countries of this world, NONE can protect even one of their people from unwelcome advances from those in space! What in essence this hypothesis says is that ALL on this world are the property of AMEN RA, or YH2UH, and except such "aliens" have permission to be here, this is a planet to be avoided. And those who are of the Christian denominations (while they work for Peace) are indeed under his wing. Those who are not of such, again if they work for Peace, are likely to be deemed to be under his wing. However for such other categories, they have not done as Christ asked, that they declare him to the Father, and that puts them at considerable risk from being declared NAHETRA DYAN IS [Not my people, by AMEN RA]

Like Pitcairn Island, this planet is probably in a remote and largely uninhabited part of this galaxy, so that "alien" action is not likely. At least in the terms of 10's of thousands of years.

In terms of this hypothesis, I am writing this because I would like those in Heaven to visit and to bring with them the miracles. However even as I write and revise this I am conscious that many on this world do not want the miracles, and they and those in Heaven are MOST unwelcome. As it was in Christ's time, so it is now.

Many, mostly in poor countries, need the miracles. In terms of this hypothesis these are entirely possible. All it takes is one Chariot of fire. However in asking for example, for the Grey Cats to visit, I have to bear in mind that they are likely to be unwelcome. Given my feeling that I may be unwelcome within certain Christian Churches, how would the Red or Grey cats be viewed? Almost certainly as hostile, which is unfair ; especially when they are in a position to perform the miracles. And they are after all, part of God's creation, creatures of Heaven and with more in common with God in Heaven than humanity.

The message of this text may be viewed as unwelcome by the Churches, because it challenges cosy dogmas, and seeks to give to my Lord the Krystyesus, ALL AUTHORITY, as was required by the King of Heaven, rather than to place it in the hands of Governments and politicians, who over the centuries have murdered many, and in some cases, millions of their own people!

Essentially it is all there, and has been for millennia, but it has been greatly misunderstood and greatly misused and abused. Revelation essentially means that something which is hidden, is revealed. Daniel (DA NY EL) is instructed to seal up the words of the book until the end comes [Daniel, 12 vs 9].

I for my part do not wish to open a book I am not supposed to. And yet I am now much more comfortable with this work than ever I was before.

I have a brief look again at Ezekiel. Chapter 30 is interesting, with its list . Watch also a little phrase in Ezekiel 20, vs 22 about not bringing dishonour to the Name of the Lord. And in terms of that text it is spoken by the "Sovereign Lord himself!"

Like DA NY EL it is, I consider, a super communicate text. Thus while its tends to suggest times which may be "times Future" relative to the writer, and times "past" as of this date, it may be "repetitive" or indeed speak of "future events "yet to come! In super communicate terms it may have another purpose entirely!

In super communicate terms, "ES E KY EL", I might take means, as is said several times, that the "Sovereign Lord speaks", that the King of Heaven speaks. Perhaps that is also done in Revelation. However, before turning to Revelation, I am going to look briefly at three options with regard to my Lord the Krystyesus. And of him, in Christian terms, it can be said "God Spoke!"

16
The Lord the Krystyesus

In this chapter I am going to look at him in three forms. The first is as "God". That conforms with Christian teaching quite nicely. The second is of him the "Son of God". That likewise conforms to Christian teaching. The third, and potentially the most dangerous, is him as a "human" individual, into which the spirit...the Holy Spirit has been put for a "short time".

I had not really considered the last as being the most important when I first thought of it, but that ties in nicely with A to Z and of "Alpha and Omega." I have considered the super communicate and "AhuraMazda", as "RA MA Z DA". The One God"

What then of Christ? First as God.

Essentially that is the most straightforward. It does not tie in with text as written particularly where Christ refers to "Our father which art in Heaven". It could be said in that connection that he is descended from "atenists" and that when he went into Egypt he went to relatives who were of that persuasion.

But God, in the sense of "God with us", the creator of the whole universe, would NOT make such a comment. However I have to be careful. I have, for the purpose of this hypothesis, put my Lord the Krystyesus in Heaven and at a Distance of 15,000 light years, and in huge city of SY ON .

In repeating the Lord's prayer, it is to the King of Heaven that prayers are offered. In the sense that that is Christ, that is fine, but the difficulty here is how does "God" pray to "himself". That could be said to be the difficulty with the "Trinity" concept. However, if the individual can be "split" then the "father" may indeed be able to manifest himself as a "small man", thus the MaTT individual which is RA seated with "the two feathered crown". He does not cease to be God simply because he looks like a little man, and is unchanging, although he appears to "grow old."

But "GOD" in the sense of the individual who created everything knows exactly where he is going, and would be much more able to speak plainly, and yet at the same time hide from his actual audience the real meaning. That is not done in the gospels.

Matthew 18, at verse 4 is interesting. Jesus says, "the greatest in the kingdom of Heaven is the one who humbles himself and becomes like this child."

I can take that in super communicate. The "child" in that sense is humanity. The "greatest in the Kingdom of Heaven" is the one who gives up the power of Heaven and "becomes like a child" (that is becomes human). Taken in that light, God can then become a human, while leaving his "troops" in Heaven. But is that a proper application of the super communicate?

The passage in Matthew 17 about the transfiguration is interesting. The voice from Heaven says, "this is my own dear son, with whom I am pleased-listen to him." Note the super communicate use of "I AM". But the words are there at the end. "Listen to him" are pure super communicate. I would translate from the Atlantyon as "Amen daren sy asta kata". "Amendaren" is the verb to listen. Sy, of course I have already said is "peace" and "kata" simply means "at present". "Amen" of course has connotations with the god of Egypt.

Now "Syastakata" and "Suyaka" are two super communicate Atlantyon words in frequent usage, and their position in a sentence is important.

"Amendaren Suyaka" has a similar meaning to "amendaren syastakata, but because of the "sy" element the latter super communicates quite differently.

If access was required to a "super computer" such as the type which was voice activated, and it was commanded to do something "suyaka" it might operate for a time, but it would ultimately cease to respond . Thus in the use of the shield generator, for example, a command for it to operate "now" [Ya Kata] would doubtless operate it for a short time. But to ask it to continue using "Ya kata" would cause it to fail, because that is not correct super communicate.

In Western Europe, and in America and Nippon, when using electrical equipment in particular, "passwords" are used which have to be input to make the equipment work. If a mistake is made the equipment will shut down. That is what it has been designed to do for security purposes.

If I take that concept to the equipment used by RA, it is entirely possible- (most certainly is the case) that the equipment contains various levels of passwords and the POSITION of the USE of the PASSCODES is IMPORTANT. This relates to < PROTOCOL TERRITORIES >.

Now if I take "God" as the man Christ, he does not make a mistake with his "super communicate" unless it is a DELIBERATE mistake. He can input to his computer what he is required to say, so that "apparently contradictory" phrases are in the text simply to "protect" the Password. It is probably possible to shut down the computer, "by Accident" so that in an unfortunate incident, the computer may not recognise "its masters voice". I would regard that as "unlikely" but in the concept of "God with us" and certainly with regard to the life of Christ, I have to allow for him to have a MUCH greater understanding than even the most intelligent individual on the planet today.

It is not reported if anyone asked him, "How does the star work?" That in many respects is a question for today [< PLASMA >] and would have been way over the heads of the Israelites of Christ's time. However, if I am correct with this hypothesis, to make such comments in Egypt in particular, would have been likely to rouse the interest of the RA priests, especially if they were of the old tradition.

In that connection with "god" as "GOD" he may have wanted to see Egypt, and possibly as a child to interact with some of their people. He would have known, even before setting foot on the planet, where he could go to find those who understood. He would also have known where to go to get even an old piece of equipment which he could use to perform some miracles. But why in his capacity as GOD should he go to such lengths to "hide" from his people? In the sense as Christ, he did not hide from them. He spoke so plainly that he was judicially murdered. [I make no apology for using that term, which I am sure some judges might find offensive. It is used because it is a super communicate term. It should not make a "just" judge uncomfortable.]

Pilate made a serious mistake in his judgment. In Matthew's gospel, at Chapter 27, verse 24 we have Pilate washing his hands and saying, "I am not responsible for the death of this man"

Oh, yes you are Pilate. And it is not a pantomime! <u>How many had you murdered judicially before, and how many after? Hand washing will not do.</u> It has assisted symbolically to tell future generations about "miscarriages of Justice", but like Pilate they have just done the same! And they continue to this day with human blood sacrifice, quoting sometime the "eye for eye rules", conveniently forgetting about Daniel's warning about the "abomination of desolation" which in any event they have not understood.

But most telling of the figure of Christ being "God" in that sense, is in Matthew Chapter 27, at verse 45, when at the moment of Crucifixion Jesus cries out, "My God, My God, why did you abandon me?" <<< FFT >>>. The words do not mean what they say. It is a <<< AGREED PASSWORD >>> which <<< HIDES >>>.

The God who made everything does not say that. If he has forgotten his password for access to the chariot of Fire, he might have cried out in utter frustration that he was rejected from the matter transfer equipment, which would certainly have enabled him to step down from the cross. To have used the equipment to step down from the cross would have seriously frightened those watching. Doubtless it would have given a heart attack to quite a few! Consequently such a move would not have been a good idea!

Mark 15, gives Jesus at verse 34 with a similar phrase, "My God, My God, why did you abandon me?" Not much apparent super communicate in that. Two versions with the same comment.

Luke 23 at verse 44 gives a different view. His version is atmospheric. He begins thus :- "It was about 12 o clock when the sun stopped shining and darkness covered the whole country until three o clock; and the curtain in the temple was torn in two. Jesus cried out in a loud voice, "Father into my hands I place my spirit! He said this and died."

<u>The emphasis here is quite different, and here is the beginning of "super communicate".</u>

Firstly to modern eyes there is an eclipse. But that would only last a short time. This lasts 3 hours! It does not look like an eclipse. With our modern technology we would ask questions, but in Christ's time, it would be seen as an eclipse, except that it lasted a bit longer than usual. However if this hypothesis is correct with a number of its suggestions, what is happening here is the "chariot of fire" or a number of them have positioned themselves between the planet and the sun, so as to blot out the light for 3 hours. Alternatively they may have activated the wormhole, to depart, and that would have caused a drain on the brightness of the local star causing it to dim markedly .

From a super communicate point of view, this passage would have been written some time after the event, and it is likely the writer was, with assistance from others, trying to recall the various events which happened. Thus the comment about the veil of the Temple (not a thin thing) being cut in two. [An easy thing for those with matter transfer equipment and laser weapons to do!].

In John 19 at verse 30 Jesus is quoted as saying at the crucifixion, "It is finished" That begs the question as to what was finished.

If I am looking at it from a purely "God " point of view, is it intended to mean that the whole of creation- the whole massive programme, which created the Universe in the first place, is finished? What then of God, who has just been murdered?

I need to look at the Resurrection. Taking the words from John, I look to see what he says.

He reports Mary as saying to the risen Christ, "Rabboni" [John 20 verse 16.] But RA ON NY is super communicate for "the Voice of Ra, Director of SY ON" from the "AD ON NY" and in longer form for AD in super communicate ATLANTYON is "ADATRAN". And note Mary makes the comment in response to the VOICE of Christ; the NY element.

Christ himself says to her, verse 17, "Do not hold on to me, because I have not yet gone back up to the father."

Again, in the person of God as God, he would not be talking in terms of "going up to his father." As part of a trinity he might say that.

However if he is returning to the SY ON in the sky, he might possibly be using the wormhole, using the "path through the eye of RA to SY ON." In the sense of a people to whom RA is real, he is telling her that all is well. RA is real.

I will now consider Jesus as the "Son of God" and in two senses. As a real son, and by "ad ro ga da" [Adoption] [Ad op TY ON] to use an English word in super communicate!

II

I had regarded this as my preferred option. Looking at Matthew, 1 18 -22[p4 GNB and Isaiah, 7 at 14 [p673 GNB], there is the story of the virgin birth, and Isaiah' comment. The passage in Isaiah does not specifically relate to a "virgin" but to a young girl. That is consistent with Mary being with child -in the normal way- and Joseph being rather unsure. The angel of the Lord reassures Joseph and he is with Mary when the child is born, in Bethlehem. Why then the importance of the "virgin" birth?

To the people I am describing in this hypothesis there is no problem with a "virgin" birth. With our understanding of human fertility, it is possible today for "in vitro" fertilization to take place, and for "sperm" to be inserted- and that despite objections from certain Christian traditions.

That still leaves this Hypothesis with the individual in Heaven "donating " his sperm! [I can see some church official squirming at the thought, but such an attitude displays a complete lack of understanding.] In that situation it is a fantastic "gift" given to Mary, and she is indeed particularly "special" to be chosen as such.

Matthew also tells of the visitors from the East with their gifts of Gold, Frankincense and Myrrh. They had seen the star. Well if they were watching the night sky it is entirely possible they would have seen the "Chariot of Fire", and it would have looked like a star to them! And it is likely to have been in place for the 9 months of the gestation period, just to ensure that there was no problem with the delivery of the child, Jesus.

Now in Matthew 2, verse 13 to 15, Joseph is instructed to take the child and his mother to Egypt, and "to stay there until I tell you to leave" Verse 13. I find that strange. The Chariot of Fire could destroy any individual who made any unwelcome approach to the child. It possesses matter transfer equipment and while that can be used creatively, it can also be used "destructively". It could reduce an individual to less than single atoms; less even than "strings" of the so called "string theory!"

For the Child to be taken to Egypt there has to be a purpose and that offered in Matthew 2 at verse 15 [KYV page 4.], while it may be technically correct, so that what the Lord had said through the prophet would come true; "out of Egypt I have called my son" I would consider only to be part of the story.

Given that in terms of this hypothesis RA and YH2UH are the same individual, it is likely the "Father" wished the child to see the foreign territory of Egypt. It may also have been important, and in terms of this hypothesis also necessary that he was introduced to Egypt with its many "Gods" so that Christ would be allowed the opportunity to "Understand" what his father wished him to say.

Again in that connection if he is made up from semen taken from a heavenly individual it is likely that the genetic make up would have been slightly different, and he may have understood that what the Egyptians talked of as "gods" were nothing but "NY TY R", which is "messengers of his father in Heaven". As such it is even possible that on one occasion he met one of the "Red" or "Grey cats". Given such a meeting, while he might have been inclined to feel they were indeed "gods" the < TYGER > in particular of Tyem, would have been specific that it was a "human type creature" and ATLANTYON, who was The I AM THE, in essence the one who was God.

Again in Matthew's gospel, Jesus is brought forth from Egypt and settles in Nazareth, and in due course is baptised by John, at which point at Matthew 3, verse 17 there is the famous comment, "this is my own dear son, with whom I am pleased."

Again the words "I AM" in the translation. Very important.

Matthew then leads on to the temptation of Jesus. In my translation the word "devil" is used rather than the terms "satan". But for the purposes of this hypothesis I am taking the individual as "Tansarduron".

Now Tansarduron will have access to a Chariot of Fire at this point and it would be possible for him to make the appearance of changing "stones" into bread using the matter transfer equipment. But it is not a straight swap. Stones are "in organic" whereas bread is "organic". He would require to remove the stones and "replace" them with bread which would need to be taken from the Chariot of Fire's on board stores. Yes it would look like stones into bread, but by a very advanced technology. However Matthew records that there was no such transformation.

There is then the passage about Jesus being "taken" to the highest point of the Temple PYLON. If that was done "in fact" it is a demonstration of the matter transfer equipment, and one which would have been frightening for Jesus ; except that with the "heavenly" genetic make up, he might not have been too bothered. This text here about throwing himself down is interesting, because without the matter transfer equipment to protect him, it would have been likely to produce a human blood sacrifice if he had thrown himself off! Possibly a very early test of Jesus by those in Heaven to see if he really did understand about NO human blood sacrifice.

The next he is taken to a "very high mountain". But even from "Everest" it is not possible to see the "whole world". To see most of it, you have to be in "space". Was he then taken into the Chariot of Fire, and allowed to see the whole world spinning in space?

That is a very best test that could be made. Not only Israel, but Rome, America, Asia, the pacific continents. The whole world is offered to him.

From that vantage point high in space, Jesus is presented with a powerful individual. He may even have seen the red cat, Tansarduron.

Christ's reply is given, "Go away Satan! The scripture says, "Worship the Lord your God and serve only him!"

Matthew then reports the Devil left Jesus.

Presumably, although it is not said, if Jesus had been matter transferred, he was put back where he was. However that may not have been the case, because it does then say; "and Angels came and helped him [Jesus]". Jesus is away for 40 days and nights. With a Chariot of fire, 40 days is a long time. The journey to Dras, at 15,000 light years takes but 5 days! In 40 days it would be possible to cross this Milky Way Galaxy!

Now it would be part of this Hypothesis that the Milky Way Galaxy is ruled by the Red < TYGER > but it is just one of Millions of Galaxies in the Universe. The Grey < TYGER > is in charge of M 31 in Andromeda, but at 2.2 million light years distant, it would take a little more than 40 days. And yet again, for those who have "overcome Apep" and who can operate a "wormhole", perhaps not. However I do not think that likely or necessary.

Now I am quite comfortable with Matthew 5, which is the Sermon on the Mount (verses 1 to 12). However, I have to be concerned with Verses 17 to 32. This supports Leviticus, and that as I have said previously is of considerable concern because of the Human blood sacrifice in Leviticus.

In terms of this hypothesis, when such comment is heard, particularly by those in Heaven, there is a serious concern. How much does Christ understand? It is fine to say, verse 18, not the least point nor the smallest detail of the law will be done away with- not unto the <u>end of all things</u>.[The alternative ending I am offered p5 GNB is that -not until all its teachings come true." Not terribly helpful that!

Matthew Ch 5 at verses 38 and 39 is much more helpful. Commenting on the "eye for eye rule" Jesus says not to take revenge on someone who wrongs you. But even that causes problems. < Context>. That you <u>RESIST</u>. DO NOT EVIL. It is intended to mean that for minor assaults, one minor smite might be forgiven, so turn the other check. But if then hit on the other, RETALIATION IS APPROPRIATE, probably after a delay and much thoughtful contemplation. See comments on SPARTA and ALEXANDER and < HOSTING >. < FVRECKRAN >.

What is the father's reaction to the Judicial murder of his son the Christ? It is as Christ says, he does NOT take revenge.

He does not "immediately" flatten Jerusalem, nor vaporise Rome, both things which with a Chariot of Fire he could easily have done. No he simply demonstrates his power by resurrecting his son, and then giving to him "all authority in heaven and on Earth" (Matthew 28 vs 18).

As a comparative exercise I check Mark's gospel, and I pause at Mark 7 at verse 6. In marked contrast to Matthew 5, verse 18, we have at verse 6

"How right Isaiah was when he prophesied about you. You are hypocrites, just as he wrote."

"These people honour me with their words but their heart is really far away. It is no use for them to worship me because they teach man made rules, as though they were God's laws!" Clear criticism here of the rules of Leviticus;certainly from this hypothesis point of view when they try to justify human blood sacrifice.

The four Gospels give "different" views of the same scene, and that is probably vitally important. Each individual as they heard Jesus words would have reacted to them differently.

Earlier in this text I was ready to throw out all of Leviticus, just because of the blood sacrifice aspect. However certain "rules" which are good from a "hygiene" point of view merit consideration. But as Jesus pointed out, they are only sensible man made rules, NOT God's law. What then do I make of the passages in Matthew and others which conflict?

I have no doubt that it was difficult for Christ. With a direct link to his father, he would have been able to check the rules and be much more critical. But I suspect that was NOT the purpose of this mission. He was not to "break" the people but rather to give them hope, and hope to millions elsewhere who were suffering under the yoke of oppressive rulers.

In essence the real words, the super communicate words, are there. They may appear to be disguised, but in the actual events as they happened the super communicate words are there. The miracles are clear evidence, in terms of this Hypothesis, of the interaction of the beings of Heaven! Mark 8 at verse 12 is interesting. This passage records Jesus comments about the Pharisees demand for a miracle. It is reported that Jesus gave a deep groan, and replied, "Why do the people of this day ask for a miracle? No I tell you! No such proof will be given to those people."

The demand for a "miracle" is much stronger today than it was in Jesus time. And in terms of this Hypothesis, I would suspect that those in Heaven will be equally determined that they will not provide such.

"How dare the panel for doctrine ask us for a miracle" might be a comment made by a "NY TY R" in charge of a Chariot of Fire, perfectly able to perform the miracles!

But again in terms of this Hypothesis, the father's anger was very great at the murder of his son. He allowed the Romans to enter the city some years later, and to destroy his Temple, and to this day it has not been rebuilt!

For whom are they waiting? ME SY YA?

From the viewpoint of the NT TY R Jerusalem today is not an acceptable place for them to set foot, far less is it acceptable to he who is ME SY YA!

III

What then of the third option, Jesus just as a little man.

Essentially that is the same . What is worse is that the "feeling" of the Spirit is much weaker within the figure of Christ, so that he is far less certain of where he is going. He is very much "in his father's hands" all the way. To that extent it is a much more severe test for Humanity. Accordingly I am going to discount that one, for if such a test was set, it is likely humanity would fail. In many respects the warning is given, "Beware He who comes like a thief in the night!" That might be trying to warn of such a test!

It is my view, and part of this Hypothesis that Heaven is not trying to be difficult with humanity, rather it wishes humanity to learn, without force. To that extent with the figure of Christ they have set an example, whether it is option 1, 2 or three. And three allows also for the individual to be come "son of God" by adoption! It just leaves it where Heaven wants it.

What then of the four versions of the Gospels? Where is the super communicate?

In essence it is part of this Hypothesis that Heaven wants the people to learn, and to learn by example. The people must "find their way" and to that extent Heaven will only assist once the way has been disclosed.

Matthew, Mark, Luke and John, which super communicates best? John talks in terms of the word, but I do not think that is the version Heaven would prefer as being "most accurate". I have already established here that Matthew contains some passages which support Leviticus, which clearly this Hypothesis cannot support. That leaves Luke and Mark. Luke has within it the "K" letter which is material from a super communicate point of view. So also does Mark. If I change "Mark" of the English, to the form "MA R K US", it brings it much closer to the super communicate. To that extent, "us" being equivalent of "Son" "K" being of SY ON, R being of "RA" and "MA" as the number One.

Son of RA, < AMEN >.

This one tells most accurately of our presence. This one is closest to a "video" of the whole scene! And its text reflects Heaven's feelings.

So this hypothesis goes with Mark's version.

I am well aware that Christian literature as of this date is vast. But in terms of this Hypothesis, I must remember that "a large library will not assist in understanding unless it works are of highest quality, while a few works of quality may be of greater benefit than the biggest library".

This Hypothesis asserts that the creatures of Space are Real, are very powerful, and are trying to assist. In essence they have left in these various texts their "calling card" but they will not respond until <u>a proper and correct understanding is demonstrated.</u>

Thus far it has taken 2000 years since Christ for this Hypothesis to be put on paper, and if I take with it over 5000 years of Egyptian history, possibly far longer, it has taken some 7000 years plus for this to be understood. And I am still concerned with it. The prospect that the old Egyptian texts have some considerable importance to the understanding of astrophysics seems to be strange. And yet this Hypothesis has made that connection.

What is important is "The Truth". I am trying to find the Truth amid a morass of lies and deceit, of deliberate cover ups and distortion. All I have is the words of "super communicate" like a "code".

I have read with interest the two works thus far written on the "bible code". As I now view it they are working with the wrong material and with the wrong code. I do not dispute that such a "code" as they seek may be in the works. However I would suspect that the mathematical code if it is there, is simply to divert those who could make use of the "super communicate" version away form that, until those who sit in Heaven are satisfied that they wish the connection made, to release the super communicate and to speak!

Super communicate does mean words of power. They can be sufficiently powerful to cause considerable distress, pain and suffering. That is NOT the intention of this work.

Rather the intention is to speak the words of Peace, and to let the Spirit guide.

17
The Risen Lord

This aspect is fundamental to this Hypothesis. Without it the Hypothesis would not have been written. It is that Kryst is risen in FACT. Not as a "belief" but in the reality as a fact. It is to deal with that as a fact that I have written this Hypothesis.

From a Christian point of view this should have been easy. The difficulty is that as part of this Hypothesis, I require to view it from Heaven's perspective. In that connection I have to deal with the days between Good Friday and Easter Monday!

The Apostles creed is a good starting point. It ends with the word: <<< AMEN >>>
While I might view it as words "adopted by man" and while I am happy to repeat, the final word is the important one. <<< AMEN >>>

This is a <<< STYLE >>> point and a very important one. Thus my insistence on the King James Version.

As I said this text is FROM HEAVEN's view and as the New Hypothesis asserts there is a SPECIFIC UNDERSTANDING.

However for the purposes of this Hypothesis, it is not a question of "belief ", it is one of knowledge; that dangerous word "Gnosis". That which nearly caused a schism in the early Church!

The early Church reacted in a way typical of it for thousands of years. It suppressed the views it "disagreed with", including brutally by human blood sacrifice!

But I hope we have come some way from that. Some 2000 years. A very short period in the time continuum of space!

So what is the position in this Hypothesis?

I could say that following on the crucifixion Christ found himself before the Tansarduron. He had *effectively* descended into hell. That parts conforms with the Apostles Creed. However since he would see the Red Cat Tansarduron, simply in a room, the reference to "descended into hell" is not entirely appropriate, since Tanarduron like Ra, was in a Chariot of Fire which was orbiting the planet!

[Since drafting this I have to be careful. My feeling now is that it was Tansarduron to whom Christ spoke first and then to Tyem; not necessarily to his father RA!]

Christ is before the Tansarduron. He is weak, since he had been brought thought the matter transfer equipment. That is done "in the twinkling of an eye"-very quickly. By the time his body is removed from the cross his spirit is in the matter transfer equipment and he is being rebuilt. The old body is of no importance. [Regretfully in terms of this Hypothesis I have to discount the "grail" stories as fiction, although one of the books mentioned in the bibliography made some interesting points . It may be that those in Heaven can use the "grail myth" as suits their needs.]

It is carried to the tomb where it is then sealed. Essentially no human can enter it. [It does not matter for the purposes of this Hypothesis if the body is "stolen" as reported in some of the texts. You can't steal what the matter transfer equipment has already taken!]

His old body, broken and destroyed it taken up by the matter transfer equipment and the particles "re used" but NOT in the new body which has already been processed from material already held in the matter transfer equipment!

Although in a new body, he is weak. He is brought before the Tansarduron, who Christ clearly sees as a human type figure, red of colour and looking like a cat ; to Christ like a Tyger headed individual.

This Hypothesis has the conversation going like this, and spoken entirely by the Tansarduron.

"Lord Krtystyesus. You think you are descended into hell. Nothing could be further from the truth! Ah, you are worried, but not too much. I do not frighten you. Indeed I have been told not to do that.

That is right, by your father.

I hate this. I so loved it when Pilate failed. It was a test set for him, and for your fellow countrymen. And they failed it beautifully. I was worried about Pilate, because the Romans think their Justice system so wonderful, but he fell for it all.

Every last bit. I loved the scene with the water. Wash his hands would he? I will get him in due course. He will be handed over to me. Then he will know what it is like to be crucified. Perhaps that is too good for him. Perhaps we could use him to fuel the local star!

Ah, you are having a little difficulty grasping all this!

You have seen a creature like me before? Where? In Egypt. But not a Red Cat. A Grey one. If only you knew how far they had travelled!

I digress. Your father, has given specific instructions, which I am to obey, that I am to make it clear to you that "all authority in heaven and earth" is to be given to you. And you are to be allowed back to the planet to tell your disciples. I have agreed to stay away from the planet with all my officers for a few hundreds of years. I will be watching. I am not really bothered because from what I have seen your followers will make a mess of it. They will not do it deliberately, but those in positions of power will not like their power, especially when your father allows them to receive the "Spirit", and they will want that power. But it will be under your control!

My proper name is Tansarduron. It has been a style for some time to shorten it to "satan". I am the head of a city of "Sarduron" and in that capacity my title is as "Tan". There are other Red Cats whom you will meet. Your father's friend is the Red Cat, Tay Ha Ty. I am military, a general if you like.

You thought he was an Ibis. That was a ruse. Done quite deliberately to hide him and to allow me a much freer hand.

In your father's eyes, you have done well. And even I congratulate you. It will not be easy though. Many will seek to pollute and dilute your words. Over the centuries to follow there will be much wickedness done in your name. But it will not be done by you.

What I can tell you is that your father will give to me all those who deny you. He may excuse some, taking them under his wing, but for the majority, they will be mine. I will be given some real horrors! Fortunately for a long time they will think that I am a fiction. But as you have discovered, I am not!

We are powerful, Lord Krystyesus. We have been here before. As you drink the Passover wine, you remember a prior visit, as do your countrymen, but they have lost its meaning.

Now your father is going to institute a New Covenant. Those who partake of this must remember your suffering and ensure that they do not repeat it. But as with much here, they will make up their own rules, and that will cause much bloodshed. More victims for me!

Why do I hate humanity? I don't really hate them. One of my predecessors did. Your father threw him out of Heaven. Took away his gift of eternal life, and he is no more. My species are still here as you can see, but that individual is not.

We have learnt much since that incident. We can assist your father. There is no need for him to exercise his tremendous power to destroy. We can be nearly as efficient.

I have agreed with your father to leave this planet and to hand it over to you. That is what I am now doing. You will now be master of it all, everything from the smallest plant to the most powerful creature. All will require to bow to your name. Your name will be made MOST Holy together with that of your Father. He will maintain his secret name, but subject to that, all authority is given to you. And I accept that.

You wonder still where you are? There is no trickery. You are within your Father's kingdom. In Heaven. And no, I am not with your father. I may speak with him and he with me .

I see you are still confused. You will have a long time to learn. Although they worshiped "Cats" in Egypt they did not understand. Not at all. They had been given the opportunity, but what with business and wars, they had well and truly lost their way. As you see I am not a "little cat" in the sense that people keep pets. I am more powerful than a Tyger. Have you seen a Tyger? They are like lions, but bigger, more unpredictable and dangerous.

Perhaps in some 1000 years they may understand what it is all about. But your father is furious. He is going to overturn all the temples to RA, is going to order to be pulled down the Temple at Jerusalem- although not immediately- and is going to destroy all.. ..well nearly all the sacred writings of RA. Again if the people are good, he may allow them to discover the text, but whether he will release the understanding in it, that is entirely different.

Today you are risen and alive, Lord Krystyeus thanks to the Glorious power of your father. You are not handed over to me. You are here that I MUST accept your dominion over me. Yes it rankles, and I don't like it, but I am not stupid like my predecessor. I value my "eternal life", which is in the gift of your father and I do not wish it removed from me!

I know you find all this strange. This is only the beginning. I am to return you to the planet. You are to speak to your disciples, and tell them that you are risen. You may say that you have seen me, or you may not. It matters not. However you are to tell them quite specifically that "All authority in Heaven and Earth has been given to you."

You have been given a new body as you see. It is yet incomplete, and while you are on the planet you should restrict others from touching you, if at all possible. You have been left with the "holes" in your side and in your hands. Your disciple Thomas does not trust what has been going on, and will require to put his hands into your side and into the holes in your hands. That you may permit. Once that is done you will be left a short while to move about on the planet; as an ordinary individual. You can eat food and drink water with this new body. After a short time you will be removed from the planet and taken up to meet with your father, or possibly some of his other creatures. Possibly the Grey cats. You may very well have many questions, but I will leave that for others to answer.

Now to return you to the planet; just outside the tomb where you were laid. Your body is gone. All that remains are the grave clothes, and they have been neatly folded by my staff. Two of your father's messengers will be there to watch proceedings and to report to him.

You are still, confused. It is the equipment. It can make you feel dizzy.

It will take between 2000 and possibly 3000 years or more for the people of this planet to better understand what has happened here over the past few days. This day, is the third day, Lord Krystyesus. You have an appointment at the tomb. The words that you speak will be noted and recorded. They will seem to you unimportant, but they will be used by future generations. They will seek to defeat me, not understanding that it is your Father who is to be most feared and he has given his authority to you. They will commit mass murder, ostensibly in his name. They are stupid. If they use his name to murder, he will not hand them over to me, as he would do with others. No he will personally vaporise them; reduce them to single atoms, and then consider their punishment for 1000's of years. Or he might be generous, inflicting no punishment at all, but removing them from his grace. One of my predecessors warned them. He used to spend time walking about the planet counting their faults. It was a waste of time. Your father was little interested. He loves this people, just because they look like him.

We have suffered because of my predecesors opposition to humanity. Now I am trying to right a wrong. Does that seem strange?

My people will bow to you my Lord Krystyesus. You shall have your name in lights. You shall be ruler of this planet!"

II

In the previous chapter, I had taken Christ as the son of the father in the physical sense. I am conformable with that, since the third option, would make matters too difficult for humanity. At this stage I have a Christ who is uncertain about his position, but who is clearly given the "authority". As written here the authority is "given" by the Father, but communicated by satan. He indicates that the Father requires it, thus demonstrating that the power is with the Father. I had at one time assumed that Christ and his father spoke directly, but for reasons already mentioned in this Hypothesis, I am satisfied that RA or YH2UH, is very reluctant to have any contact with Humanity. As a father he is distant. That does not mean that he does not love his son, just that he **does not trust humanity**.

The story of Isis and the serpent tells of the hurt to RA . Moses, in the version offered in Genesis had not come up to his standards, and as Tansarduron had just proved, the people would not give up their love for human blood sacrifice, and had done that to the "Son of God". In many respects it matters not whether he was "adopted" or not. For if adopted, he was entitled to the same privileges as a son, and by murdering him the people had shown their contempt, not for the son, but for his Father: God.

In this regard the parable of the son who is murdered by the Keeper of the vineyard is relevant. For in essence the vineyard is the Earth and the Father is Lord of the Vineyard. That could be said to be one of RA's titles!

And it has to be remembered the Gospels were written AFTER Pentecost so that it is entirely possible that the SPIRIT put into the text, in super communicate style, much of the parables; which in essence are super communicate speak, toned down slightly!

The next event occurs when Christ is taken up into Heaven. By that stage the disciples have been enabled to speak the special kind of super communicate, and the early Church is on its way. It still has a long way to go, but the way has started. The first small step has been taken, as the Chinese might say.

On the second occasion that Christ is taken into Heaven, he knows that he is not to return shortly. He is however unsure of where he is going. He might have expected to meet his father. For the purposes of this Hypothesis, he is brought on that occasion before another Cat, a blue grey Tyger headed individual, this time the "Tyem" from M 31 in Andromeda. In marked contrast to the confrontational "Tansarduron" this individual, who is one of RA's most trusted officials, and in right as controller of the vast M 31 galaxy, is much more informative and gentler.

Again the scene is on the flight deck of a Chariot of Fire. The Tyem sits in the middle of a back row of three chairs, with two in front. Present on the flight deck are 4 officials from Tyem and two who accompany the Lord the Krystyesus. The conversation is thus:-

"You look much refreshed, my Lord Krystyesus. Your visit to the planet has done you some good. You feel stronger. I am going to transfer your shortly to one of the other Red Cats. You are to be placed in the care of the Tay Ha Ty. He will take you to his city, to a country retreat of his, and from there you will go to SY ON, where you will take your Father's seat as the

Head of That City. And you wonder where I am going? I will return to my Galaxy, that is my part of Heaven. It is vast, bigger even than this part of Heaven where we now are, but it is far distant. It is, in your terms, much further than Rome, than the pillars of Hercules, further even than the "lost continent".

If I compare this planet to a grain of sand, I am further away than the moon . If I did not operate this craft properly, and caused a destabilisation of the mechanism we use, I might cause this whole planet and everything on it to be fired into the local star. In an instant everything living would be vaporised, and all trace of humanity gone! Having said that, your Father would be most displeased at that, and I have no intention of incurring your Father's displeasure.

No, your Father is slow to anger, as you rightly said, but once angered, it can take a large number of us to placate him. And HE is mightily angry at what has been done to you here!

My wife has offered him a home with us. He has been much hurt by your judicial murder. What has upset him most is that the Romans feel that their justice system is the best on the world. They were not to know that that would draw his attention. But they failed badly. When Pilate had an opportunity to show how good his justice system was, he failed the test miserably. All he had to do was say that you were the Emperor's property and to have you removed to Rome, and the crowd would have been placated. There would have been nothing they could have done. If they had tried, he would have put his troops on them. Not that we would have approved of that. Far from it, but it would have demonstrated to us, and to your Father in particular that they understood that you do not convict the innocent. And Pilate compounded it. He let the guilty go free! In two decisions he showed that the Roman justice system was worthless!

However his real anger was reserved. You are his son. That is what you said, and still they murdered you. They did it in his name!

Now that is one thing which you must try and ensure that those who follow you do not do. For as you said, the Father is unlikely to forgive those who abominate his HOLY

NAME. And sometimes they do not see that is exactly what they do.

YH2UH is a term we sometimes use for him, and is well known to you. But we prefer to say "AMEN RAY". The Red Cats use a different form of speech, and usually say "AMEN RA" but we are both talking of the same individual. He is a small man, my Lord Krystyesus, but he can make himself appear like any one of us. He usually does not choose to do that, preferring his < ATLANTYON > form. For long periods, and I mean long periods, it could be millions of years, he does not appear in any form. He is just simply "Spirit". We have had him for some time in his <ATLANTYON > shape and he likes that. We would wish to keep him in that form; in so far as we may ever hope to contain one who is essentially pure of Spirit and who created everything that is, even Tansarduron, whom you have met.

I have been asked to speak with you. Your father wishes to reserve his meeting with you to a future date. You feel a little strange talking to a large grey skinned cat. But we have met before. In that temple in Egypt, where you went in with your friend. He was frightened, your friend, but you were not afraid. You were of the one true God. But you did not expect to see me! And that gave you a bit of a fright. I was able to hide that incident from you, although I suspect you have a lingering memory of that incident.

You correctly said that in your Father's house there are many mansions. I am in one of them, if you like. A galaxy, it will be called in future time.

I am not an "Egyptian" god. I am a THRENS and in this connection a Messenger of your father. Sometimes we are called NY TY R as the Red Cats would say, which translates as Messenger. We say it differently, but it is the same thing.

Your Father's ways are many and **mostly mysterious**. Even I do not presume to know his will! You have worked his will, and you know it is hard. But he is above all a creature of love, who would not knowingly seek to hurt others. And yet within him a terrible contradiction, that when he is angry, really angry, he is a force for terrible destruction. Fortunately he spends most of his time "creating". This Kingdom of Heaven(

His collection of galaxies) is vast. Mind bogglingly vast, and getting bigger every day!

Some of the philosophies on some planets have it that there was once a "big bang" and that there will be one day be a big crunch. Such have not reckoned with your Father, nor the < APPLIED METAPHYSICS > which he employs!

In the Egyptian mythology, which incidentally some of your followers are shortly going to substantially torch, there is much knowledge. It is not immediately apparent. Your Father has taken great care with it, and was intending to allow it to be used by the people to advance their society. Not now!

Essentially what he has done is to split his teaching into two parts. The Old Orthodoxy is in Egypt, which is why you went down there when you were young. You had friends there, who were Egyptian. Your parents did not like that visit to Egypt (and by that I mean your father Joseph, and mother, Mary, who looked after you while you were on the planet), but you did not bother. Still you were loyal to your father, referred to by you as YH2UH. What you did not see, and what may take many years to understand, is that YH2UH and AMEN RA are one and the same individual.

Hidden yes. Unseen yes. The local star is sometime called "RA" but that is merely a physical tool. It is not the metaphysical RA, the Creator of the Universe.

Even I, who control a whole galaxy, which is millions of millions of planets like this one, find it difficult to comprehend that which is your Father. Physically, while in the shape as a little man, I could tear him to pieces. But what does that prove? Certainly not my superiority. It is quite the reverse.

I could gently touch him, but to do so is to be more familiar than I might feel appropriate. It is not easy.

He feels so alone at times. That is why this planet was created! He has created millions of civilisations in space, most far from this planet, but this was to be his jewel.

When he asked for assistance, it was gladly offered. Many planets came together. This planet was selected. We had various attempts at creating a "this " species for this location. They all did not come up to his requirements. It took us a while. In craft like this < Boats of Millions of Years > as we call them, time can pass as in the blink of an eye. We can shorten time and speed it up.

We thought we had it with the "dinosaurs" creatures yet to be discovered. But he was not happy. I think he always knew what he wanted but was just not willing to try. So finally he did. He said he wanted people he could move about with, as though they did not know who he was!

One of the Red Cats a particular Tansarduron, said that was absurd. Given RA's sometime violent temperament, to put that into a creature was just madness. But your father insisted. And in the way of things we thought it was not so bad.

The Tansarduron was not happy. Although not supposed to do so, he came to this planet and spoke with one of Ra's daughters; one of the new creatures he had created. Unfortunately she listened to the Tansarduron, and with his help set a trap for Ra.

You have heard it. It is the story of Ra, Isis and the snake, as told by the Egyptians. It was re written with the names of the individuals changed, as the garden of Eden and flood story in Genesis. Your father was furious, as that Egyptian story tells. But his fury was unquenchable, when he thought of the damage that might have been caused. He exiled that Tansarduron to this planet, threw the planet into a spin, nearly wiped what was left of this his pet project, and departed to a far flung part of the universe. We were fortunate to find him, and brought to him to our galaxy. He was distraught. He would not speak to anyone. His favourite home with us is a palace, but he lives far far underground, and yet it is filled with light. He can watch everything which happens in every part of every galaxy, but mostly he remains hidden. When we are able to calm him sufficiently he will take < ATLANTYON > form, but he has to be treated with care. From a medical point of view he can give himself a very severe mental breakdown. For a human it might last a few months, a few years. In his case it can last thousands of years!

And our fear, even as I speak, is that this incident will have done just that to him! His staff have persuaded him not to vaporise Rome and Jerusalem, but I fear the punishment for both will be dire, probably running to thousands of years.

Millions will feel his wrath, not because he attacks them but because his face is turned from them. He will not hear their cries, and will not listen to their prayers.

In giving all authority to you, we hope that you may be able to intercede with your Father for them, and to bring to us, the little man, who is the King of Peace, the King of Love who we all so much adore.

The Egyptian texts will be virtually destroyed. He will provide a thread, in the shape of a stone, so that in the fullness of time they may translate some of the hieroglyphs and understand the philosophy. Given that he is giving all authority to you, the temples to RA and the other cats, such as myself are to be closed. The TAY HA TY, and MY Y Dras will ensure that their shrines are all reduced to ruins, so that it may be seen that all authority is to be given to you. But be careful with it. It is your personal property, not to be delegated.

Your father fully expects that some will not give you Glory, and he will deal with them. If they are lucky they will be handed over to Tansarduron, who is relishing the prospect of being handed millions of the defective humans, even if the time scale is long!

And now I have said enough. If you would care to follow me, I will transfer you from this craft to that of the Tay Ha Ty who will take you to SY ON that you may be installed there; as King of Heaven. And one day there, in the Mighty High Temple, you may join with your father, and the Spirit, to make, in the presence of the elect, the ONE who is the MOST HOLY TRINITY .

[NOTE: When I originally wrote this I was working with the material as I understood it. The grey cats, indeed the Red cats, were viewed as "pussy cats" able to be manipulated to what I wanted them to be . That is NOT the way the < Applied Metaphysics > works. Fundamentally it is Not for me to tell the Threns what they can say and do. That is a matter for them. The basic genetic make up has to be the same but matters MUST BE AGREED. As said elsewhere this is not a text for the Genetic Science, but simply to provide and introduction to the REAL TYGERS of Threns and of the < SYSTEMS of BARRED SPIRAL +SYFERT + SCULPTOR GALAXIES >

and their Individuals. Much of the text before this note shows its errors because events with Christ are FACTUAL. It is NOT a belief exercise nor one which can be manipulated to suit particular Christian or other viewpoint, including the Anti Christs of various persuasions.]

18
The 2 Rs

I have substantially covered the Resurrection in the last chapter. However I have to make a comment about it before passing to consider Revelation.

And it is a major point. Unless it is accepted that Christ (preferred spelling Kryst) was the son of the father then Revelation is meaningless. For in essence Revelation deals with various views of < SYON > and the interpretation of it.

Standing as I was once in Malta, overlooking Grand Harbour, I was struck that the walls of Valletta so resembled the Walls spoken of by John in Revelation. And while I was able to enjoy the sunlight on that Mediterranean island, I recalled also Paul's visit there, and I was at a loss to understand why he had gone to the catacombs. Was it because of some hurt, of some failure on his part? Was it because he could not perform the miracles?

Another thought came to mind. Given his presence at the murder of Stephen, had his conversion on the "road to Damascus" perhaps not been quite the glorious event that is reported in biblical texts. Suppose for a moment that he had simply changed sides to head off the Christian Religion in its early development. He has supported much of the Levitical teaching, teaching which to this day condemns many to suffering. As a consequence of that it is necessary and appropriate that this hypothesis should consider the motives.

Certainly as viewed by those in Heaven they would not have been misled. If the attempt was to upset the early Christian church they would have seen that. And in that situation perhaps it was time to keep secret, that which they had intended to reveal. Yes Revelation was written, and its montage of scenes is difficult to read-still is-but behind that montage is the physical presence of those in Heaven as a reality.

There is nothing which Heaven allows to be left if it does not wish. It was not an "accident" that the Rosetta stone was "left" and is "not" an accident that is sits in the British

Museum. It is not a "coincidence" that the British have a vessel called the "Ark Royal". All is watched by those in Heaven!

To Malta was given a medal. The George Cross. Their flag, red and white has in the corner, a small design of that medal. It may seem a minor addition, almost absent if viewed from a distance, but it is very important. It tells of a great suffering by the Maltese people, but also of great triumph.

Standing at Grand Harbour, I recalled the Ship Ohio, which had come from "Tail of the Bank" to Malta. It ought not to have arrived there in Malta, but it did. As I understand it, it arrived on the feast day of the patron Saint of Mosta; itself a victim in the war.

Coincidence? No it bears all the hallmarks of a mighty hand at work; mighty to save.

Mosta is one of my favourite places. Its Cathedral preferred by me to St. Pauls in London. Different denomination though. And at least in the case of Mosta I did not require to pay 50 p to enter! As I walked around Mosta as a visitor, of course, I looked at its wall painting and that of Isaiah in particular. What would Isaiah make of me? Would he lift the stone to throw at me?

And now at this stage what would he make of my, and this hypothesis, and my use of his words? Another stone in my direction? All very relevant. To me the only relevant question is whether my words are "faithful and true". And what would John, who wrote Revelation, make of me, for the use of the words of Revelation?

I stand in St John's Co Cathedral in Malta. I look at the famous painting, of the murder, again Judicial, of John the Baptist. Not an acceptable picture in my view within a Temple to the Most High God. But then in technical terms, that Cathedral is a Church; not a Temple to The King of Heaven. The Temple to the King of Heaven, is in Heaven, and there the only acceptable "sacrifice" is of PRAISE.

As a vision of SYON, I would expect, if I was able to walk there, that in part of that city would be a church similar to Mosta, so that when in Mosta I could recall, SYON, and *vice versa*. And the walls of Valetta I could also place perhaps in SYON or elsewhere as in Hermarut.

But SYON is a vast city. Perhaps not quite as vast as that now measured in John, as thousands of miles square, but large none the less. I say it simply has a population of 25 Millions, and would make it about the size of modern day Los Angeles.

Unlike modern Los Angeles, SYON is peaceful. No gun crime there, for guns are not required. They are "harmful" in the terms of Isaiah, and accordingly not permitted. "Bees" despite the fact they may sting, would be allowed in SYON, for they are not intrinsically harmful. Honey is most pleasant; particularly "Acacia" honey. That was after all the wood with which the "Ark" was built. And that was a tree to be found in the Temples of and associated with RA.

I can go to particular passages of Revelation. Sometime when watching the television, I appreciate what is happening. It is as though John was allowed to see a piece of equipment, like a television, where the pictures were flicked from one channel to another. In consequence when he tried to write down what he saw, in a flat and word sense, what he wrote was quite strange. But taken as little snippets of a much larger picture, and a moving picture at that, his text provides a glimpse of those powerful Galactic Civilisations.

How much of it is real?

Given my perception of the people of space and this Hypothesis, all of it is real! But what purpose does it serve?

Does it, as has been suggested, like other parts of the Bible, contain a code? And if it does contain an Apocalypsc code, what does it say?

This Hypothesis is not concerned with a mathematical code. That is far too basic. Yes, such a code may be there as a "guide" to indicate that the text is important. However in super communicate terms, it is a reality which has to be looked for and investigated.

The figure in Revelation, who has on his clothes a name that no man knows save he himself, is a real figure. It is, in terms of this Hypothesis, symbolical of RA, and his secret name. This Hypothesis has put RA and YH2UH together as the same individual. And in that combination might properly be called < AMEN RA >. That "Trinity" is there in that two have been joined to make the THIRD and ALL are in ONE. And NOW the ALL POWERFUL as a small HIDDEN individual,[a < VISIBLE INVISIBLE >] he can EASILY come like a "thief in the night". Again as is said in Revelation.

As I watched on the television a dramatized account of the battle of "Meddigio" as fought by the Pharaoh, Tothmoses, I was again reminded of "Revelation" in the real sense. It is not necessarily that an "actual final battle" will be fought at "Meddigio" but it may be *that when the dramatisation of that battle is shown on the television*, THAT is what John recorded, and it is THAT which then signals the "end". But the "end" in that sense comes and goes unnoticed. The programme has been broadcast many months prior to this text hitting any book stall. Nothing "Apocalypse" type has happened.

However, I require to be careful, because *what heaven sees is quite different*, and it may regard what is considered minor here, as a major affront to it! As always it is Heaven's view which is important.

Heaven may be checking out the "justice systems" just as it did with Pilate. And it will be particularly annoyed with any system where the Government loads on to the back of individuals loads which the elite of the Government are not themselves willing to bear? <u>There is biblical text on that point already</u>!

Watching a programme on Charles II, I am again reminded of the history of human blood sacrifice within the United Kingdom. Television has also drawn to my attention, that James VI(I) of Scotland, (responsible for a translation of the Bible) apparently made representation to Elizabeth I not to make of his mother, Mary Queen of Scots a Human blood sacrifice. He did not put it in those terms but he did ask for the life of his mother to be spared. History records that was not done.

And in the case of his son, Charles I it was "Parliament" which performed the Human Blood Sacrifice. Like the Jews at the time of Christ, by asking Charles I to sign his own death warrant, there was perhaps an element of side stepping, of trying to shift the blame. It does not really matter because it was done from good "Christian" and "Protestant" convictions. The years which followed the death of Charles II pitted once again the

Protestants and the Catholics against one another. Not acceptable conduct from Heaven's point of view! Do the Churches not realise that? Do they consider the Lord the Krystyesus would approve of such conduct?

Did either of those two groups stop for even one moment to consider the views of the King of Heaven. Doubtless as far as they are concerned HE is a complete irrelevance. It is all a question of power!

Such views will irritate RA, as YH2UH, < AMEN RA > if truly that is the view they take. It will be checked of course. But if it is correct, there will be trouble. Slow is AMEN RA to anger, but when roused he is fearful. His "Awesome Holiness", if I recall from what I wrote earlier, is what HE said .

Now who among that group would like to take on RA and his local < Fire Disc > and other < FIRE DISCS > ? Because that is also what this Hypothesis is about. I have written about "overcoming apep" in the sense of the power of Super light travel. I have been very critical, highly critical of the practice of human blood sacrifice in its many shapes in many cultures, past present, and "possibly" regretfully, yet to come. I have elevated my Lord Krystyesus to as high as I can possibly put him. I have given to him as much power as I can imagine, and I am resolute, resolute, in my conviction that human blood sacrifice is not to be performed.

In contrast to Paul, communion is not a mystery. It is simply the recognition before God, and in a reasonably pleasant exercise, (for can eating bread and drinking wine be viewed in any other light), that those who do it know, and understand that human blood sacrifice is not to be performed. There was to be NO more sacrifice after the judicial murder of Christ. Many have ignored that, and some have gone quite deliberately "Anti Christ", trying to dispute the miracles. This Hypothesis supports Christ (the Lord the Krystyesus) as he is described. That I "question" does not make me anti Christ, where I am searching for the "Truth". In essence I am doing exactly what was done by my Lord the Krystyesus. Unfortunately I do not appear to be quite as well connected to those in Heaven. That is for those in Heaven to determine.

I know that to make progress and to keep myself right with God, I must treat my fellow humans carefully; asking as far as I can for the King of Heaven to "take me under his wing" and to "protect me from evil".

As I have said earlier, with their matter transfer equipment they can as soon scramble my atoms, as make for me a new body which is "incorruptible". And it may be that that equipment is set with a test on "No Human Blood sacrifice". If that is the case it would be dangerous for those who have performed such to use.

However, I am satisfied that those in Heaven have a serious interest, in justice, peace, love, possibly summed up as "MaTT." They are all difficult concepts.

Justice does not mean for a moment that the "guilty" be allowed to walk free. That is as bad as convicting the innocent. Forgiveness may be divine, but care has to be taken. Christ said, "Father forgive them, for they know not what they are doing". The text does not record his father's (< AMEN RA > in terms of this Hypothesis) comment. In this text < Tyem AM > made it clear that he had to restrain and persuade RA not to vaporise Rome and Jerusalem. The fact that both these cities currently exist does not mean that the anger of < AMEN RA > over the judicial murder of his son has been assuaged. He may be biding his time. Revenge is his, again without quoting it specifically, a comment which can be found in biblical text.

Justice may require a punishment. The punishment in terms of this Hypothesis is that AMEN RA turns away. By doing that he may bar the way to progress and effectively leave the way open for destruction by others.

Equally he may be watching very closely, as in the case of particular individuals in the Concentration camps or on the "Burma" Railway. That the vaporisation of a city should occur because one individual was "murdered" may seem to some excessive. In terms of this Hypothesis, such individuals were "special to < AMEN RA >, albeit unseen" and there is therefor in this text a clear warning to those whose business is murder. Tansarduron, as the military official of the Dras Red cats is held on a leash waiting for instructions for the assault. He has been promised many who are not going to SY ON; those who hate it.

Revelation is not easy to interpret, and the interpretation I have given to it here I accept is one which assists this Hypothesis, and I make no apology for that. However that leads me on to the next aspect. That of < AMEN RA .>

[Note. I have now started to use the term < AMEN RA > in chevrons. That is because of the New Hypothesis and the Particular Scientific Context of the Visible Invisibles and of < HOSTING > in particular. The text which follows will now be adjusted to reflect that < Understanding >]

19
Strange Books

While Revelation may be difficult for me, it is not half has difficult as some of the texts relating to "RA" and while by making RA and YH2UH the same individual it might be thought that I have given myself, in terms of this Hypothesis, quite a headache, the opposite is the case once the concept of the < AMEN RA > is fully appreciated.

I can ask patriarchs, priests or ministers of the various Churches of their opinions with regard to Revelation, and some who read this may criticise my interpretation. I cannot ask the Egyptian priests of Ra anything . They have long gone. Now while I might have regarded that as a problem, it is Isaiah who supplies the answer. The priests of RA were supposed to help the people understand. Instead of that they did not. They may even have done the opposite. So if that is the case, and Moses was partly instructed by RA, or at the very least assisted by him, then there must be more in these texts than is at first sight appreciated.

One of the major works of "RA" theology is the writings on RA as left by the Egyptians. Again I am taking my text from the work of Budge, volume 1 "The Gods of The Egyptians." And then there is the "book of the dead."

When I first read that text as translated, I found it all gobbledygook. Yes I can relate to the TAHATY and to Sekhmet, to Tyem and others [all as changed to the super communicate pronunciation, if not the spelling], but all those other names and hours of the night. Is it not all absurd nonsense?

I consider super communicate again, but here I have to consider Super, super communicate. In essence this Hypothesis says, as Isaiah says, that the Egyptians themselves did not understand. And it is part of this Hypothesis that < AMEN RA > exists......well if I take Genesis 1 literally, I could slightly rephrase and say, "Before the beginning I AM." But that may not be altogether correct!

The grey cat < Tyem AM > has access to a boat of Millions of years. < AMEN RA > has access to the boat of millions of years. If then millions of years are simply a "short" expanse of time, then both < Tyem AM > and < AMEN RA > existed before the beginning. In terms of Genesis, God made the world. That is not so impossible if the "time" element of millions of years is taken out of it. And watch the "GOD" is in many respects the < HEAD OF THE GALAXY > where the "O" represents the < GALACTIC DISC > or < SEVERAL OF THEM >. That is the Science part and < UNDERSTANDING >.

It is as though the local population have grappled with the ideas and the words not fully appreciating exactly what is being talked about because in technical terms it is complicated.

So when the book of the dead talks in terms of RA journeying through the "hours of the night" it is merely talking in terms of various different gaps when "RA" was travelling. If an hour of that text is in fact "millions of Years" then what I am dealing with is the various ages of the planet since before the "Dinosaurs". The various monsters of the "book of the dead" are nothing more than EITHER the various dinosaurs who existed previously OR are other GALACTIC BEINGS which are not compatible, as for example in the case of the Gorgons! [In the case of the Gorgons it might simply be talking of the RED TYGERS, if I recall correctly from a photograph I saw of a statue of Sekhmet!]

< AMEN RA > while a mighty individual CAN TAKE THE FORM as a "small" individual.

When they crucified "Christ" did they appreciate just exactly who they were trying to "kill"?

This current age could last for "millions of years" before < AMEN RA > returns. And again, as Revelation says, he may come like a thief in the night!

In 2003 AD, < AMEN RA > is not welcome. The United Kingdom while notionally a "Christian" country, is viewed by many as "Multicultural" [but to that extent excluding < AMEN RA >!] Most of the Far East would defer to theories of Buddha. Even Kwetlskoatels, the feathered plumed and painted serpent whose followers "erroneously" indulged in human blood sacrifice may be allowed to < GALACTIC SY ON > PROVIDED it is made clear that all authority is with Christ. And to that extent the massive statue in Brazil of "Kryst the Redeemer" says that of the Americas.

But all the world does not give authority to the Lord the Krystyesus. The communist countries deny the existence of God. For them there is no < AMEN RA >. Perhaps it is they cannot see the sun, or are blind. But even a blind man knows when the light of the sun has risen.

And what of the Land of the Rising Sun? Kay FA RA. FA RA in super communicate is a colour, and that colour is blue. TA HA, FA RA would make it light blue, which would be the colour of < AMEN RA >. He has other stars in the heavens and those would be denoted by a "blue" in their spectrum. Thus in Scientific terms I am talking < BLUE and BLUE WHITE STARS >

I have here < AMEN RA > as a very powerful < INDIVIDUAL >. I am aware that that power can be "shielded" and he can appear as just a little man. But he is NOT ever that. For he keeps his power in Heaven in <u>< HIS GALAXIES ></u> at his disposal. And if push comes to shove he will use it. But he has to be really provoked!

If < AMEN RA > visits, and appears as just a little man, the risk may that he has nearby, but shielded by its powerful shields, a Chariot of Fire (boat of Millions of years), OR ADVANCED OTHER TECHNOLOGY and that if he decides to depart, that departure may trigger a destabilization of the < FOOTSTOOL >, causing it to spin. The < UNDERSTANDING > of the < INDIVIDUALS > such as < AMEN RA > and the < TYEM AM > is staggering, and by comparison, this planet is like a droplet of water.[Compare with boundless watery mass!]

Like a Jumbo jet on the tarmac, as it powers up its engines, the hot gasses shove away the water droplets lying on the tarmac. And in a few moments the Jumbo jet is gone, up into the sky, the water droplets moved far away from their position at rest. It is as nothing for they are only water droplets, against that Jumbo jet with its 200+ passengers.

What of < AMEN RA > with his passengers and if the planet is "pushed" out of the way, to or from the SUN? Certainly in terms of this hypothesis, < Tyem AM > has already indicated that < AMEN RA > would be displeased if a planet was destroyed. But a planet and its people which loves and lives by human blood sacrifice is no friend to < AMEN RA >. He may apply his "Mirror" rule, and allow them to become as they wish, human blood sacrifices.

It is not the intention of this hypothesis to frighten. Merely to demonstrate the power at the disposal of the < RA > of this hypothesis. Far more likely in terms of this Hypothesis that < AMEN RA > would depart unseen and his Chariot of Fire would also be unseen. But even in that there is a problem. For the planet may lose its designation as being of < AMEN RA > SIMPLY by failing to use that NAME! And the consequence? With his wing removed, his protection withdrawn there may be at real risk from other violent beings in space. And if there was a "second attack" on RA, like that done by Isis, Tansarduron might consider himself to be assisting RA by attacking the planet. He might be able to do that, until RA told him to stop. Indeed that might be the position as it applies today. All the human blood sacrifice of which I am complaining may be done to the instructions of Tansarduron, because < AMEN RA > left some time ago. 2000 years ago perhaps?

So perhaps with this text I am asking the < TRINITY INDIVIDUAL > < AMEN RA > the combination of RA and YH2UH to put a stop to the murder and violence. As I said earlier, I have the feeling that my lines of communication with those in Heaven are "not too good".

As I listen to the nonsense about making areas "nuclear free", or of the risks of "global warming" or a "new ice age", I am slightly staggered at the complete lack of understanding.

The < AMEN RA > of this hypothesis can and HAS moved the local star about. Can the people of this planet move the local star? Can they supply the light and power for the whole planet if it moves a fraction...a tiny tiny fraction further away from this planet?

Many will say that is not going to happen? Was it a meteorite which destroyed the dinosaurs? Look at the evidence?

Not at a version which suits current tastes, but at the whole picture. What causes earth Crust displacement? What is the importance of the volcanoes in the rotation of the planet? What is the importance of the magnetic field? So many questions which MUST have ACCURATE and CORRECT ANSWERS. That is the SCIENCE PART. It is TRUTH which is VITAL in understanding the Science.

Astrophysics? In terms of this Hypothesis the local population are not going anywhere in deep space until they have a CORRECT UNDERSTANDING, and NO HUMAN BLOOD SACRIFICE is an ESSENTIAL ELEMENT of that. I ask the questions, because I am interested in the TRUE answer.

The perception of those who wrote the story of RA was of an Individual who could move the "big yellow disc" as I sometimes call the local star ! But I understand that the term < FIRE DISC > with its chevrons is a < TECHNICAL SCIENTIFIC DESCRIPTION >.

If individuals thought of that power and misunderstood the "God" concept might they not indulge in "human blood sacrifice" or much worse to prevent the removal of the local star?

Current understanding of even basic physics means that such a view is regarded as absurd nonsense. It is ridiculous..... Absolutely ridiculous..............absolutely impossible.

The Dinosaurs were killed by a large rock from space. That is story currently taught. That I now suspect, is VERY VERY VERY far from the Truth.

With evolution the planet can make "new" life. Again I suspect very far from the Truth.

As for the understanding of "DNA". Even if the Dna is "mapped" that will not do much good. It is wrong science.

The real science is how life is made, and that <u>HAS TO BE</u> in the old fashioned way. I think the common word for that is SEX !

II

A very miffed and annoyed < AMEN RA >. He wants nothing more than to return from whence he came. He will NOT take the Star away, nor collapse it. This time. His presence as the < VISIBLE INVISIBLE > is not seen. How could it be? As a little individual he is still < AMEN RA >.

He was responsible for all the various ages and moved the water over the water, as rain. He can arrange for < HIS FOOTSTOOL > wrongly called a planet to be moved a fair bit! He can create oceans where there had been deserts and *vice versa*. He has enjoyed making this < FOOTSTOOL > and its creatures. He has enjoyed working with the design team in making humanity in his image. Moses got that right!

And yes he could be arrogant, and yes he could be violent, but all those feelings he had taught himself to suppress. And with suppression, and the desire to progress had come vast leaps. He had built, and was continuing to build, within his < GALAXIES > in this Universe, vast civilisations, the most powerful of which were the most peaceful because they had the greatest understanding.

Humanity was yet young, in its terms. A few million years yet. And yet, to "walk among them". Always a risk as Tansarduron had said to him. He was after all one of < AMEN RA' s > Military advisors. And it was prudent to listen to the military, to select them carefully and to teach and train the military properly; and as in the case of Sparta and Alexander, to look after the military.

The Book of the Dead and its monsters ? Science, not simply previous and dangerous designs.

Some of these designs had been "IMPROVED" and they had "evolved" such as the crocodiles and the sharks, to name but a few. And the snakes.

With the snakes the warning is there, and it concerns the technology which apep" represents. It is NECESSARY to be wary and careful. Indeed < AMEN RA > knows that much that appears dangerous and is IN FACT dangerous is there for a specific purpose. To protect. The nuclear weapons fulfill exactly that purpose, BUT they MUST be kept by those, like Sparta and Alexander, who know how NOT to use them. That again is Science. The real test is to keep the technology secure.

And so he picks up the funny little wooden stick. It is simply an exercise tool, but that little stick says plainly that this <

FOOTSTOOL > is EXACTLY THAT, that it has < EXTENSIVE GALACTIC CONNECTIONS > and like Sparta and Alexander, when roused, they can fight. The < GATES OF FIRE >.

But while it is important to know the heat of the sun and how dangerous it is, the real understanding is of that soft, soft balmy heat and the gentle breeze. And it is in that soft heat, that gentle heat, that the < LIFE GIVING PLASMA > is safely delivered and received.

And < AMEN RA > is pleased with his Elegant, Sylised and Sculpted Galaxies and he has < BARRED and SECURED > them to keep them conform to HIS DESIGNS!

III

< AMEN RA > is pleased with < HIS GALAXIES > and with many of the creatures in it. And he is always pleased when a New Civilisation reaches that level of development, of understanding, that they may piece together all the various pieces of the jig saw puzzle he had left for them to enable them, like a child, to develop their own mind and to join with his Galactic Civilisations.

IV

There is another super communicate aspect to the " Book of the Dead" and the various journeying of RA. Given the super communicate aspect of it, while telling on the one hand of the various evolutions of the dinosaurs, it might also give the various passages through the "Tuat", except that the "Tuat" is in fact regions of space and all the various "hours" are just the times it takes for the Chariot of Fire to travel though some regions of space. The various "monsters" are simply regions which are either "friendly" to RA, or areas where he is "Not willing to go" because he is unwelcome. The problem is how to make the text relevant to a "Star Chart".

I can be comfortable with the Hebrew text of the Torah containing a "Star Chart". Indeed that might explain some of its inconsistencies, especially if it was "back engineered".

Why do I say star chart? It is written linearly and with various sectors, as laid out flat, and with a plotter or it, each letter representing an elevation, above or below the galactic plane, it might be as various slices taken out of a galaxy; and in one instance, this galaxy. Various separate books may then represent different galaxies, some being larger than the others, some friendly and safe, others not! But where to begin?

Clearly the marker for this "Galaxy" is with the phrase "I am who I am". That would then be taken to be the region of space immediately adjacent to this star.

In these terms it is immensely complicated. Yes there may be a code in it, but it is at so many different levels that it is difficult to see. And it is not made any easier by those who to satisfy their own requirements, would destroy all the hidden knowledge. But then again the knowledge must be kept hidden from those who, if they fully appreciated what it was, would try to use it destructively.

And what of Revelation? That certainly qualifies as a strange book. Perhaps a trap for the unwary! On the other hand perhaps an essential tool to provide the vision to enable the other various books to be linked.

Within the scope of this Hypothesis I can only speculate. I may be far from the mark, or I may be very close. I cannot accurately say. For that I need the proof, and that, regretfully is sadly lacking. It has all been so skillfully hidden, that I probably need a super, super computer; far more sophisticated than anything on this planet!

However, even if it is hidden it may yet be possible to find it. And if that is done the Hypothesis may be proved, and those vast civilisations in space may respond.

The current efforts to speak to those in space, such as with the "Seti" programme are limited. I would view it as being equivalent to someone standing on Pitcairn Island and shouting into the wind to attract the attention of someone in say London. In the first place the individual in London has little interest in what the individual on Pitcairn has to say, and indeed given that some of the inhabitants of Pitcairn were "pirates" as viewed by some in London, they were not welcome there. It would be a virtually pointless exercise. In that situation the people of this planet MUST CONFORM to the Civilisation which is < ATLANTYON SYON > with its millions and millions of inhabited < FOOTSTOOLS > or they simply will not be permitted to understand how to travel such vast distances. With the current levels of violence there is little hope of developing or of discovering the technology which would enable this Galactic travel; assuming that is that some would wish to do so! However with that analogy, I greatly oversimplify, and I understate quite considerably the love of a Mighty God, who has stretched forth his hand to touch and assist this poor people in times past, present and yet to come.

What then of the proof. What would be needed?

V

This Hypothesis now proceeds on the basis that RA and YH2UH are one and the same individual as < AMEN RA >. I have changed the "spellings" of the "Egyptian" Hieroglyphs, because it does not correspond with the super communicate, which I say is a language which pre dates by "Thousands" if not "millions" of years that of the Hieroglyphs. If as has been suggested by others there was an attempt to back engineer the hieroglyphs and that produced Hebrew, then it may be much closer to the super communicate than is appreciated.

While I can reproduce the super communicate "font" as I understand it, I am reluctant to do so. I am very reluctant.

My reluctance is caused by the various comments I hear on television, particularly the news programmes. If this hypothesis is correct, there is much knowledge which will be released; albeit that it may be a slow release. Questions of timing arise.

If this Hypothesis is correct, what I say here will not change, it will merely be that with the passage of time more discoveries will tend to prove what the text says. If it is not correct, I have wasted my time. But at least I did try.

For the purposes of this hypothesis, I do not dispute for a minute that Champollion did marvellous work. However it does seem to me, in super communicate terms, that those in Heaven are still concerned about the release of much of the super communicate text and THEIR SCIENCE . Even now in 2003 AD, I am concerned about the super communicate text. I note of the hieroglyphs that the vowel sounds "e" "Y" and "i" are similar, and I am satisfied that I am correct in my moving around the phonetic sound. The "Two feathers" would tend to suggest a "Maat" influence, which ties in very neatly with the super communicate. The single "feather" of Hieroglyph is therefore a partial sound.

When I started to write this on previous occasions, it was the super communicate aspect which made me recoil from attempting publication. This time, I am much more comfortable with it, but still apprehensive.

Perhaps I ought not to be, for if a mind such a Sir Isaac Newton did not find any bible code despite devoting a great amount of time to it, perhaps the super communicate can be discarded as just fanciful thinking on may part .

I am quite satisfied that those in Heaven will ensure that this text is seen only if it assists them to make progress at this time.

I have to say that when reading the late Mr. Budge's work on the Gods of Egypt I was surprised that he did not make the connection with the I AM. Perhaps he did, but it would have been too dangerous or harmful to his academic reputation to make such a comment during his time.

In my case I have been brought here by the super communicate and by an understanding I have of events concerning the life of "Kryst" in the real sense, and very strenuous efforts by me over a long period to try and make some really meaningful understanding of the events of the life of Kryst. Not in a belief sense, but in a real sense in terms of his life of as real man. That is one of the things this text is about.

At the time of Kryst, he could not comfortably talk about RA nor the other "gods", particularly in the country where he lived; even if it had been to suggest, as I am, that far from being gods they were simply "messengers". The anger of the people is demonstrated in that blood sacrifice which they required Pilate to make of him, and which regretfully, Pilate allowed to be made.

In this year of 2003 AD, and with the assistance of past generations of Christians who have thirsted after the knowledge, I am able, within the confines of this modern secular democracy to consider the reality of what actually happened, free of the fear which would undoubtedly have restricted me in other countries or at other times.

Of the various old Egyptian messengers, I would regard those whom I can "translate" in super communicate as "real" in the sense that they are <Heavenly Beings>, from different planets and galaxies.

With the messenger Neith, I would change that first "e" to "y", and there is again a connection with the Red Cats, in the figure of "NY Tay Ha" which of course has to be contrasted to with the "Tay HA Ty". While appearing as almost the same figure, it is not, and the fact that the figure of "Ny Tay Ha" is feminine is perhaps shown in the reverse word order of the super communicate. Like the TAY HA TY, it is similar words which are involved. Given the power which was attributed to "Hathor" and her connection with "Ra", it would be my submission, contrary to what Budge suggests, that "Hathor" is a localised form of NY TAY HA which was more acceptable and more accessible to the "locals" than was NY TAY HA.

But in the super communicate it is talking of the terrible damage which these beings can inflict; in essence the huge voice of Light; a mighty explosion, as in a nuclear blast. Given that "Neith" is described as one of the primeval "messengers" who created the Universe, am I not back at the "big bang" theory again, this time dressed up in "people" form?

Not easy this Biblical code! Not easy this Egyptian code!

The I AM THE, has been working VERY hard with this < FOOTSTOOL > and its populations.

There is not enough proof in these texts though. It is speculation on my part. It may be accurate, but I need proof!

If real, I NEED the people of Space to put in an appearance. I am sure that they have done that in the past. The problem is that it is my assessment that they do not trust humanity. And I would consider that to be a very PRUDENT view to take!

NOTE: On reviewing this text I have had to make substantial adjustments. As should be clear from the New Hypothesis that is because of the Science. The figure of < AMEN RA > is now correctly identified. This chapter could be cut considerably, but the fact that it is not cut, but adjusted simply shows the level of disinformation which exists and the difficulty of separating the "wheat" from the "chaff". Essentially once the HIGH, IMPERIAL and UNION GALAXIES are indentified, much of the technology slots into place. It is in fact like a massive jig saw puzzle, multi dimensional and very < TIME SENSITIVE > and < PLACE SENSITIVE >. Thus it is correct or say that Heaven will only release what it considers to be appropriate.

The more important aspect for the technology operation is that it REQUIRES input from the GALACTIC CIVILISATIONS and at a PRACTICAL and REAL LEVEL by their INDIVIDUALS. Certain civilization can thus trip themselves up, as with Imperial Japan in the 1930's and 40's but now corrected. And likewise those societies which were < PROTOCOL> such as the United Kingdom, may make themselves unacceptable to the High Imperial and Union galaxies, simply by the policies which they adopt. Thus with the case of Cromwell and indeed with others; even in Victorian and Edwardian times. This really relates to the standard of living and how safe it is for visiting Galactic Officials to visit.

Again with Newton, having regard to the time when he lived and the local practices, there is simply NO question of the HIGH IMPERIAL and UNION GALAXIES releasing to him other than very basic information.

The technical science is that this is a < BARRED SPIRAL GALAXY > and while that term is currently used in Scientific texts, it has a < PARTICULAR > meaning. And that is that these galaxies have MANY INHABITED and HIGHLY DEVELOPED FOOTSTOOLS which they HIDE from prying eyes and telescopes; especially from other Galaxies UNLESS they are FRIENDS.

Thus in the case of Messier and his catalogue, he might simply not have seen certain galaxies because they did not wish him to see them. And it is not a matter of having bigger and more powerful telescopes. All that means is that the galaxies are as viewed "through a glass darkly".

The Galactic Science is called either <APPLIED METAPHYSICS> or <ATLANTON GALACTIC PHYSICS>. There is an exercise for both which is called < SPORTING > and which has particular Science aspects to it! It involves the small < HEADPIECES > which are sometimes designed to look like the < ANKH > of the Egyptians. That is IN FACT THE symbol for the HIGH, IMPERIAL and UNION SYSTEMS GALAXIES !

[The last chapter of the Old Hypothesis which follows I have adjusted likewise to take account of this note.]

20
RA

The RA of this hypothesis is not the RA as understood by the Egyptians, but with the association now made with YH2UH, has much more to do with that individual. And I now use the term < AMEN RA > for the particular individual and the technical Science to which that description relates. He is "Masculine" in the sense as the "YA" figure, and is the individual who is in charge of <<<HIS GALAXIES>>>. As such he is "The King of Creation" or the "King of Heaven" and KEEPS OUT and REFUSES those who do not meet the required criteria to join his system of Galaxies

In that sense, and as indicated in Revelation, he has many names. The personal name is, in terms of this hypothesis, that which is written on his clothes, and upon his thigh. He is the MaTT individual.

As Lord of the local < FIRE DISC > the Sun and < FIRE DISCS > and < GALAXIES > he is massively powerful, but as I hope I have shown thus far, he can take the shape of a small individual and to live within his creation, enjoying as an individual especially the light and heat from the local star. In terms of this hypothesis he is a REAL individual, and an <ATLANTYON>.

KY FA RA MA RA, is an adapted super communicate form of the name Kephra Ra Amen to describe him. But a question still remains. Did he talk to Moses, or was it someone else? Again the suggestion that Moses or the Pharaoh's made it all up causes a difficulty. But not to the RA of this Hypothesis.

While YH2UH is a "secret" name, and the name on his clothes remains secret, the REAL secret is the OBVIOUS ONE that the individual is in fact < AMEN RA >. And that is very cleverly done. It is done in the repetition of the name "AMEN" and of the teaching which goes with it. It is done in the Trinity context, as I have done bringing the YH2UH and RA together as < AMEN RA >. And it is very real in the sense that the LOCAL STAR is well aware of what is going on, on its <

FOOTSTOOL >. It is Isaiah which holds the keys, and the keys are the < WOODEN SPORTING STICKS > with their < HEADPIECES >. They are not high technology, although they may conceal that. They are exercise tools, both PHYSICAL and MENTAL. They are < ATLANTYON > and disclose membership of the HIGH, IMPERIAL and UNION SYSTEMS GALAXIES.

And as for that script on the thigh?

It has to be < ATLANTYON >. As I view it modern Hebrew is similar to it so it does look as though someone saw the Atlantyon words, but could not correctly read them nor understand accurately what they meant.

The RA of this Hypothesis is BOTH able to look down from Heaven on this < FOOTSTOOL> and to walk among the people and creatures as a < VISIBLE INVISIBLE >.

This is not the text to go into that concept, as I am sure a number of Visible Invisibles will be well aware, as indeed will the local star.

Whether < AMEN RA > is actually present, or one of the other < Visible Invisibles > is not clear. In terms of the Christian teaching, and in terms of this hypothesis, this planet is within the control of the Lord the Krystyesus and he has no need to visit or to watch.

But it may be that a < VISITING > Galactic Official may transit trough this Galaxy and this < Footstool > simply to check on development and to report back, including to the Lord the Krystyesus in < ATLANTYON SYON >, which is on another < FOOTSTOOL > in this Galaxy. And likewise that Galactic Official may be required to < REPROGRAMME > both the < FOOTSTOOL > and the < LOCAL STAR > so that they may again join with the HIGH, IMPERIAL and UNION GALAXIES .

That official will almost certainly EXPECT and REQUIRE that ALL authority is with the Lord the Krystyesus, ON THEIR TERMS, otherwise they may arrange for the < FOOTSTOOL > to be thrown. Indeed Edinburgh may retain < RESERVED STATUS > as a city simply because of a lady who threw a Footstool, explaining, although not in those words, that this IS AN ATLANTYON FOOTSTOOL and their RULES apply in this THEIR TERRITRY. She was simply repeating what Hadrian had already been told. This is ATLANTYON TERRITORY and they are watching.

This text makes it quite clear that authority is with the Lord the Krystyesus, that he is alive and well and sits in MIGHTY ATLANTYON GALACTIC SY ON . That does not mean that any one "Christian" tradition can dominate all, but it does mean that authority rests with The Lord the Krystyesus .

As this text earlier said, in the comments by the < Lord Tyem AM >, when speaking to the Lord the Krystyesus, "the ways of your father are many and mostly mysterious."

Where then do I put < AMEN RA > the < ATLANTYON LORD >?

Threns? Or even further away, at the boundary of the Universe at Llycot Lleydran? Or has he again assumed his pure energy state, and will not reincarnate himself for many millions of years as < AMEN RA > and as the "MaTT" individual?

This world, with is philosophy based on the violence of evolution has no place for < AMEN RA > . Within the physics as taught in the most important universities, and with green global warming, there is no place for < AMEN RA >. But all that does not make him unreal. Neither does the 6000+ million of this planet who say he is not real. Can they not see the local fire disc? Can they not feel its heat, or the absence of its warmth?

The truth as I said earlier, is OBVIOUS. So is the Science.

A < FOOTSTOOL > crack appears in the Galapagos. Why not? It is a volcanic island.

They have other Gods now, like Darwin and various modern climate scientists who are much more powerful than < AMEN RA >.

Really, and I question?

I do not think that the < HIGH, IMPERIAL and UNION SYSTEM GALAXIES > will be much impressed with such so called "scientists".

In terms of this hypothesis considerable care should be taken since the fundamental science does not change. This Hypothesis with its science is < STAR > based and

< GALACTIC >. In essence with RA and YH2UH merged as one in the < TRINITY > figure of MaTT, there is indeed a New Heaven and a new Earth!

It has not been exactly painless, and may not yet be finished, for the mechanism may require that SPECIFIC volcanoes are set off and earthquakes take place in PARTICULAR locations, <u>if very carefully controlled</u>! That is after all what the < ATLANTYON GALACTIC PHYSICS > teaches!

I am satisfied that the warning; "Beware he who comes like a thief in the night," is a warning about the < VISIBLE INVISIBLES > who come to check out the < FOOTSTOOL > and to < REPROGRAMME > as required to meet their < CRITERIA >.

And that < Visible Invisible > in terms of this Hypothesis can be PUT into Christ, either BEFORE BIRTH, as in the virgin birth <u>OR AFTERWARDS,</u> but in BOTH CASES, even if unknown to the individual concerned you are dealing with a < VISIBLE INVISIBLE > like < AMEN RA >.

Now it is perhaps appreciated how big a mistake Pilate made!

Allow for < AMEN RA > or another < VISIBLE INVISIBLE > to leave most of their knowledge in space(for he or she has no need of it in practical terms while they are "on holiday" on a < FOOTSTOOL >),and they can indeed make themselves just like a small insignificant individual. From the inside looking out they can leave their knowledge with huge holes in it, so that looking to the stars, they cannot even recognize the star patterns which they as < GALACTIC INDIVIDUALS > put in place! In that situation the figure of Kryst can easily become confused as he speaks on a day to day basis. But that does not make that individual any less < AMEN RA >. I have said that in terms of this hypothesis, Kryst was the SON of God; RA's son in terms of this hypothesis. What of the two daughters? And what of Israel?

In terms of this hypothesis, by the time of the judicial murder of Kryst, it was proved to the satisfaction of RA that his people wanted nothing to do with him. He simply turned his face away. In his time scale 2000 years is a very short space of time. And the suffering of Israel? Not his problem. He simply has to look at the words spoken of in the Good News.

What of the Christians? Have they gone the same way? Have they lost their way? Time scale is shorter than with Israel. The risk to the Christian community is that they do not appreciate what they have, and allow them selves to drift into no religion at all..........or to misunderstand entirely that which they were given.

That is not the case at present but there are tensions with the Christian community ;talk even of schisms! While one holds to a strict line, like the Pharisees, another is criticized for being too soft. While in RA's terms he may see it as a matter for the Lord the Krystyesus, he will be conscious that by adhering to strict rules, the people of the planet, lose the spirit and the message, and distance themselves from him!

As an isolated < FOOTSTOOL > there is no need for < AMEN RA >to visit. Indeed there is really nothing to interest him. Those in <ATLANTYON SYON> may have pointed favourably to a particular justice system, hoping perhaps to entice him back from Threns, at least to watch and possibly if satisfied to < UPRATE > to < FOOTSTOOL >. Given that he is comfortable in Threns and can comfortably watch from Threns, why travel here at all?

A visit might be necessary, if not from him, at least by one of his officials, if it was intended to allow the people to see Space Aliens in a contact situation. In that situation, < AMEN RA > would probably allow for the local inhabitants to say how they would regard "first contact" to enable him to compare the fiction against the reality. Certain films which have dealt with "first contact" give a glimpse into the mind of the local population and their reaction to such contact. Equally there is still a palpable sense of fear in the "War of the Worlds" scenario, although the hope is that Humanity can fight off such with a simple "cold" virus.[Unfortunately not understanding that the "virus" are part of the programming and reprogramming mechanism].

He can even arrange to feed to the "Seti" programme the Mathematical signals for which they are searching; while keeping from Earth his VAST HIGHLY SECURE GALAXIES because thus far, they have not made the necessary connections and have not developed to the required level.

Certainly educated "Western" culture in the developed world can take the contact with real aliens, provided they are peaceful. Which is perhaps what the Red Tyger and Grey Tyger of this hypothesis are not. Rather unfortunate then that the Red Tyger are described in terms of this Hypothesis as being in control of this galaxy, and being real!

This galaxy is massive and they are in control of it! But it is only one of millions....billions of billions of millions which make up the Universe.[Watch here that while the Universe is large, there are SECURITY PROTOCOLS for the HIGH IMPERIAL and UNION GALAXY and their GALAXIES are SECURED and it is THEY which are effectively called the KINGDOM OF HEAVEN. This DESCRIPTION is TECHNICAL SCIENCE.]

Smashing atoms to find yet smaller particles is NOT the way to progress in terms of this Hypothesis. What does that prove? The capacity to destroy! That will not impress < AMEN RA > and his Galactic Civilisations. No he in interested in MaTT (Truth) and Justice and in the DESIGN, the compatible design of the species on HIS FOOTSTOOLS.

These are TECHNICAL DESIGN POINTS which MUST BE MET .

This hypothesis asserts that the creatures of space are real and VERY powerful, but are controlled by < AMEN RA> as an < ATLANTYON > who delights in taking that Atlantyon shape, which is similar to human shape but with several technical UPGRADES, not least of which is the upgrade to allow Galactic travel. This is again is SCIENCE BASED and has to do with the COMPATABILITY of DEPARTING and RECEIVING STARS and their footstools .

< AMEN RA > and his < GALAXIES > are willing to defend this < FOOTSTOOL> but NOT when population and their Star set out to attack him. Thus the problem with Isis. He will retaliate, if attacked, and with his tremendous power, the results can be devastating. He can remove his protection, and in so doing, allow others to cause devastation. He may be slow to anger, but he can become very angry.

I am not here going to deal with the Anger of RA. But I am satisfied that the flood story was much more massive than is currently contemplated, (except by a few who talk in terms of earth crust displacement) and all within RA's power.

It has been hinted by me, (by the Tyem AM in this hypothesis) that at the time of the Crucifixion of Kryst, RA required to be pacified. It is convenient, in this culture to say that "forgiveness is divine" but with that care must be taken. Where forgiveness causes injustice, it is entirely inappropriate, and that cannot be said to be "divine". There is a place for forgiveness, and there is a place for retribution. In the case of the < AMEN RA > of this hypothesis, he EXPECTS and REQUIRES balance and fairness in the Justice system and that justice flows like rives of pure clear crystal water! The retribution is almost always the result of an attack on < AMEN RA > or his < TERRITORIES > and it can appear quite disproportionate; particularly since the gap in time may run to hundreds and indeed even thousands of years.

Has the existence of and the physical presence of That Vast Galactic Civilization been proved by this "Hypothesis"? That is what is at the core of this Hypothesis, and which it is submitted, is "encoded" within the Egyptian Hieroglyphics and within the "Torah". It is not a simple mathematical code, for the beings who devised it are way ahead of the "pure maths". They are "builders" of this universe. The maths will explain to a certain extent how it works, but it is NOT the matter which makes it work!

I am still a little uncertain. It is all so tenuous, although I do accept that is the way of super communicate. While I still worry about the "script" which I have disclosed and which I can use, I am now satisfied that it is not super communicate. While I had a suspicion that it is a "Threns" script, it is in fact Atlantyon, and is in daily use at Tyem on the < FOOTSTOOL> in M 31 . In that regard it is much like English, Spanish or Chinese. There is an added element, which they need because of their level of development; and more particularly to give to "Truth" its proper importance. Equally they are very deferential to THE I AM THE, whom they refer to as < AMEN RA> and he is an < ATLANTYON >. He can also, as if to state the obvious,

< SHAPE SHIFT > to different Individual designs; as in the THRENS TYGERS!

That is in itself a warning. Shape shift to different designs. I see a large White Tyger pacing up and down his enclosure. He is NOT pleased. The Volcano, which is a large ATLANTIC one, is fortunately AT REST!

Again I am aware that < AMEN RA > may be RA, RE, RAY, RAE. If I understand correctly it is RA 1; or more commonly written as RA MA. The one and only. The I AM THE. The figure of RA in India? Possibly. And the RED TYGER?

While I am treating < AMEN RA > as an individual, albeit in a Trinity context, it would be entirely wrong to view him simply as a spaceman. My description of him as having an individual persona, while making him more accessible HAS A GALACTIC SCIENCE UNDERPINNIG IT. It should be borne in mind that he can take "many shapes" including that of "pure energy" as a < SPECIAL KIND OF PLASMA >. There is also a suggestion that he may be "asleep" for a long period of time. While this may appear to be a contradiction with him "neither slumbering or sleeping", it should be remembered that where the mechanism is working, it may not need an input at all times. This spiral galaxy spins, but in terms of this Hypothesis, it is < AMEN RA > who determined the program and the mechanism which makes it spin. And not just this galaxy! For the present I am comfortable with < AMEN RA > as an individual, because that state is currently pleasing to HIM, and of him being on DAL in Threns, in M 31 Galaxy!

And I am aware that I can have him walking off the pages of Revelation. He may not be what I expected. Indeed he may not be what anyone expected, but that does not change the fact that he is " THE I AM WHO I AM",to use that term.

He is powerful, but in a very controlled way. With the story of Kryst, whether that is believed or not, he has told the world PLAINLY what he can do. It is just that this World has chosen not to listen; to make up its own theories about the life of Kryst, and in certain instances to be entirely Anti Kryst and his message. Certain of the Christian Churches would probably refuse Kryst entry (if he was to return again) without him first submitting his credentials to the Panel on Doctrine (and doubtless with the demand for a miracle.) Some things do not progress in 2000 years! I have no doubt that is the view which RA would take. Such would not impress him!

In terms of this Hypothesis, in Heaven's terms, the Truth is VERY important and is a < PARTICULAR SCIENTIFIC UNDERSTANDING > relating to < INDIVIDUALS > . There is indeed a beauty in The Truth. But if any attempt is made to make "truth" conform to doctrine or dogma, any beauty, and more particularly the science is likely to be lost .Truth is the English word, *Veritas* the Latin, and Maat the Egyptian. In this Hypothesis that last word is changed to MaTT, but it means something different and SPECIFIC. It relates to the INDIVIDUAL and to the < HOSTING > of the < STAR PLASMA >.

"Pentecost" which is an English word, and which does not at first sight appear to super communicate, does possess the "super communicate word" "Ko" meaning Mouth. [Py Ny Ty Ko S T]. Thus the bread eaten in America which is called a "taco" [Ta Ko] does incorporate into it super communicate. And since "bread" is part of the "Holy Communion", I suspect that it is indeed a correct translation. I accept that it is obtuse, but that is in the manner of super communicate.

The power involved here is colossal, and there is no doubt that it must be shielded. I can sympathize with such as Moses if he did, as some writers suggest, destroy very advanced equipment because the people were frightened of it.

For a civilization or group of individuals to possess the keys to a wormhole, effectively super light travel, and not to understand what they had, and to destroy it, hardly bears thinking about. If it was done deliberately and maliciously, rather than to protect, then serious questions would arise as to whether they were entitled to have that advanced technology restored. While I had previously thought that its misuse would be similar to a gross misuse of all the hydrogen bombs currently on the planet, so as to destabilize the planet, in terms of the Atlantyon Galactic physics, that it NOT how the system operates.

It is not about destroying the Earth, in that sense, but rather of ADJUSTING its orbit round the sun, CAREFULLY and in a CONTROLLED MANNER so that what is currently Earth, with a very limited understanding of Atlantyon Galactic Physics, is SUBSTANTIALLY UPGRADED so that it become a < FOOTSTOOL> in strict Galactic terms. That requires as a FUNDAMENTAL the approval of the local star which is NOT simply a big ball of Hydrogen gas!

The warning of the Apocalypse is correct. If the science is used incorrectly it can cause a serious destablisation, but it will usually ONLY be done by an AUTHORISED OFFICER and WITH AGREEMENT of the LOCAL STAR! Very, very, very BIG SCIENCE. Talk of Global warming caused by man and carbon emissions is entirely erroneous and WRONG SCIENCE.

While the "Ankh" which was held in the hands of the Egyptian Ny TY R might at first sight just seem like a fancy symbol of the "neter" (Ny Ty R of this Hypothesis) it is in fact < THE KEY >. It <DESIGNATES > the < GALACTIC and ATLANTYON OFFICIALS > . Not only is it small, but it is like the baton as used in relay races, and IN THOSE RELAY RACES and in the EXERCISE ROUTINES is the SCIENCE. It can be used like a conductor's baton, as if conducting an orchestra, and in exercise routines, but it is IN FACT as PAINTED UP, the SYMBOL of a PARTICULAR GALAXY or series of Galaxies. It is light, usually made of strips of wood such as balsa (native to the Americas) and therefor it could be easily concealed within a Pyramid or beneath the large monument of a < RESTING TYGER > or indeed in a small tomb! As carried and passed from hand to hand it carries the message. If damaged it needs to be repaired and might be given to a carpenter to repair or to replace! As part of a cargo and placed at the bottom of an ocean; part of a cargo which did not reach its destination, it would simply disintegrate and its meaning lost! Carried on a ship or a plane WITHOUT proper authorization, the ship or plane might not reach its destination!

The symbol is the "ankh". I would call it in Super communicate "Ta An K............" While I thought that in super communicate the word was split, "AN" translating as "key", and the single "K" as the key to the Chariot of Fire; that is a wrong understanding. The "AN" is short for the word < ANANAN > which is Atlantyon and translates as "Living" the "K" is for the Atlantyon word which translates as "Director" and in the context of < HEAD of GALAXY >. The last letter is "H" which is short for the word "HA" meaning light in Atlantyon so what it is in fact is the SYMBOL for the HEAD of GALAXY; as I said above. While it may contain gem stones, and indeed is likely to contain both silver and gold coins, or even computer data on a chip, it is not of itself anything more than a fancy painted and weighted piece of wood.

But that painted wood and the STYLE, determines the STYLE OF GALAXY.

If the design shows it as the "ANKH" symbol that is of a < SYFERT > <GALAXY, OR COMBINATION > of the < HIGH, IMPERIAL and UNION SYSTEMS GALAXIES >. If however there is a substantially plain cover, with a blue outline, that is of a < BARRED SPIRAL GALAXY OR COMBINATION >, again of the <HIGH IMPERIAL and UNION SYSTEMS GALAXIES >. If it is both cut and styled and <SCULPTED> that is for a < SCULPTED GALAXY > or combination again of that <HIGH IMPERIAL and UNION SYSTEMS GROUP>. Just a fancy piece of wood, yes. Essentially worthless, apart from the gold or silver coins, but in the Science terms, very important. And the coins are placed in it in a particular way and to PARTICULAR and SPECIFIC WEIGHTS, each weight of silver coin representing a level of development of a particular < FOOTSTOOL> and its suitability to be part of the < HIGH, IMPERIAL and UNION SYSTEMS GALAXIES>.

Those < HEADPIECES> and the < SPORTING STICK > on which they are usually screwed is personal to its owner and user, and contains the encoding of its owner in the DESIGN. Again for security purposes, it is useless to all but its rightful owner. Its apparent uselessness can cause it to be thrown away; or hidden away. It is the < STAR > and in particular the < SEQUENCED STARS > which know how to make it, who designed it, and who is < AUTHORISED > to use it.

Those societies which seek to collect biometric data on their own people should proceed with caution, and ensure that they have safeguards which would satisfy the King of Heaven.

DA TA is a super communicate word, and abuse of that is likely to anger <AMEN RA>.

Before writing even one word of this hypothesis, I simply proceeded on the basis that it was all wrong and of no interest to anyone save myself. I have fought hard for this Hypothesis, and despite my doubts, I now consider that it does explain quite a lot; albeit that it appears obtuse.

I do not wish to upset the < Tyem AM >, nor indeed any of the other galactic INDIVIDUALS, particularly their < VISIBLE INVISIBLES >. However it is THEY who check this text, and who assist me with the revision of it. And I have been especially conscious throughout the whole of this work that I do not upset <THE I AM WHO I AM>.

There is a small phrase I use in super communicate. "Y (pronounced "EE") Va Da Mut Amut", which means "without intending yet causing".

With this text I am trying to avoid human blood sacrifice, stating plainly that it is NOT acceptable. And yet, in terms of this Hypothesis I am aware of the massive power of < AMEN RA > and of the < HEADS OF GALAXIES > and their < COMBINATIONS >.

In the sense of the "Sun", the local star, it is obvious; albeit kept at a relatively safe distance. Fortunately most often that power it is used creatively.

The position in terms of this Hypothesis is clear. If human blood sacrifice is performed, it is the abomination of desolation, which is performed, and that directly challenges not only < AMEN RA > but the entire collection of Galaxies of which that individual is a part!

Essentially that allows and AUTHORISES the release of the Military Dras commander, Tansarduron and to bring about the destruction of which Revelation talks !

Murder is NOT excused, just because there is some apparent Biblical reference to "permit that". That is the message of this Hypothesis. And I would submit it is not my message, nor indeed a new massage. It is a message which has the full backing of < AMEN RA > as I trust I have now accurately described him to HIS satisfaction .

In terms of this Hypothesis < AMEN RA > can operate a "Mirror Rule". That is some time expressed, as "do unto others as you would have them do unto you."

So, for those who love Human blood sacrifice; of mass murder, then for them Heaven is just that. They in their turn will be murdered by others of their kind. It is the words of Isaiah which warn. If they hate SYON and all it stands for, then the doors of SYON, the < MIGHTY SEQUENCED FIRE DISCS > are locked barred and bolted to such. Nothing which is HURTFUL or HARMFUL will be admitted to the < HIGH, IMPERIAL and UNION GALAXIES>.

For some there will have been a realization that what they did they had to do. They did not like it. They do not approve of Human blood sacrifice, but it was something which was unavoidable. Sparta are admitted, because they did not willing seek the conflict AND because they walked and FOUGHT in the manner of < AMEN RA > . Turn the other cheek and do not immediately retaliate. Make the < FORMAL COMPLAINT > to < AMEN RA > and seek guidance. Do that and it is the < SEQUENCED STARS > which will < HOST >and which will gently guide. It may be a path like that trode by Alendander, but take care to be < HOSTED > correctly!

That is where the passage in the "Lord's prayer" is relevant. "Lead us not into temptation". As Kryst said, "If the cup of suffering may be removed, then take it away." Unfortunately for him it was not possible. The test was of the people and their love of Human blood sacrifice. However, in terms of this Hypothesis, the Communion is now the symbol that it is understood that Human blood sacrifice is something which is not to be done; at least by those who seek to uphold the "Spirit" of the teaching of the Lord the Krystyesus.

[Note here. I am dealing with < VISIBLE INVISIBLES>. They are quire capable of listening to Kryst and removing him from the Garden of Gethsemane and replacing him with a < VISIBLE INVISIBLE >. That done Kryst can watch his own Crucifixion from the comfort and security of a Boat of Millions of years. That however means that Pilate and Rome made an exceptionally serious mistake in <u>dealing with a Galactic Director,</u> and puts <u>ROME</u> and <u>its eagles</u> at risk of serious retaliation AT A FUTURE DATE! These individuals are well able to set off Volcanoes and to cause earthquakes! Note also that this interpretation does not take away from the actual event, and is indeed more likely since they do not approve of Human Blood sacrifice!]

In that light the sleeping Dragon of Revelation might not be CORRECTLY APPRECIATED . For dragon read < DOUBLE HEADED SERPENT > and < FIRE DISCS > in the Scientific context.

I see < AMEN RA > watching, and not best pleased, about to unleash the lightening of his terrible swift sword! Admiral Yamamoto, remembering 7 December 1941 may have thought of the sleeping dragon as the United States. He would have been most unlikely to be thinking of Revelation, and of the power and might of the King of Heaven and the local < FIRE DISC >. In that context the sleeping dragon is the < FIRE DISC >; a pit which some film makers appear to have understood, even if only faintly! I presume the local fire disc has been "playing" with those films, in much the same way as with those who make and produce the Science Fiction!

I am reminded of the word "ToRAH" sometimes used to describe books of the Old Testament.

T O R A H. < TYEGA ON AMEN RA TYEGA DA HA >. Super communicate ATLANTYON translation:

< LORD of the PEACE CITY AMEN RA, THE LORD of LIGHT >.

So I have looked with this text for the Word of the Lord of Light, of the King of Heaven, and I have set down plainly what in terms of this Hypothesis, I consider that I correctly Understand . The Trinity concept is there, and that comes from the Atlantyon word Tyega for "Lord".

<THE I AM WHO I AM> is there because he IS HEAD of the GALACTIC DISC and of other SEQUENCED DISCS!

Heaven's requirement, as spoken in terms of this Hypothesis and in New Testament terms IS that All AUTHORITY IN HEAVEN AND ON EARTH WAS GIVEN TO KRYST. That means that someone gave it, and in terms of this Hypothesis that someone IS < AMEN RA > who is "The Father"; the DESIGNER!

Revelation talks in terms of the NY TY R being sent forth again, and like the "First" Passover, appearing again, and striking down those who are not "for the father". In that sense there is an instruction to leave those who are "sealed on their foreheads". A clear reference to the "Baptism" which is operated by the Christian Churches!

In Heaven's terms, and in terms of this Hypothesis, baptism is the symbol of the Trinity concept of < AMEN RA > and of the < VISIBLE INVISIBLES > which clearly and easily takes in The Lord the Krystyesus.

II

The proof of this Hypothesis? That is a < HOSTING EXERCISE >.

Although I cannot at this stage see them, my suspicion has to be that the TYGER, both grey and red are VERY real and like < AMEN RA > in the < VISIBLE INVISIBLE > concept watching closely both what I am writing and HOW it is received! In addition he will monitor events on the planet and as they require will <REPOSITION> the < FOOTSTOOL >.

Again I am satisfied the < FOOTSTOOL > is technical advanced science while Earth is not.

In considering this Hypothesis, long before I put pen to paper I used the terms "Tyem Am" to describe the grey cat race of space creatures. It is probably no coincident that "Grey Aliens" are used to describe extra terrestrials, and in that style are even shown in Science fiction.

Where did I get the grey cats from? I drew it from my mind. Then in Budge's work I noticed it in print. It is very obtuse, yes. This whole Hypothesis has been difficult for me. It still is. But I have tried. I would suspect that in "super communicate terms" Budge's work was kept from me until I had sufficient information to write this Hypothesis. And for the present, the mention of the <Tyem Am's> is the only proof that I am allowed. That and the change to GERY TYGERS and the understanding that that famous resting Egyptian cat does in fact ACCURATELY depict the THRENS TYGERS and that it is the < FOOTSTOOL IDENTIFIER > like a lighthouse warning Alien visitors who are unwelcome and not conform to design to < KEEP OFF THE GRASS >.

III

In terms of this Hypothesis there is a New Heaven and consequently a New Earth, because the understanding is now quite different. [Revelation 21]

That which was previously misunderstood, has now been "revealed", and there is every chance of it being properly understood.

This text is probably not what was expected. It is communication up close and very personal. No obtuse radio signals, just the written word. The Threns have no need or desire to contact seti sending a signal relating to "hydrogen". What they need to see is a CORRECT UNDERSTANDING of what they have LEFT, before they lose interest and <u>REMOVE their property!</u>

IV

I am aware of my vast shortcomings, and of the culture in which I live . It does not live by Truth, and has lost confidence in the real message of the Lord the Krystyesus and the SCIENCE which in terms of this Hypothesis has now been disclosed and BROUGHT OUT OF EGYPT!

The < AMEN RA > of this hypothesis is a very complex and private individual. He is old and yet he is young, like a baby! He is not just 2000 years old, 20,000, years old. He is yet millions of years old. As a small man, as he can make himself appear, he is approachable. As the individual Kryst, crucified and resurrected, he has allowed some of his power to be seen. But it is only a fraction of it.

For Threns to have him as a small <Atlantyon> individual and on one of their < FOOTSTOOLS > is a triumph for them and a severe criticism of this < FOOTSTOOL >. There was indeed no room for him at the inn; rather unfortunate that in his terms the inn was and is <HIS FOOTSTOOL> as Isaiah said!

And while I put him in Threns I am aware that he has NOT NECESSARILY turned his face from this <FOOTSTOOL>. I am aware also that his patience is running out. He does not want all these sacrifices, and especially he does not want the human blood sacrifices. And yet they continue.

While I might have said that in his anger with the people of this planet he has caused all his temples to be overturned, to make it quite clear that authority is with his son, that may be slightly inaccurate. The technology was left and the defacement and the ignorance of it has been SELF INFLICTED by the local population and their incessant blood lust. Reprogramming is certainly required!

The Anti Christian sentiment will be spotted for exactly that. And while Kryst may have said; "Father forgive them for they know not what they are doing," that does NOT apply to those who are deliberately pursuing Anti Christian policies with a view to undermining the Christian Church and those who are part of it. A matter fully appreciated by < AMEN RA > and CHECKED by HIM.

As I said I am dealing with < VISIBLE INVISIBLES > who have their own agenda, and who regard this as < ONE OF THEIR HIGHLY SECURED FOOTSTOOLS >

Leaving < AMEN RA > in Threns I am aware that he can watch there exactly what is transmitted locally here and that I currently have a very, very angry < AMEN RA > who is NOT PLEASED at the dreadful conditions on this one of < HIS FOOTSTOOLS >.

If they require global warming he can certainly melt the Ice caps in a very short space of time, simply by rousing gently the sleeping dragon which is the local < FIRE DISC >.

Many years ago, before the flood, they did not think < AMEN RA >would take action. But he was so angry at what was done, that he did take action. So again now as he looks, he is angry at the levels of violence, at the human blood sacrifice. He is well able to open the pages of Revelation.

He is so powerful that in essence he does not need to take any action. He can simply turn his face away, remove his staff,but he can also move the < FOOTSTOOL> and adjust the population to meet his requirements. And still he can stay <HIDDEN>. He is, after all, a < VISIBLE INVISBLE >, HEAD of GALAXIES >.

NOTE: I have had to substantially adjust this text from that originally written in light of the New Hypothesis. As said in the Preface it is the NEW HYPOTHESIS which contains the Science; and it is that Science which has required the text adjustments. Some errors in understanding still remain, and these are examination points in < ATLANTYON GALACTIC PHYSICS > or < APPLIED METAPHYSICS > .

The bibliography which is added, is added at this stage since it is not appropriate to the New Hypothesis. At the end of the New Hypothesis I will provide design details of the <HEADPIECE> which is referred to. That has been registered by me as a registered design, and that is part of the Technical science. It is called < APPLIED METAPHYSICS > because it does require that certain things are DONE and SAID in a particular way. They are thus < APPLIED >.

The < STAR CHARTS > likewise added at the end of the New Hypothesis are < STYLISED > for the < HIGH IMPERIAL and UNION GALAXIES > they are again designators and the < FOOTSTOOLS> are identified as < RESTING TYGER >. That is < THEIR STYLE POINT > and a < WARNING >.

THE OLD HYPOTHESIS
Notes and Bibliography

I   Notes

I have provided a list of books from which I have read and which have assisted me with the preparation of this work. It is important to me that I give the references so that the quality of my text may be examined by others to check my conclusions. That said I almost certainly will be said to disagree with those who feel that they cannot accept the terms of this Hypothesis. Some of the works have been quoted in this text and others may be quoted in future texts or are otherwise considered relevant by me simply because I have read them.

Where the works deal with science the fact that I make reference to them does not mean that I accept their "theories" or "hypothesis" as accurate. Simply that they were considered by me when working with this text.

The Biblical code books have attempted to draw attention to a possible code; and it may be that the use of material in this Hypothesis may assist with further efforts with that code. That will really depend, in terms of this Hypothesis, whether the code they have apparently found was put there in the first place.

I am <u>uncomfortable with copyright rules</u> because they can clearly restrict progress. That said the copyright in the names I have used in the Hypothesis including particularly the term < VISIBLE INVISIBLE > and the stylised use of the chevrons REMAINS with me, <u>particularly on super communicate ones</u>, since I am satisfied that is a < GALACTIC REQUIREMENT > and is not restricted to the short time scale of current copyright. The personal aspect of my copyright should also be noted! I am satisfied that the < VISIBLE INVISIBLES > will be watching and it is they who require of those who publish any part of this work for me that they protect my interest. The bibliography is not long, and the various works may assist with an understanding of this text. My many thanks to the various authors to whom reference is made.

II   Bibliography
1. The Good News Bible ISBN 0 564 00301 8
2. King James Bible
3. CH3 Hymnary (Church of Scotland)

(Note here the various Church song books of different denominations may assist, although not known to me because I am confident that the "Spirit" and by that I mean the "Holy Spirit" should be contained within them.)

4. Secrets of the Exodus, Messod and Sabbah ISBN 007133315 4
5. In search of Zarathustra, Paul Kriwaczek, ISBN 029764622 2
6. Cracking the Apocalypse Code, Gerard Bodson, ISBN 186204730 8

7. The Bible Code, Michael Drosnin, ISBN 0752809326
8. The Bible Code 2, Michael Drosnin, ISBN 0297842498.
9. The Ark of the Covenant, Roderick Grierson & Stuart Munro-Hay, ISBN 0297841432.
10. Lost Secrets of the Sacred Ark, Laurance Gardner, ISBN 0007142951.
11. The Gods of the Egyptians, E A Wallis Budge, Vols 1 & 2, ISBN 0486220559 ISBN 486220567.
12. Akhenaten, King of Egypt, Cyril Aldred, ISBN 0500276218.
13. The Elegant Universe, Brian Greene, ISBN 009928992x
14. The Hunt for Zero Point, Nick Cook, ISBN 0712669531.
15. Secret Chamber, Robert Bauval, ISBN 0712680489.
16. The Ra Expeditions, Thor Heyerdahl, ISBN 0045720207

THE NEW HYPOTHESIS

21
Finding Atlantis

I said in the preface that I am a member of a Christian tradition. That tradition has been welcoming and I am essentially both comfortable there and pleased to be there. That I was placed in their care I now know was not a detail. That applies to ALL those in that tradition. That tradition does require a fair degree of protest, including in particular in the < THROWING OF FOOTSTOOLS > if required, although I now accept the technical nature of such a comment.

I do not like revisionist historians who are trying to re write history or biblical text for political expediency, or those who are trying to persuade that it is in error, such as the scientists. I am well aware that much of the text has been carefully and skillfully written and other parts of it have been deliberately distorted. I investigate works which suggest the Bible may be looked at in a new light and I protest at those who tell me it must be viewed "their way", and to their heavily doctored and selected text.

Once I have picked up a book I like to finish it, but I will be aware fairly early on whether it is technically correct. I am a lawyer by training and that means that on many occasions I look at books and texts in a very different light. I enjoy a good detective story and an intricate puzzle. And in many respects the Bible is such intricate puzzle, as indeed is this text. This is not intended as revisionist, but rather at correctly identifying and understanding the very advanced science.

The "Preface" and "Two" subsequent texts is a style matter. It is much the same as the Biblical Style. That Style TELLS me that the Bible is VERY ACCURATE as to particular Science even although those who wrote it had little idea of what they were writing. Indeed even if they attempted to "doctor" it, it will STILL provide the information.

At a scientific level, for < ATLANTYON GALACTIC PHYSICS > the Preface is the TEXT to check. It provides the accurate information. It is or should be the correct answer. The two subsequent parts are the explanation as to how I arrived at that answer.

The application of the Human Rights Legislation is factually producing much wrong. In terms of the preface that is to be expected, since it is NOT ATLANTYON! It is a FUNDAMENTAL of the < JUSTICE and MEDICAL PROTOCOLS > that there is < FAIRNESS and BALANCE > in the justice system and where that is NOT the case, including where the justice system REGRESSES, such a society will be assessed as < NA SY > and < WITHDRAWAL of MATERIAL > is a likely consequence. Such Nazi societies whose legislation brutalizes their own people are likey to fall foul of the < SEQUENCED STARS >. That has EXCEPTIONALLY SERIOUS CONSEQUENCES.

<<< STARS >>> such as <<< THOR ARRAN ARGHAARTH >>> <<< HEAVILY RESTRICTS >>> who can do what with its <<< TERRITORY >>> and <<< INDIVIDUALS >>> living there and runs EXTENSIVE checking exercises over long periods. They will NOT TOLLERATE Human blood sacrifice nor anything which looks like it, notwithstanding that they are quite capable of vaporising cities far more effectively than Hiroshima and Nagasaki. Indeed in terms of these Hypothesis it is THAT STAR which is < PERMITTING > this text simply to convey its < FURIOUS ANGER > before arranging for delivery of < HOT PLASMA > in an Insecure and < HIGHLY DANGEROUS MANNER >. The view taken concerns the past 1000 years!

As a lawyer I preferred dealing with houses because the houses did not "run away" and "did not change their history." I have even purchased and sold in Arran blissfully unaware of the importance of the < STAR > < THOR ARRAN ARGHAARTH > and indeed of its <<<< HIDDEN GALAXIES >>>>.

When the new Land Registration system was introduced in Scotland I took to it like a duck to water as it was geography and plans based. Regretfully I did not appreciate a material defect which in part has led to the dramatic financial crisis currently affecting the entire United Kingdom. Like Heyerdahl with in his Ra I, I thought the Land Registration booklets preferred to the "unsightly cord" and bundle of titles. But what I was not aware of was the defect introduced in the 1800's when the Land Registration system was modernized and the Notarial Instruments changed. The change to English from Latin did not cause the problem. In fact it corrected the problem. The history, the cord of property ownership, is VERY IMPORTANT as is also the fact that individuals are involved in the transactions. The modern attempt to make it computerized, may suit the large Public Limited Companies, but it fails to understand the VITAL IMPORTANCE of <u>CORRECT DESIGN NAME</u> and the INDIVIDUAL. A point fully appreciated by the <<< STAR >>> <<< THOR ARRAN ARGHAARTH >>>. And the < STAR > notes the CORRECT and CORRECTED IDENTIFIERS and technical adjustments as to < PLACE > and < EVENTS > concerning < ATLANTIC TRAVEL >. And that < ATLANTIC TRAVEL > includes specifically < ATLANTYON GALACTIC PHYSICS >.

    The word "Thorn" in this connection is important. Using the formal name in chevrons if I write it as < THORNON > it can perhaps be more readily appreciated the connection with word "thorn" and individuals. If I relate it to < TERRITORY > and take the extensive territory of Amenhopis III and transpose that to a modern map, a certain incident before Pilate takes on a slightly different appearance, <u>and a much more dangerous appearance</u>. The £1.00 sterling silver Scots is thus FAR MORE DANGEROUS than it appears! Especially with its Latin words. This is a < FAMILY MATTER > and < GRANNY's RIGHTS are APPLIED > <<< HA KA PURE BLACKS >>>. <<< HIDDEN WARRIOR FVRECKRAN TYGER >>>.

    Part of the difficulty is that sometimes both the DESIGN and the "cord" are not seen for what they are. In the case of the first RA boat it was the tensioner which kept the stern up. If the stern was allowed to fall, the boat would sink. That is a DESIGN point. That, however, depended on the < ATLANTIC >. In good weather a badly designed boat might succeed, BUT that would not prove the Science! The Science is proved sometimes not at the first attempt but on the SECOND when the CORRECT DESIGN is used!

I am dealing with this material VERY, VERY, VERY carefully. The < BLUE WHITE STAR > <<<< THOR ARRAN ARGHAARTH >>>> IS in a different Galaxy, but both it and the Local star know exactly what I am on about and are watching! THE ≤ JUSTICE and MEDICAL > < Protocols ≥ AND a footstool throwing exercise. While this text is now < AVAILABLE > <<< THEIR GALACTIC AMBASSADOR TY KANSAL >>> <<< IS FORMALLY IMEDIATELY RECALLED >>>.

On a Global basis this territorial aspect and star involvement can be difficult to appreciate. Very difficult in fact. While I currently live in the United Kingdom, in the Northern part called Scotland, and Scotland has a specific history; very often apparently forced upon it, it is the < SEQUENCED STARS > which take a < DIRECT INTEREST> particularly in the case of < THOR ARRAN ARGHAARTH > with its < SPECIFIC REQUIREMENTS > disclosed by its < OPEN STYLE SYFERT HEADPIECE >.The correct clothing is THUS VERY IMPORTANT!

Some would doubtless like to currently "revise" it to make it "politically correct" and expedient. When the leaders including political and religious leaders do that, as was the case with the writers of the Bible sometimes the politically correct adjustments actually act like the unseen cord. They provide the spring tensioner, which keeps the ship afloat; they make obvious what they really waned to conceal.

Technically the United Kingdom is a Christian country. Its coinage currently says that with the letters D.G. Of course there is the wish to move to the Euro, but such coinage does not contain those words. Then there is the other argument that the gift D.G came from Rome and that it is not appropriately held. It may indeed be correct to say that it did come from Rome and THAT may make it < UNACCEPTABLE > in < STAR TERMS >. The Euro is thus Roman coinage and in < STAR > terms severely polluted on account of the practice of human blood sacrifice! I draw attention to the crown of Thorns!

The < BOUNDARY MARKER > for the <<< STAR >>> <<< THOR ARRAN ARGHAARTH >>> is on the Ground. The word < THUN >. Where even part of the <

ARGHAARTH > is in the name that is the < TERRITORIAL BOUNDARY MARKER > or < NEAR to IT> . The marker in fact is Hadrian's wall. Currently that is NOT in Scotland, but that aspect is not relevant, since the wall MOVES as a Boundary marker in time to do with the STAR SCIENCE. But it is the < STAR > which determines HOW and WHEN the boundary is moved. It is the < STAR > which < MARKS >. It < ANANAN NY ON TY IS >. It places part of its < PLASMA > < SAFELY > on the Head!

James the 1 and VI was aware of that. But like many before him and after he made a real mess with his Star Chamber! He was just not well advised on that.
Technically he required the services of an Egyptian VY SY R, who would have put him right at once on that and set him on the correct path. But the decision to print the King James Bible was not coincidence; certainly not in the style with its preface AND two parts. It is just that it is not understood the VERY ADVANCED SCIENCE which is within those pages. So it is not a coincidence that I select and insist on the King James Version when dealing with biblical references. There is no real problem with the Good News Version. Indeed a comparison in wordage is a worthwhile EXAMINATION question. But there is a MATERIAL SCIENCE ASPECT with the King James Version [VER SY ON]. That I had not appreciated when I wrote the Old Hypothesis.

While in this text I will make reference to the actual pages, I am not going to quote the particular words. That requires, failing all else, sight of a copy of The King James Bible to work out exactly what I am saying. I am not being difficult. Yet again there are TECHNICAL SCIENCE ASPECTS in that.

I pause here with my typing, now corrected. I had previously picked up a copy of the King James Version, but at this stage in revision I do not need it. I do not need to know every word as if drawn from a computer disc. No what I need is the SPIRIT, the DISTILLED essence of it. <u>But it is more than that</u>. I am conscious that my uncle had a similar version with a light blue cover. I have misplaced that copy, but I last saw a similar one in Valetta, Malta and on that occasion the cup was given to me, and I partook of the bread and wine. A short time later, perhaps even a year or two later I purchased a copy of a Book on Tut Ankh Amen, which I read on the plane back. It may have been the time when we passed by Etna and I could see the plume of smoke billowing out. It was like a giant chimney. In that book I came across the word "Apiru." I had not previously seen it. I was familiar with the term Hyskos, but that did not mean much to me. I was aware that there were two groups of Pharaoh's, the North and the South, but I was always confused by those terms.

A teacher teaching me to remember the difference would have asked me to remember it using a mnemonic which is the grammatical term. "SMHEA". Some men hate eating onions.
For those who have studied Geography it should be immediately apparent what I am talking about; I hope. For others it will seem utterly peculiar. But it is necessary because these mnemonics are important.Some are < VERY ADVANCED> and some are straightforward.

[There is a < HIGHLY COMPLEX MNEMONIC > in this text at this stage concerning the < STAR > < THOR ARRAN ARGHAARTH > and the Blue covered bible. It is to the effect that Rocket Science in the WRONG technology for Galactic travel BUT that the correct science has been and is being ABUSED!]

The Star <<< THOR ARRAN ARGHAARTH >>> notes the position and IS SATIFIED with the notation.<<< CORDED and TRILBY >>>.

This is called the ATLANTIS Hypotheses (in the plural) and this is the NEW HYPOTHESIS. As such this part is dealing quite a lot with TECHNICAL SCIENCE. And one of the important aspects of that science is Gravity and Anti Gravity. In this connection the "Flags" which the airlines carry and display are important, especially if they are in mnemonic form. And the mnemonic may be "advanced" and "compound". This is similar to the mnemonic "some men hate eating onions" but in the modern developed world a little easier to see and appreciate particularly for those familiar with airlines. These mnemonic "codes" allow detailed information to be stored in short form and "hidden" among other largely irrelevant text. In part that is done with this text. As of 8 May 2009 I have revised this text here to explain the < COMPLEX MNEMONIC > rather than to specify a specific airline. The earlier mnemonic which is to do with the order and list of the Great Lakes between Canada and the United States, [Superior, Michigan, Huron, Erie, and Ontario] HIDES the < ADVANCED GRAVITY MNEMONIC >. In these "Advanced" mnemonics COLOUR is important.

As I said this is the NEW Hypothesis, or Ra 2, if I take the reference from Heyerdahl's boat. And so I have to be taking about the "Boat of Ra". And in that connection the A 380 is a very good example. A double decked four engine piece of anti gravity equipment; commonly known as an aircraft, or airplane depending on which "spelling" is preferred. But it is NOT the spelling which makes it fly. True if the manufactures text are not correctly understood because of a spelling mistake, the actual plane might not fly, but for reasons such as that they have test programs. And in like manner Heyerdahl's first K ON TY KY voyage was such a test flight.

Heyerdahl's hypothesis was that off Cape UBY similar Egyptian boats had snapped their rudders and drifted across the Atlantic. Quite good as a Hypothesis and his "proof" of that stands. However, as I said this is the NEW HYPOTHESIS, RA 2, and his journey in RA 2 was MUCH more than he appreciated; indeed than even I appreciated initially. For the Egyptians did not "accidentally" snap their oars. They DELIBERATELY set out to the RED SEA with view to crossing it. For the RED SEA in question was the sea of the "SETTING SUN". That is a PHYSICAL MATTER. The current Red Sea is simply a diversion from the real text.

As I said this is Science, and it is like a mathematical proof. I may HAVE ALREADY provided the proof and I do not need to write another word. I have to appreciate also that BRIEF WORDS are best.

While word processors are a useful tool, further words may obscure the relevant parts and may cause material points to be missed. But further words, although brief, are required for proof purposes to show the correct scientific proof and that it is correctly understood.

[When considering gravity, it is NECESSARY at a GALACTIC SCIENCE level to consider the WHOLE SPIRAL or SCULPTED GALAXIES and THE STAR COMBINATIONS. To talk in terms of zero gravity in space discloses an entirely incorrect understanding of the Galactic Science and indeed of the Stars!]

In the case of Ra 2 Heyerdahl brought the boat builders from America [Spanish usage] and from Lake Titicaca [using Anti Gravity equipment] and asked them to build the boat on this side of the Atlantic.

[An Applied Metaphysics Professor would have marked me down at his point if I did not make some specific points about the construction of Ra 1 and 2 before blandly saying "He then sailed it (Ra 2) across the Atlantic successfully because he had correctly understood the technology; even if he did not appreciate it."]

Yes he had BROUGHT the builders to this side of the Atlantic, and because of Egypt, but there were MORE than subtle differences between the two boats. It was to do with the TIME, the manner, the DESIGN and BUILDERS, the PLACE and the REASON.

The Original Ra 1 was the Old design and like the Old Hypothesis here, built to the wrong design, in the wrong place and to a certain extent for the wrong reason. That had to be corrected and was substantially done with Ra 2, and which, with assistance, I have NOW done with this text.

The builders were brought [first] FROM lake TY TY KATA, which was an ELEVATED location by ANTI GRAVITY EQUIPMENT to a LOWER location at MO RA KO, which has an Atlantic Coast, but where the boat was built in a SECURE and GATED LOCATION to enable the completed journey to be made and for their theory to be "proved". The first one could be built in Egypt, but the second had to be built at or near the Atlantic Coast.

The A 380 is a piece of Anti Gravity equipment, and it is similar. As a "Boat of Ra" it is like the Ra 1. It is not fit for purpose. I do not mean that in its "flying ability" but as a "Boat of Millions of Years."

That is the ancient Egyptian reference to the Boat of Ra. The flying disc is sometimes used and the reference is to the Phoenix; which is the firebird. A "Sunderland" or "Catalina" flying boat AGAIN conveys that reference. The "Sunderland" because of its "location" reference, the Catalina because of the "Cat" reference.

Now the obvious fire bird to those in the developed countries is a craft like Concorde or a fighter pane like a "Blackbird" especially one using "Stealth Technology". Not a lumbering A 380. But while Heyerdahl safely crossed the Atlantic, those on the Titanic were not so lucky. Some did. Like Heyerdahl on the first Ra they were rescued and some of them doubtless crossed the oceans thereafter, as indeed Heyerdahl himself did on Ra 2. But in technical terms the A 380 in a Galaxy context is like the small papyrus boat. That the airframe is built shows TECHNICAL ABILITY to build a craft of suitable size. However current physics, particularly the use of rockets and explosive technology, discloses that the connection between Aircraft and Galactic travel is NOT APPRECIATED. The same can be said of the way that the Egyptian writing and drawings are NOT appreciated for the ADVANCED SCIENCE they contain. These are <u>HIGHLY TECHNICAL and FACTUAL MATTERS.</u> That can be checked quite easily from ordinary television transmissions where the WRONG UNDERSTANDING is regularly given in transmissions.

I said here that it was not an "accident" that the boats set out from Egypt. What were they doing? Where were they going? Who sent them?
HO RAM HEB.

He stopped the painting of his tomb so that the painting is unfinished. After all what was the point of all those Egyptian NY TY R, if when you needed them, they were not there. He was a military commander, and was upset by the taunts about the NY TY R and because he considered that he had lost a valuable piece of technical equipment which had considerable military significance and which could not easily be replaced. So instructions were given secretly. Two pieces of specially marked Black Diorite had to leave Egypt. They were under threat from the ABRU PER SY. [This term might be taken to be "unbelievers" but it really means those who are NOT our design and who are AGAINST us. It highlights a different understanding, a point well appreciated by the NY TY R who would be inclined to regard such as "evil". Thus the ABU [GATES] by which they mark and designate their territory. Certainly in their terms SY NA, from which the word sin is derived.

The < BRICKS > were not very big, but equally not very small. They fitted together to form a seat. It was a mission from which there was likely to be no return. They were chosen men; some of them excellent seafarers. The instruction was to take the Diorite Bricks and return them to the Lord of the Great Southern Kingdom. As the bricks departed Egypt Horamheb had given up. He was angry. He was aware that Boy King Tutankhamen had been used and was aware of the missing NY TY R exercise stick, < THE AdSY >. He had been left with only TWO < HEADPIECES >. That loss was painted on the walls of Tut's tomb as ONLY TWO are shown, and they are NOT on the AdSY, but loose. That painting is there to this day and has been reproduced in a number of books. TWO unattached AdSY HEADPIECES. They can be hand held as in the exercise routine. On the AdSY stick there had been other < Headpieces > all attached. HE KNEW that the AdSY stick was used for exercise purposes, but it was as far as he was concerned the symbol of their and his Authority; as given by the NY TY R.

[A < LARGE WORKING AdSY > swung inappropriately might cause a head injury of the kind on King Tut's skull because of the screws at its base. That it had been forcibly taken is SELF EVIDENT as it was not in the tomb, nor correctly shown on the Tomb paintings! They are not just fancy stylized drawings.]

But what Horamheb did not appreciate was that to work the AdSY's properly the < INDIVIDUAL > had to have the correct < STAR APPROVAL > without which the AdSY would not work. And even if it appeared to work initially, it would soon stop working if the underlying science was not properly understood or if it was misused. Indeed if misused, far from acting as a kind of compass, would simply leave those holding it wandering aimlessly and coming to regard it as a worthless tool.

[The small golden figure of Tut Ankh Amen found in the tomb shows him holding the AdSY with the TOP to his chin, AND elevated from the ground as it rests on his feet, and with the top as in his beard. That AdSY is for a TRIPLE BARRED, representing a BARRED SPIRAL GALAXY, which is CORRECT for THIS Milky Way Galaxy AND < PTAHAARAN>.]

What HoRAMHeb did not appreciate was that the Lord of the Great Southern Kingdom was WATCHING EVENTS CAREFULLY.

The Lord of the Great Southern Kingdom is very partial to red meat, beef cattle or lamb and fish. Indeed one of his favourites is *Ruraskaradon* (wild boar). It was not a matter of what to eat or what not to eat. Safety is important. Wild boar, may be delicious, but they can be dangerous, and for that reason, not a good food source. So with other animals and fish.

But he would not find the Lord of the Great Southern Kingdom where he was sending his messengers and their sailors. They might find him in America, but it was more likely HE would find them, and then only when their journey had ended. And in any event, meeting the Lord of the Great Southern Kingdom could be dangerous. Horamheb knew the "secret" name for the Lord of the Great Southern Kingdom. Like all best kept secrets it was open to public scrutiny and was available to many. It was just that if you did not know what you were looking for you would not find it. As he looked upon the figure of the resting Tyger he mentioned the name KYEN TY AMEN TY. That would translate as the Most Mighty the Most High, The Amen, of the City of Kyen. And the Pharaoh's cloth headdress of DARK BLUE and GOLD reflected the colour of another TYGER. It was not in the slightest obvious unless you KNEW what you were looking at.

Horamheb had not seen the White Tyger nor the Blue Grey Tyger and it would be many years before the White, the Blue Grey and the Black Tyger would be seen or understood. I use the present tense for the Tygers because I am conscious that in the case of each I am talking about < AMEN > and I am talking about REAL INDIVIDUALS who have been around for a VERY, VERY, VERY long time and who are known in technical terms as < VISIBLE INVISIBLES > .

In many respects that is what the Pharaohs tried to be and that is what King James was on about with his Divine Right of Kings. That is what the Middle Kingdom [China] is talking about when they talk of the Mandate of Heaven. *It is NOT a piece of paper. It is an INDIVIDUAL.* It is encapsulated beautifully in the words <<< I AM WHO I AM >>>. King James Version Page 62 has it as <<< I AM THAT I AM >>>.
That is FUNDAMENTALLY a description for the LORD of the VINYARD where the VINYARD in question is the FOOTSTOOL. The < TA AT >. The word < HA > in Atlantyon without a gender, would be taken to be in simple form as a light, but its use in a name is GENDER SPECIFIC and is to IMPLY ENLIGHTENMENT . The letters TT again in Atlantyon refer to the LORD of the GALACTIC DISC. (The TY KANSAL is the MIGHTY GALACTIC DISC). Thus Moses is being told that he is SPEAKING with and to the LORD OF THE FOOTSTOOL to use the Isaiah term.

But face to face with The White Tyger, The Blue Grey and especially the Black Tyger. Nose to nose with a Tyger! VERY DANGEROUS. Thus the line about what would happen if he saw the face! A sound barrier or other SHIELD may be prudent for safety reasons. And millions of "light years" distance might be preferable to their HOME FOOTSTOOL; unless that is, that THEY are to OUR DESIGN and they are BIG PUSSY CATS and we are THEIR FRIENDS!

In LIKE manner when Moses conveyed those words to the Pharaoh, the Pharaoh should have UNDERSTOOD EXECTLY WHO WAS REFERRED TO .
However, MUCH EFFORT has been put in to DELIBERATELY CONCEAL and it needs to be DECONSTRUCTED and INTERPRETED, especially if the intention is to understand the correct science.

Thus the < STICKS > with < SNAKES > has NOTHING WHATSOEVER to do with actual serpents. It is to do with the < AdSY'S > their < HEADPIECES > and the < GALACTIC TRAVEL > where the snakes in question are the routes to footstools and might be taken to be the < ONE

PANEL > < TWO PANEL > and < TRIPLE PANEL AdSY UPSTANDS >. The "double headed" serpent is thus the symbol for the understanding of this < WORMHOLE > or as I call it < SUPER LIGHT > travel. It is the < ATLANTYON GALACTIC PHYSICS >. The "many" headed serpent is thus the "HYDRA" which in fact is the references to the NUMBER of HEADPIECES on the AdSY.

This < HYDRA > is a COMPLEX mnemonic since it contains the letters < HY >. Note also that I have used the words <<< I AM WHO I AM >>> and within TRIPLE CHEVRONS. That usage is to DEFINE with DUE DERFERECE to the LORD OF THIS GALACTIC DISC and to OTHER LORDS of THEIR GALACTIC DISCS. This is NOT a detail. This also highlights the CONSIDERABLE CONFUSION about the whole LORD of the DISC since the Egyptians had been CORRECTLY TOLD that there were DIFFERENT GALACTIC DISCS and not all of them worked to the same understanding. <u>Most of that has currently been Lost thanks principally to religious intolerance.</u> On that aspect the scientists are correct.

The word < THAT > while it MOST ACCURATELY conveys the SUPER COMMUNICATE of the Lord of the GALACTIC DISC, in modern English usage tends to convey a "thing" as opposed to an Individual.

The < INDIVIDUAL > aspect is < MATERIAL >. The < KING of HEAVEN > in that sense is the < LORD of a GROUP OF GALAXIES > which work to a < PARTICULAR > < SY > <AGENDA > when SY in Atlantyon is < PEACE >. This is a SCIENCE ASPECT and it can be difficult to understand. It likewise is SEEN TO BE LOST by individuals whose only interest is in MONEY, since the PARTICULAR GROUP of GALAXIES, which are indeed wealthy, have OTHER INTERESTS rather than money, not least of which are TRAVEL and the DESIGN of INDIVIDUALS! But they can spot the misuse of money and will < WITHDRAW THEIR ADVANCED TECHNOLOGY > for such misuse, leaving former < FOOTSTOOLS >as isolated and sometimes lifeless planets!

In terms of these Hypotheses the Individuals are called < VISIBLE INVISIBLES > and they are also called < AMEN >.

The < THREE AMENS > has to be treated carefully since that is likely to mean a < PARTICULAR GROUP OF GALAXIES > to this < PARTICULAR DESIGN > and the < HEAD > of such group as an < INDIVIDUAL >.

The LONG AMEN [AMENDARAN SYASTAKATA] is an Atlantyon phrase which a teacher might say to a class. It translates as "Please pay careful attention to what I am saying."

The CORRECT NAMES and the CORRECT UNDERSTANDING is FUNDAMENTAL. It has the ability to be LOST in translation.

However with < ULTRA > mnemonics the information is actually straightforward. The < ULTRA > mnemonic for the < SPECIFIC GALAXY COMBINATIONS > of < TEN > < GALAXIES > in the correct sequence is < THE TEN COMMANDMENTS >. It is actually straight forward once it is know that it is a very sophisticated mnemonic < AT ULTRA >.

To return to the voyage by Horamheb's messengers. When they arrived at the Americas Horamheb's messengers knew where they were going; even if the crew did not. They had to follow the course to the south and they would be CONVEYED to the lands of the Southern Kingdom, to the land of the RTUR. [Now RTUR is like an AMEN and has been around for a very long time.] A minor typographical error makes me type Ryur because of the spacing on my keyboard. So I see how easy it is to adjust the spelling so that only those who are in the "know" know exactly who is being talked about. Thus "Arthur"!

Thus the "Consul" who enters Egypt might be taken for the < Kansal >, since the pronunciation is as a hard "C". Spanish does not have the K, except until recently so uses the letters "Que". KWTLS KO ATLS, is therefor written Quetlsokatels. And I have already explained the importance of the Atlantyon word < KANSAL > and the use of Chevrons.

The Atlantyon does not have a "J" nor a "Q". The capital "Q" written as a 2, might highlight an Atlantyon word with its Number 2 Tone Control! [Quantum is thus 2Uantum or

WANTUM and does not super communicate to Atlantyon]. In all of these "spelling mistakes" the <<< FOOTSTOOL at the LANAST STAR >>> is conveniently "Lost." Those who KNOW exactly what is being talked about are quite happy at the confusion and the nonsense story of the Lost Atlantis.

But the FOOTSTOOL MARKER is there ON THE GROUND. Horamheb looked at it and said the name KYEN TY AMEN TY. He sent the stones to the RTUR and in due course at the end of their voyage the stones indeed were delivered . < FVRECKRAN > [M 51, Whirlpool.]

Which brings me back to Heyerdahl and to Kweensland and NORTHERN TERRITORIES and most importantly the < AT LAN TY K > ocean.

For as Horamheb understood it, as the Kyen Ty Amen Ty understands it [Note the tense and that name is used with permission], the Polar ice cap is to the NORTH of AUSTRALIA, effectively the SOUTH POLE and the bricks had to be delivered to the SOUTHERN KINGDOM. That Southern Kingdom is what is currently called NORWAY, and part of it is the ORCADIA, now part of Scotland. The land of the ORCA. I will try to define the territory later.

The ORCA may not be visible there all the time but that is THEIR area and that INCLUDES Scottish waters and the < AT LAN TY K > ocean. And they can travel to the Polar (Antarctica) if they wish. Who can lift themselves clear of the water if they wish using those tails to demonstrate an understanding of ANTI GRAVITY! As for digital, someone should examine those "clicks" of theirs. Sounds of highly advanced digital data, communication and language !
Humans can also lift themselves clear of the water. They do that by climbing steps, including steps to an aircraft, even if those steps are a "finger". Now they can not only Walk on the water, they can fly over it. It is all part of the same technology.

But the Great Southern Kingdom is not just Norway. It will take in A CONSIDERABLE DESIGNED and DESIGNATED TERRITORY, including Scandinavia and even to Russia, where there are indeed SY BY RY ON TYGER ! It TAKES NO ACCOUNT OF POLITICAL COUNTRIES. It is a <<< STAR MATTER >>> with <<< INDIVIDUAL STAR

DESIGNATORS >>>. The <<< STARS >>> and the <<< NY TY R >>>have <<< GATE MARKERS>>> and < PROTOCOLS > of what is < PERMITTED> and what is NOT. A Political Government which makes errors will be < OVERTURNED >. This is NOT easily identified and may take hundreds of years. It can be done quickly, as in the collapse of the Berlin Wall!

Atlantis has "risen from the sea". It was ALWAYS here. What it lacked were its < GALACTIC CREDENTIALS >. I am dealing here with VAST and POWERFUL GALACTIC CIVILISATIONS who like to do business with their FRIENDS but who will deal FEROCIOUSLY with their ENEMIES and those who threaten them and their < FAMILY STYLES >. For their friends they will RE PROGRAM and UPGRADE the so called "dna" in effect re writing it, which is a <u>MUST for serious GALACTIC TRAVEL</u>, even in this Galaxy .

To CROSS the < AT LAN TY K > ocean CORRECTLY is a MUST for serious Galactic travel. As I have said Heyerdahl did do that CORRECTLY with Ra 2. That he set out in K ON TY K first was a pre requisite for the correct crossing of the Atlantic.

The word CORRECT is important here. While his crossing was correct, others have pushed the point. In certain respects it is a minor inconvenience, but in certain instances the FAILURE to CORRECTLY CROSS the < AT LAN TY K > <u>has serious and long lasting consequences</u>.

The Titanic is one such incident. The "boat" in question was the "White Star". That is a < Star > designation. Ty and Tan do not go together in Atlantyon terms. It did not just "happen" to hit the iceberg! That was in 1912. This is now 2009. I said Heyerdahl was CORRECT with his voyage and that was after 1912. But the problem with Titanic persists. And now it is not just Titanic.

When dealing with serious Galactic travel it is the < SEQUENCED STARS > which are involved and they are the < GATES OF FIRE > .

Permission is required to < CROSS > the < AT LAN TY K >. Thus in certain respects < TREATY > obligations with regard to air travel. But it is NOT a detail. < WINTER

NORTH ATLANTIC > is < APPLIED >. That is a < FOOT EXERCISE > as is evidenced by the "Plimsole" line.

Where the <<< STAR >>> <<< THOR ARRAN ARGHAARTH>>> is incorrectly said it might appear as the "dog star". It is in fact not < SY RY US > but in a < DISTANT and HIGHLY SECURED and HIDDEN BARRED SPIRAL GALAXY COMBINATION >. The mnemonics have to be worked carefully! < KHUN AARON>, individuals and location < KHUN AARAN> [M104.][Letter "K" is mainly silent as with "F" in < FVRECKRON >; individuals!]

These mnemonics are VERY VERY VERY advanced. Blue and White are < STAR COLOURS > so that airlines with those colours should be CORRECTLY BADGED. That however depends on the mnemonics and a correct understanding of them! A correct understanding of the Galaxies is ESSENTIAL as is the understanding that a number of large Volcanic eruptions are caused by the delivery of < HOT STAR PLASMA > and that some weather conditions and minor crust cracking are caused by the < SAFE DELIVERY > of what would otherwise be < EXCEPTIONALLY HOT and DANGEROUS PLASMA >. As in < PLASMA > from <<< THOR ARRAN ARGHAARTH >>>!

The RTUR sits on an adjustable seat. It is not his judgment seat, the DIORITE BRICKS, but it is none the less his seat. And he does not need his seat to take a view and form a judgment. That he is more likely to take after a brisk walk and with a PROPER and CORRECT ADDRESS to the LOCAL STAR!

The < GLASS BRICKS > were smashed. It was done deliberately and maliciously. That might not appear to have involved the ATLANTIC but it DID. Not as obvious, but there none the less.

The < LANAST STAR > notes the position, marking < AT PROTOCOL>.
<<< THOR ARRAN ARGHAARTH >>> notes the position marking at <<< WITHDRAWAL CONFIRMED >>>.

22
Keeping Atlantis

While it is one thing to FIND Atlantis and to understand what is meant, the main problem is to keep it and to KEEP IT SAFE.

The individual Kyen TY Amen Ty is not easily seen. General Horamheb, looking at the resting Tyger Monument may know that is who is represented, but that Tyger keeps many secrets, and over time the name has been well hidden.

I found his name in Wallis Budge's dictionary of the Hieroglyphs. But I had to change the spellings and FIRST I had to understand and appreciate that Kyen is a LARGE CITY on a footstool in Threns Galaxy [M31]. It is not a telescope I use. The distance is too great. It is <u>THE CORRECT UNDERSTANDING.</u>

I have used here the reference to Heyerdahl's Ra 1, as a "cord" in this Hypothesis and one aspect which has been touched upon is that the design was wrong in respect of the stern tensioner. In fact it was much more than that. It was incorrectly built. <u>And that is a DESIGN matter</u>. As I said that was rectified by Heyerdahl for his boat Ra 2. In respect of this text I have RECTIFIED a MATERIAL ERROR in DESIGN.

With the Old Hypothesis I did not have the correct BLUE PRINT and was NOT aware of the HIGHLY TECHNICAL and NON NEGOTIABLE POINTS.

To do that correctly I required instruction from the REAL NY TY R AND ATLANTYONS and their GALACTIC PHYSICS which means that I needed the assistance of the Local FIRE DISC; the Lanast Star and the < STAR SEQUENCED GALACTIC ALLIANCE > < CORRECTLY NAMED and DESIGNED >.

This is HIGHLY TECHNICAL. I now APPRECIATE that that delivery is done over TIME PERIODS and at DIFFERENT LOCATIONS. It is much like a MOVEABLE DIMENSIONAL JIG SAW PUZZLE. Thus the understanding of and the permission to name the WHITE TYGER INDIVIDUAL the KYEN TY AMEN TY.

Like Heyerdahl, I have to BRING the TECHNOLOGY from M 31 and M 51 in particular! That is MORE than a bit tricky, for while Heyerdahl was dealing only with local boat builders, in terms of these Hypothesis I am dealing with The Kyen Ty Amen Ty the White Tyger and MANY others in HIGHLY EVOLVED and MASSIVELY DEVELOPED FOOTSTOOLS and EXCEPTIONALLY POWERFUL SPECIES DESIGNERS AND THEIR INDIVIDUAL FIRE DISCS in CONTROL of HUGE HIGHLY SECURED POPULATIONS and MANY GALAXIES, including in particular the, SCULPTED, SY FERT and <u>BARRED SPIRALS</u>.

These INDIVIDUALS the AMEN and the RTUR can WHERE they WISH be in MORE THAN ONE PLACE at the SAME TIME and at DIFFERENT TIMES and over VAST DISTANCES. <THE BLACK TYGER FVRECKRAN>.
<u>That is the difficult part to understand.</u>

The Kyen Ty Amen Ty does NOT NEED to appear here in his TYGER shape. Indeed I am not sure if I could take the Tyger Headed two legged individuals who I call Threns. Yes they can appear here as a WHITE TYGER, but that is NOT the kind of Tyger he is. That is what the RESTING TYGER MONUMENT REPRESENTS. He appears here ONLY as a TYGER HEADED individual WHEN and ONLY if this FOOTSTOOL is COMPLIANT. Otherwise he is simply a little Atlantyon, MALE or FEMALE.

He can SHAPE SHIFT. <u>That is what the RESTING TYGER MONUMENT SAYS</u>.

But this is not FICTIONAL SHAPE SHIFTING. It is DONE BY THE LOCAL STARS and OTHER STARS in the SYSTEM. <u>CONSIDERABLE CARE MUST BE TAKEN when dealing with such individuals. They are very powerful; as if to state the obvious.</u> It is partly for that reason that they are < HIDDEN > and their < GALAXIES > are shown as < HIDDEN >.

They MARK their territory with BOUNDARY MARKERS. Often they will arrange for others to do the building. Thus Hadrian's Wall. It marks THEIR TERRITORY but while the Wall is fixed their territory is MOVEABLE.

It extends around what THEY regard as the GREAT SOUTHERN CONTINENT. [Effectively much of what is currently the North of the Footstool, Globe]. Their NORTHERN TERRITORY takes in Australia, New Zealand and Antarctica and a chunk of America [Spanish] from the Antarctic side. Thus the Falkland Islands are designated.

The RESTING TYGER is their FOOTSTOOL MARKER. It is also used on their STAR CHARTS. You do NOT THREATEN these TYGER and MOST CERTAINLY do not attack LARGE AKUA TY K VOLCANOES and MOST CERTAINLY you do not do it in the name of the THREE TYGERS, collectively KNOWN as the THREE AMEN [although one of them an RTUR as well].

HADRIAN had other Northern borders. One leaked like a sieve. It is the RHINE DONAU line, and is STILL the border today. And He was TOLD that EGYPT was their GATED TERRITORY and that he had to act there in accordance with THEIR MANDATE. A matter duly noted in a building he built in Rome with some of their material and to their design!

In German, if I remember correctly the word order is TIME, before MANNER before PLACE before REASON. This chapter is called Keeping Atlantis. If Atlantis is the WHOLE FOOTSTOOL, why the Borders?

It is to do with the NY TY R and ATLANTYON DESIGNATED TERRITORIES and CERTAIN DESIGN PRACTICES for their INDIVIDUALS which are MATERIAL. These are <u>THE NOT NEGOTIABLE</u> MATTERS. Out with these designated areas other designs may be allowed but these MUST NOT interfere with or THREATEN the NY TY R or ATLANTYON ones and their territory. Where that happens the NY TY R and ATLANTYON will take action.

It may appear to be a sluggish response, but it can be very terrible, for they can cause the Volcanoes to be set off and the Footstool Plates "adjusted."

TWO items which are ESSENTIAL and where <<< THE HIGH IMPERIAL and UNION GALAXIES <u>AND</u>

COMBINATIONS DESIGN PROTOCOLS MUST BE MET >>> are on < MEDICINE and JUSTICE >.

Where the Justice protocols are NOT met, the individuals are NOT conform to NY TY R and ATLANTYON design and WILL BE REMOVED. Essentially, they are THROWN OUT or REFUSED ENTRY to the NY TY R and Atlantyon Territories, which includes the < HIGH IMPERIAL and UNION SYSTEM GALAXIES and their FOOTSTOOLS >.

The ATLANTYON term for those out with their territories and NOT to their design is NOT PROTOCOL (which means not acceptable) and the NY TY R one is ABRU (not Apiru as mentioned in one text.) Which means [Out with our designation-beyond our gates]. The GATE MARKERS are ABU; thus ABU SY M BAL. These Gates are MOVEABLE and indeed ABU SIMBAL demonstrates that. With the recent building of a dam the Gate was raised. This is TECHNICAL and is a WARNING that they are WATCHING UNFOLDING EVENTS VERY CLOSELY.

The ABOMINATION OF DESOLATION is one of their terms. It basically refers to ALL MURDEROUS PRACTICES, including judicial ones and MOST PARTICULARLY to HUMAN BLOOD SACRIFICE. And CIRCUMCISION falls into that category. While they can accept that for MALES they will NOT for FEMALES. It is PROHIBITED. In like manner the age for adulthood is 18 for BOTH MALES and FEMALES. <u>SEX MUST BE CONSENSUAL.</u>

In good "Scots" parlance NO MESSING with that.

Alexander the Great and (E) L (N) Y ON NY DES of Sparta know the FATAL BLUNDER, for Nagasaki, Hiroshima and KOBE. It is the DIVINE WIND. UNDER NO CIRCUMSTANCES do you sacrifice your own troops. The odds may appear insurmountable but there MUST be some prospect of success. <u>YOU MUST look after your own troops</u>. Alexander knew that. That is why he was so successful. But that is <u>also why he failed</u>. L Y ON NY DES of Sparta knew that and BECAUSE they KNEW that they held the PASS as the GATES OF FIRE.

Which brings me neatly to "Keeping Atlantis". The GATES of FIRE. That again is a NY TY R and ATLANTYON term.

Any Physicist reading this should know what is coming. If one of the GATES is at ABU SIMBAL on the Nile and another is the RHINE DONAU line, then the fire is <u>WATER MADE</u>. The word FUSION comes to mind! There are MANY TYPES of FUSION, some of them VERY DANGEROUS, others VERY SAFE! The <u>PLASMA FUSION PRESERVES and DEFENDS LIFE</u> and is usually provided by the BLUE and BLUE WHITE STARS.

The whole of the NILE from E TY O PY YA and Lake VY TY KO RA to the Mediterranean is ALL NY TY R territory and ALL GATED. The "Gator" symbols are obvious! Any dams which are build MUST HAVE NY TY R approval. Aswan is permitted for it serves the NY TY R purpose to RAISE the GATES of FIRE. I am dealing here with <u>GALACTIC INDIVIDUALS WORKING with and LOOKING AFTER THEIR TERRITORIES.</u>

Sometimes the NY TY R arrange for a particular brick to be MOVED and in certain instances placed in a WALL. It may be quite small, so difficult to identify. But they will know it was put there and by WHOM. Thus Hadrian's Wall. Thus Hadrian's building in Rome. The granite came from Egypt. He needed NY TY R approval for that. If he did not have it <u>the building would have long gone.</u>

The same applies to the <PYLON> OBELISKS. None are where they are by COINCIDENCE including the one at the bottom of the Mediterranean! And some which have not come from Egypt MARK the NY TY R and ATLANTYON boundaries CLEARLY. TRAFALGAR, KOBENHAAVON and ABU KIR. The last name gives it GATE REFERENCE CLEARLY. Most words with ABU in them are SPECIFIC GATE MARKERS. That includes PLACES NOT TO GO and NOT TO BUILD. Build in such locations and the buildings will be taken down. They are like HOLES on the ground!

The boundary is not a straight line and has many twists and turns in it.

To the NY TY R their territory which is EGYPT INCLUDES the PROMISED LAND and that is as defined at the time of AMEN HO PY IS III, BUT moved to the MODERN MAP. [My spelling and my pronunciation. Amen o Fis is an incorrect pronunciation]. That makes many individuals PROTOCOL who might otherwise fall to be classed as ABRU. But watch. Individual < FAMILY > practices are RELEVANT.

The NY TY R and ATLANTYON marking is WINTER NORTH ATLANTIC. The GRAVITY is increased + 2, so while the line on the ships remains the same, the safe cargo loading means that the loading on the ships should be LIGHTER loaded so that there is TWO FEET gap between that line and the actual load. The date 2 January 2009. And the period is extended so that only May and June are NOT in the Winter period. There is No obvious change, but the < STAR > notes the position and < HOW > and < WHY > it was < CORRECTLY APPLIED >.

II

In many respects this text is like a Math's Solution or a physics solution and at examination level. It is a VERY SCIENTIFIC solution, WHICH MUST draw from local events to show that I CORRECTLY UNDERSTAND EXACTLY what I am talking about. The subject? Super light travel from <Footstool to Footstool>. <<<HOSTING WHITE AU FVRECKRAN>>>.

It is WAY BEYOND current physics and astrophysics. Putting on a FEDORA or TRILBY and with or without the < SPORTING HEADBANDS > I might add, AT this TIME they have the WRONG EQUIPMENT and are LOOKING in the WRONG PLACE with the WRONG UNDERSTANDING.

<u>NY TY R and ATLANTYON PROPERTY MUST NOT BE MOVED or ATTACHED WITHOUT THEIR EXPRESS PERMISSION and at the CORRECT TIME.</u> And that applies ESPECIALLY to their BRICKS. Horamheb knew that but he had PERMISSION. He was trying to send them to the Lord of the GREAT SOUTHERN KINGDOM, the KYEN TY AMEN TY. And the Lord of the Great Southern Kingdom was WELL ABLE to see where the RTUR's SEAT

was being taken and was well aware that it was to be moved AWAY from those who are ABRU PER SY.

They were NOT pleased to discover aircraft engines were being sold to ABRU PER SY territory in the late 1930's and made Mr. Churchill aware of their anger. And in like manner they do not approve of the Great Southern Kingdom providing ABRU PER SY with advanced technology. The KURSK incident in "North Atlantic" and "AR TY K" is a similar warning to NY TY R territory. There is no problem dealing with territories formerly part of the Great Southern Kingdom, such as the RAGH, but care should still be taken to ensure that they have not become ABRU PER SY.

Note here, as should be obvious that the term ABRU PER SY is VARIABLE. That aspect is HIGHLIGHTED by the PASSOVER and by BAPTISM. The BAPTISM makes INDIVIDUALS PROTOCOL. Those not baptised are likely to find themselves classified as ABRU PER SY. But it is NOT as simple as that. This is to do with the STYLE of INDIVIDUALS and FAMILY PRACTICES. Individuals taken into a PROTOCOL FAMILY are PROTOCOL.

Business practices are ALSO INVOLVED. If balance and fairness are NOT FUNDAMENTAL to the JUSTICE SYSTEM such system will be regarded as ABRU PER SY. Such system is NOT entitled to the HIGH IMPERIAL and UNION GALAXIES technology, which includes DNA and substantial medical and scientific technology and they will WITHDRAW their material from such .

If a Government indulges in SHOW TRIALS and MANIPULATES the EVIDENCE to secure CONVICTIONS, if its punishments are HARSH and OPPRESSIVE and involve human blood sacrifice such GOVERNMENT is CLASSED as ABRU PER SY. It is a NY TY R and ATLANTYON GALACTIC classification by the HIGH IMPERIAL and UNION SYSTEM GALAXIES. <<<FVRECKRAN>>>.

This text is to do with KEEPING ATLANTIS. And it is the GATES of FIRE which can be used to do that.

The < FAULT > lines on the map are clear as is the < RA D ON > gas. The GREAT GLEN and the lines

HELENSBURGH to   STONEHAVEN and GIRVAN to DUNBAR.

This is to do with the SAFE STORAGE of PLASMA from such as RYGEL and ATLYR and SYRYUS. Not surprisingly this PLASMA is DELIVERED SAFELY as <<< MIST, RAIN, SNOW or FOG >>>.

I am not going into the technical detail here. That is detail for < ATLANTYON GALACTIC PHYSICS > or examination questions on this text.

When it is delivered there will be certain "unusual" and local weather systems and conditions; very cold or very hot; most frequently as a result of ATLANTIC conditions and usually only + or - about 10 degrees Celsius.

PLASMA DELIVERED SAFELY from ALTYR and certain OTHER STARS in the HIGH IMPERIAL AND UNION SYSTEM GALAXIES is STORED SAFELY under the control of the "Sleeping Warrior" the local Volcano centered at < AR RAN >.

That is what the STARS in this TYPE of GALACTIC SYSTEM are all about. The <u>SAFE STORAGE of the PLASMA</u> and the <u>PROTECTION of their POPULATIONS</u>.

Each of the stars ALTYR, RYGEL, SYRYUS and LANAST, may ALLOW an INDIVIDUAL to SAFELY FEEL THEIR PLASMA. That is what the TERM <<< HOSTING >>> MEANS. It sits on the head GENTLY like a FEDORA or a TRILBY or in the case of ladies a large wide brimmed hat, with or without feathers. The < PLASMA > is IN FACT STORED SAFELY INSIDE THE HEAD because that is what these STARS REQUIRE. To MOVE from this footstool to a RECEIVING FOOTSTOOL that RECEIVING FOOTSTOOL STAR or STARS MUST PUT THEIR PLASMA SAFELY into the INDIVIDUAL INTENDING TO TRAVEL. This SCIENCE is CALLED <<< APPLIED METAPHYSICS >>> and the RELEVANT STARS KNOW EXACTLY WHAT I am writing about and THEY CHECK this TEXT for ACCURACY and that it is to THEIR REQUIREMENTS.

Alien visitors are ONLY ALLOWED on this FOOTSTOOL if the <u>LOCAL and CORRECT SYSTEM STARS PERMIT.</u> The RESTING TYGER and the substantially damaged Hieroglyphs are the STARS WARNING to KEEP AWAY unless the STYLE REQUIREMENTS ARE MET.

In certain respects easy stuff but potentially very tricky.

One of their MNEMONICS is "Some men hate eating Onions." This is a GATE marker for NY AGRA ; another GATE OF FIRE. Quite obvious actually at the HORSESHOE FALLS. The Northern limit of the Great Southern Kingdom is at the shore line of these lakes to the SOUTH (that is the USA side). It is part of the KWEENSLAND which with the other KWEENSLAND NORTHERN TERRITORY explains AUSTRALIA, NEW ZEALAND, with some <<< SCULPTED >>> PACIFIC ISLANDS and KAR I BEAN and <<< AT LAN TY K >>> islands. And of course < AN TA R TY KA >. The TSAR is male while the CSAR denotes female. Makes it easier to see the NY TY R TERRITORY. It might even take in the RAGH although there is some < VOLCANIC CUTTING and FOOTSTOOL CRACKING > to be done.

The <<< IN FAMILY >>> arrangements are what are MOST IMPORTANT and they are MONITORED CLOSELY, particularly by pilots of Boats of Millions of years observing PROTOCOL PERIODS to check that they are <<< CONFORM to DESIGN before making CONTACT >>>. While variety is allowed and indeed desired, particularly with EXTENDED FAMILIES, there are <<< VERY DEFINITE and DISTINCT and SPECIFIC STYLES >>>. MALE and FEMALE is a FUNDAMENTAL DESIGN MATTER. Cloning is NOT PERMITTED and artificial means of reproduction are SERIOUSLY FROWNED UPON!

III

This is referred to as Keeping Atlantis. While I have touched on "local" events over some 5000 years I am aware Atlantis is MUCH OLDER. And in many respects the LANAST STAR is well able to look after itself and its <<< STYLES >>>.

This text is about COMMUNICATION and TRAVEL within this Galaxy and out with. As such I have to consider the position of "visitors".

Some visitors are PERMITTED, others are NOT. Some are permitted to certain areas BUT not to others. In many respects it is controlled by the local LANAST star. And is NOT the remit of Governments and politicians. Where governments make a mistake on that point, they put at risk HUGE numbers of individuals. The < PASSOVER > is NOT a FICTION. It describes the a REAL EVENT of REPROGRAMMING the LIVING "DNA" when Local stars and Others are checking individuals and can be VERY FRIGHTENING. It is NOT a door marker exercise. It is a REAL SCANNING to ascertain if the INDIVIDUAL is PROTOCOL or NOT and to be UPRATED or REJECTED. There is NO HIDING PLACE.

It is acceptable in certain fictional texts to talk of monsters, but when dealing with the science and that includes Dinosaurs certain aspects MUST BE ACCURATELY REPRESENTED. Thus in this text I have to deal with it like the answer to an examination question in <<< APPLIED METAPHYSICS >>> and I MUST HAVE in it the REQUIRED ELEMENTS.

One of those required elements is the < INDIVIDUAL VISIBLE INVISIBLES >, such as the Kyen Ty Amen Ty.
For physical equipment another is the A 380 type aircraft. In essence it is Heyerdahl's Ra 2.

In that connection I am dealing with a factory outside the City of HAAL and a new craft being built. That new craft can reduce the journey times as the PROTOCOL PERIODS have been shortened. Only ONE MONTH outward from THRENS and ONE MONTH HERE at ATLANTIS. A 12 month journey is cut to 8 months and the round trip is 16 months instead of 2 years. A substantial time saving. Note the ROUND TRIP aspect is MATERIAL.

The craft need to be the size of an A 380 for technical reasons. A 747 is the wrong shape and too small. But even if an A 380 can be built here, which is part of the PROTOCOL TEST REQUIREMENTS for GALACTIC TRAVEL, the required question is; "HAVE the JUSTICE and MEDICAL PROTOCOLS BEEN MET?"

That is ENTIRELY a FACTUAL ONE.

While I have "distilled" this text, [and revised it wearing my TRILBY and without and with corded headbands and < SPORTING >] I have also CUT it substantially since certain material is the area of both <<< APPLIED METAPHYSICS >>> and <<< ADVANCED APPLIED METAPHYSICS >>>. In fairness I have added some HIGHLY TECHNICAL MATERIAL and EXPLANATIONS while wearing my Trilby.

Essentially it is for the LOCAL LANAST STAR in PARTICULAR to be satisfied as to PROTOCOLS.

I am reasonably satisfied that the TECHNICAL PROTOCOLS are SET UP CORRECTLY for a BARRED SPIRAL GALAXY COMBINATION of the MILKY WAY TYPE which this one is and as part of the HIGH IMPERIAL and UNION GALAXIES WITH THEIR ASSOCIATED GALAXIES. The <<< NUMBER >>> is a <<< SPECIFICALLY ORDERED TEN >>>.

The Star Chart is in colour on the rear cover as is required.

On these charts the PART OVALS represent < FOOTSTOOL STARS > of the BLUE TYPE. The FULL OVAL over the BLACK RESTING TYGER shows < THIS FOOTSTOOL AT THE LANAST STAR > and the black represents a < HIGHLY SECURED FOOTSTOOL >. From both charts and the rear cover chart, the MIDDLE CLOSED GALAXY is seen with its YELLOW DISC. In the light blue spiral the Black Line to the Red at the top represents the MOVE from GALAXY to GALAXY. Thus the BLACK and RED from this GALAXY to the NEXT. But the Black and RED to the lower Blue oval represent this GALAXY since the red has pale blue either side. The DARK BLUE is the GALAXY PATTERN. When the DARK BLUE is in the ROUTE at RED and BLACK that signals a Galaxy change. While the rear cover says TWO galaxies, there are in fact THREE; this DRAS galaxy, a TRANSIT GALAXY < POWER CLOSED > which is REFUSING COMUNICATION and TRAVEL LINKS, and the TOP, THRENS.

The white rectangle is the GALACTIC PLANE with this star bottom right. The HIGH IMPERIAL and UNION

RECTANGLE represents the ROUTE MAP, from BOTTOM RIGHT to TOP. It stops with BLUE, but from that Star location would move to yellow, as SYRUS is to LANAST for example.

IV

There are certain aspects here which are difficult and certain which are very easy. To show a CORRECT understanding of < PROTOCOL > what is required is not Rocket Science but of a CORRECT UNDERSTANDING of the TYPE of CRAFT used and the SPECIAL ROUTES to be taken.

Currently travel to NEW ZEALAND and AUSTRALIA is eastwards over territories which are NOT PROTOCOL in GALACTIC TERMS. Likewise various airlines are NOT PROTOCOL again in Galactic terms. What is required is that the < PROTOCOL > Territories route their craft along the ATLANTIC ROUTE and in a < PROTOCOL > manner. That is essentially what COLUMBUS did and THAT is what HEYERDHAL did. The Atlantic is the FOOTSTOOL OCEAN and it will ONLY PERMIT APPROVED TRAVEL. This is NOT a detail. It is < STAR MATTERS >. Likewise to INTERFERE with transit to or BETWEEN PROTOCOL TERRITORIES ACROSS THE ATLANTIC is to ATTACK the < SEQUENCED STARS >.

The < STAR GATE MARKERS > are < THORNAN > and < FVRECKRAN > and hand washing of a Judicial whitewash kind will simply NOT DO.

Returning to the Airlines, even an A380 cannot currently fly direct to Auckland from Glasgow or London. But what it CAN do is to DEMONSTRATE the CORRECT UNDERSTANDING of the technology and FLY < PROTOCOL COMPLIANT >. Thus LONDON to KY RO [Gated Protocol Territory] or to AD DIS [Gated Protocol Territory] . It can also do the more technically difficult. London or Glasgow to TENERIFE [AKUATIK VOLCANO] [GATE MARKER for BOATS], then to ASCUNSCION [GATE MARKER for BOATS]and to the Falkland Islands [GATE MARKER] before making, INVER KARGIL, CHRIST

CHURCH and AUCKLAND all part of [AKUATIK VOLCANIC ISLANDS] < SCULPTED > before making it to Melbourne and Perth, WA .

There is no need to change to those routes UNLESS it is < PROTOCOL COMPLIANCE > which is sought! While CURRENT ATLANTIC carriers could change and add to their routes, where airlines with mnemonic Names are flying those Atlantic routes, as for example to Ascension or to the Falkland Islands, that would tend to suggest < LANAST STAR > approval. But that should be neither assumed nor taken for granted! Ascension is a Large Aquatic Volcano and it and its neighbour St Helena have ALREADY made their requirements known!

Likewise with the Science fiction, substantial adjustment is required to make them MUCH, MUCH, MUCH more technically accurate. Thus the emphasis has to be on <<< IN FAMILY >>> arrangements, and the SAFETY of such and a <<< CORRECT INTERPRETATION >>>. Wrongly report < Family Styles > in the newspapers and that could have seriously adverse affects on Protocol Compliance, even if other aspects are done correctly. It really does require a substantial change of emphasis so that BALANCE and FAIRNESS are SELF EVIDENT in the judicial systems at a FACTUAL LEVEL.

In many respects that is for the individuals themselves. If the individuals do not wish to be < PROTOCOL > then they will not become such. The same applies to the Countries and their territories. It is all FACTUAL.

In respect of films and entertainment much more of fancy and elegant diner and dancing sequences, and far less gratuitous violence general brutality and incorrect sexual behaviour. As for SEX, <<< THAT is MATERIAL and it MUST BE a CORRECT understanding of it and the IMPORTANCE OF SUCH >>> <<< IN FAMILY >>>. Failure to understand that correctly and the "dna" can be SERIOUSLY down rated rather than up rated and not only will there be NO GALACTIC CONTACT for many, many, many more years, but in the interval there is likely to be serious genetic incompatibility in sexual matters following on the down rate!

<<< Hermarut >>> [pop 1 million approx] which is the luxury and Ambassadorial district of <<< Tyem City >>>[Pop 25 Million +] is similar in many respects to Valetta [except that most of the squares have obelisks in them, even small ones], although on a landscape basis and climate basis the area is similar to Tenerife between Santa Cruz and Puerto de la Cruz and Garichico.

Wet suits are often worn by the furred Threns when swimming and surfing [a favourite pastime at the beaches by the airport at <<< Palutyankeron >>>] so that the local large fish species do not regard them as fur seal food! And they have grey and white Orcas which patrol most of their surfing bays to keep the surfers safe!

As I have said this GALACTIC SYSTEM has HIGHLY, HIGHLY, HIGHLY advanced and predominately PEACEFUL CIVILISATIONS, which delight in FAMILY, PARTYING and TRAVEL and who ENJOY and INTEND to CONTINUE to enjoy LIFE in all its fullness; including over many ROTATIONS(many lifetimes).

The < PROTOCOL > is marked as < CONFIRMED >

23
Threatening Atlantis

In this Hypothesis Atlantis is the whole footstool. So the view is taken of the conditions on the whole footstool.
Currently while there is a developed western culture, parts of Africa and Asia are at SERIOUS PROTOCOL CONTRAVENTION. Where that is politically driven it is in Atlantyon terms unacceptable. It is the Lord of Atlantis who has been crossed as I have PREVIOUSLY DEFINED <<< THAT INDIVIDUAL >>> and <<< THE SYSTEM FIRE DISCS >>>.
During one revisal of this text I kept the King James Version open beside me. The pages of Isaiah. Chapter 54 at Verse 5 are interesting.
The expression the Lord of Hosts is used. I HAVE ALREADY DEFINED < HOSTING > in ATLANTYON and THRENS TERMS. That is a SPECIFIC MEANING in terms of these HYPOTHESES.
I am dealing here with ENORMOUS and SECURED GALACTIC GROUPINGS and their HIGHLY ADVANCED SCIENCE>. That science REQUIRES that it is DEMONSTRATED to THEIR UNDERSTANDING a CORRECT INTERPRETATION of the MATERIALS they have PERMITTED TO BE LEFT at this < FOOTSTOOL >. That is not done by posturing politicians or religious authorities manipulating words to distort accurate information. To the Atlantyons and others of their GALACTIC SYSTEMS such comments are GROSSLY OFFENSIVE coming in the main from ABRU PER SY politicians. Such political comments have much to do with political and religious posturing and nothing whatsoever to do with TRUTH. TRUTH is a MATERIAL ATLANTYON and THRENS GALACTIC SYSTEM CONCEPT since it relates to < VISIBLE INVISIBLES >.
Thus the comment, "I am the Way, The Truth and the Life!"
MUCH WORSE is that such comments by politicians and others often IMMEDIATELY HIGHLIGHT a FAILURE

to GRASP the <u>FUNDAMENTAL GALACTIC and the ATLANTYON and THRENS NATURE as SHAPE SHIFTERS</u> and is ACTUALLY A DIRECT THREAT made to HUGE SYSTEMS of GALAXIES by individuals, who if they had understood what they had been taught over many years, <u>should have known far better than to do such a thing</u>.

I am ENTIRELY SATISFIED that NOT ONLY will the <<< Kyen Ty Amen Ty >>> and the <<< Tay Ha Ty >>> agree with me but also many in THAT TEN SYSTEM GALACTIC COMBINATION, including their < VISIBLE INVISIBLES!

They are indeed TWO TORA from different < Footstools > but of the Three Threns, the THIRD TORA is <<< <u>THE RTUR</u>, VISIBLE INVISIBLE a REAL BLACK TYGER >>>. Somewhat of a <<< ME R L ON INDIVIDUAL >>> who can wield a <u>TERRIBLE SWIFT SWORD</u>. A bit like a SLEEPING WARRIOR who has been wakened from his "gentle" slumber.

The Tay Ha Ty who is of this Galaxy notes the TERRITORIAL MARKER excluding the City of Edinburgh. The Kyen Ty Amen Ty has been aware of it for some time. The designation was < APPLIED > and the RED TYGERS moved to [KING U SY] to CONFIRM.

Both these individuals deal with PLASMA of the KIND which is used to make PARTICULAR STARS. If they authorize the delivery of < HOT STAR PLASMA > from a < BLUE or BLUE WHITE > the effects if < NOT SECURED > will make that visited on Hiroshima Nagasaki and <u>Kobe</u> mere pinpricks! As I said if secured, is simply falls safely as an unusual variation in ordinary climatic temperature!

[Note here the Three Cities. It is the VISIBLE INVISIBLES who determine the TIME SCALE and in the case of Kobe while that was devastated many years after the end of the Second World War and by CRUST CRACKING, the MASK was still maintained. Events are NOT exactly as they appear. The word < KO > in Atlantyon is to do with the Mouth, as in Ta Ko. TY KO YA is thus in Atlantyon < HIS MIGHTY VOICE >][Note here that that virtually IMPLIES that Tokyo is < PROTOCOL TERRITORY >. Once that is <

UNDERSTOOD > it < HIGHLIGHTS > certain aspects about the Second World War which are < NOT PROTOCOL > to put it very mildly! <KO RAY FVRECKRAN >.

Almost certainly NO MEANINGFUL CONTACT would be PERMITTED until the Iron Curtain was taken down. But watch here. Much of the IRON CURTAIN countries are in fact PROTOCOL TERRITORY, so what was seen was hiding the reality. It is in fact drawing attention to the < BARRED SPIRAL > nature of this < FOOTSTOOL> and its < LOCATIONS >. VARIOUS populations were thus being SECURED. This is NOT easy to see particularly in light of the atrocities visited on Russia. Again this is to do with INDIVIDUALS and PROTOCOL. Individuals who are NOT PROTOCOL should NOT be brought to PROTOCOL COUNTRIES and INDIVIDUALS who are PROTOCOL should not be taken to NON PROTOCOL COUNTRIES.

For Example: In < PROTOCOL > terms if the UK authorities lodged an extradition request to Russia, in < PROTOCOL > terms that can only be agreed to if the UK is < PROTOCOL >. In terms of this text Russia is substantially PROTOCOL. England, however, is ONLY protocol if HADRIAN'S wall which is a NY TY R boundary marker is MOVED SOUTH as was done at the time of James VI. That wall has been MOVED SOUTH PREVIOUSLY, but CURRENTLY in 2008 and 2009, the line takes in only PART of HADRIAN'S wall and EXCLUDES EDINBURGH. It is a NY TY R and ATLANTYON designation and has nothing to do with the UK Government.

Recently a Scottish Court was held in London, and while that may be acceptable to the United Kingdom Government, it does not make London a < PROTOCOL > location if the Atlantyon's or Threns have marked it as < NOT RESERVED >. The same applies to Den Haag. What about U TREKT? Is it in the Great Southern Kingdom or not? In < PROTOCOL > terms the Supreme Courts in Edinburgh are < ROMAN >and thus < NOT PROTOCOL > for that reason but primarily they are < NOT PROTOCOL > because they are NOW in < NOT RESERVED > territory. This is a GALACTIC MATTER! The UK Authorities are likely to make Edinburgh Protocol if the business practices which they conduct there are protocol. In Galactic terms the banking system is currently 2008/9 < SERIOUSLY NOT PROTOCOL > which is < SELF EVIDENT >!

The ATLANTYONS and NY TY R are not trying to be difficult. They are well aware of the point with the Scottish Courts .

This is a < PROTOCOL > matter. If the Scottish Courts and the European Courts do not meet the required < PROTOCOL STANDARD > on < BALANCE and FAIRNESS > there can be NO CONTACT and certainly no travel in Galactic terms. Human rights are NOT RELEVANT. It is < ATLANTYON GALACTIC PHYSICS > which is involved. There are VERY VERY VERY specific requirements which must be met on a < FACTUAL COMPLIANCE BASIS >.

Hadrian is well aware that they are not to be pushed on that one and while Hadrian will hurriedly point out to them that he built the wall and built the monument in Rome to THEIR SPECIFICATIONS as requested, with the ATLANTYON and NY TY R capability for FOOTSTOOL CRACKING and VOLCANIC activity, he will be well aware of the potential significance of the damage to a Roman Eagle.

The ATLANTYONS and NY TY R duly note the position. The line is revised and taken along Hadrian's wall but the City of Edinburgh REMAINS NOT RESERVED, despite representations, as does FIFE on a vertical line just to the East of Cupar. There is considerable NY TY R and ATLANTYON anger with the location St. Andrews and its UNIVERSITY.

TREATY OBLIGATIONS are of MATERIAL CONCERN and INTEREST to the NY TY R and ATLANTYONS. They are VERY, VERY, VERY particular as to where their Protocol individuals may go and the TREATIES which PERMIT that. It is GALACTIC TREATIES which allow MUCH of the GALACTIC TRAVEL; particularly in BARRED SPIRAL GALAXIES.

Since Scotland is < PROTOCOL> considerable care should be taken in dealing when moving Scots out with < PROTOCOL TERRITORY >. Thus if the United States is not on the same < PROTOCOL> an Extradition Treaty involving Scots may have very serious repercussions. That also applies to old mistakes and might justify a < NOT RESERVED > on London for incidents in Edwardian and Elizabethan times. This is < GALACTIC SCIENCE > and it is not a child's toy! Watch since the < TIME > element may involve TWO Elizabeths, and NOT necessarily in the same way. July 7, might be protocol in the period 1953 to 2008 but not thereafter. An incident in 2009 is viewed differently. As I said in the case of James VI, London was almost certainly Protocol, but clearly it was NOT RESERVED at the time of the Plagues and the Fire of London. The latter was probably a necessary clean up after the plagues.

TREATY OBLIGATIONS have to be treated with considerable care. If BREACHED the NY TY R and ATLANTYONS will apply their GATES of FIRE simply to PROTECT THEIR INDIVIDUALS. That essentially is what was done by the Russians! The individual populations did not see it that way but that is factual in ATLANTYON terms. And to a certain extent it is the Russians, and in particular their Admiralty, their Atlantic, Arctic and Black Sea Fleets which currently may be viewed in symbolic fashion as holding the "GATES OF FIRE".

In that connection CONSIDERABLE CARE should be taken with the <<< 1707 >>> TREATY of UNION, in view of its DATE and its NAME! The separate "Scottish Jurisdiction" is actually MASKING the ATLANTYON REQUIREMENTS, as Hadrian well knows!

Although the < ATLANTYON > mechanisms may not be easily "seen" given the FIRE DISC connection, they can devastate. While I have said the Russians may hold in symbolic fashion the Gates of Fire, the ACTUAL < GATES OF FIRE > when dealing with < GALACTIC PHYSICS > are the Sequenced Fire Discs, including the Local Lanast Star! And in their case there is not a lot that can be done to stop them since the controls are with PARTICULAR STARS and with THEIR MECHANISMS.

It is correct to say that in their arsenal of weaponry they have many bows. It is relatively easy for them to move the footstool (that is after all partly why it is so called) so that the orbit is varied. Sometimes that REQUIRES to be done and CRUST CRACKING at particular locations is unavoidable. To do that or not to do that can cause climate change. Considerable climate change. They can adjust the spin speed of the footstool within DEFINED PARAMETERS, which can be very minor. Indeed they may REQUIRE to adjust the SPIN SPEED simply to SET UP the GALACTIC MECHANISMS to permit the < FOOTSTOOL to FOOTSTOOL TRAVEL >.

These are THEIR OWN MECHANISMS and < SEQUENCED STAR MECHANISMS > so there is NOTHING ANY GOVERNMENT can do except to speak kindly to them. For the most part they will ASSIST since they wish to PROTECT and SECURE their POPULATIONS.

I check Isaiah 54 at verse 9. While the waters will not be used to move the footstool, [VIOLENTLY], they can still be "Moved" carefully so that even part of what is a land mass ceases to be such and what was previously beneath the waves is raised above, or indeed the ice melted simply as part of the REPOSITIONING PROCESS. Such statements are simply TELLING about HOW the FOOTSTOOL OPERATES. It is a FACTUAL MATTER and OBVIOUS. Even a basic geography class at senior school level should be taught this and know this as ADVANCED SCIENCE and GEOGRAPHY. The correct teaching of BASIC SUBJECTS is a PRE REQUISITE to GALACTIC TRAVEL.

[When visiting another footstool it is of considerable interest to know the Geography of you own footstool since a visitor is likely to be asked to give an account of places to visit and of SIMILARITIES in locations. Thus for example a particular view at Malta is similar to the large promontory at one of the Dras Cities on its footstool where the TAY HA TY has a palace. The four main Dras cities are vast, containing in many districts like connected towns, a few hundreds of millions of individuals, although they are spread over large areas on their Continents ; one of which is similar to Australia.]

This is both GEOGRAPHY and SCIENCE and where it deals with specific locations on other inhabited footstools is the SCIENCE of < Applied Metaphysics > WRIT LARGE and CORRECTLY TAUGHT.

Isaiah 65 at 17 is relevant. Once the FOOTSTOOL is RESTORED to STATUS and <u>ONLY WHEN the FOOTSTOOL is RESTORED to STATUS</u> with its GALACTIC LINKS is SYON RESTORED. I can write this text but the proof of the pudding is in the eating thereof. Where is the Boat of Millions of years?

Isaiah 66 at 1 is appropriate. There is the clear reference to a FOOTSTOOL and to the fact that it is the PROPERTY of the SOVEREIGN LORD. When describing him as the LORD OF HOSTS, when that HOST is actually represented by a SOVEREIGN COIN it is a PARTICULAR ASPECT which is being discussed. It is the < VISIBLE INVISIBLE > and < HOSTING >.

[In < APPLIED METAPHYSICS > terms HOSTING is a REAL FEELING. The relevant Stars will know what I am talking about, and in part it is for me to explain. A soft hat like a Fedora or Trilby is good way to try and feel it. It is on the back or top of the head. It is probably the weight of about 5 to 7 gold sovereign coins, but more in a powder form like sand or a small rock. <u>Gold or silver sand in a pouch for example and balanced on the head</u>. I rests only for a time and is gone. But it is a VERY DISTINCT FEELING. It is not easily forgotten. The other similar feeling is the Animal Magnetism where that is put in. It is quite a specific feeling. It does pass, but the location of where it happened is not likely to be forgotten. It will usually involve another individual again to state the obvious].

In the < SPORTING > program of < Atlantyon Galactic Physics > or < Applied Metaphysics > that can be taught using a small cut or uncut stone, or by making a small pouch into which is placed some soft sand, and that placed on the head. And if I am not mistaken one of the Ancient figures of a NY TY R shows just that pouch of gold or sand and the outstretched arms of the exercise routine.

The Threns and Atlantyon use what is referred to as an ULTRA HEAD DRESS to designate them once these feelings have been felt. In both cases a simple cord worn on the head and with two pleats to rear, with or without two feathers. [I am not here going into detail of the full Atlantyon dress code nor the < WEIGHTING > and < HOSTING >.] If a < HEADPIECE > from an AdSY is placed to the rear of the headdress and the sun or a light strikes it from behind, the image will be similar to one of the Egyptian Crowns; the red one if I recall correctly. That would tend to suggest a < RED STAR HOSTING >.

I am doubtful if the Pharaohs knew what the various crowns represented, but it does very much look as though they were given some detail of the exercise routine, because as I said in the Preface, it is actually a very, very, very important part of the Understanding. Likewise sports such as Tennis and Squash and to a certain extent Badminton, with their rackets, backhand and forehand movement, copy the exercise movement of the < HEADPIECES > and indeed, within a gym environment, the "foot" and "towel" exercises with the hand held < Headpiece > or similar will assist the hand movements for such games.

This is partly where there was and is the wrong understanding with the DIVINE RIGHT OF THE KING OR KWEEN. It is the LORD OF THE FOOTSTOOL who HOLDS and WHO IS THE MANDATE OF HEAVEN. It is an < INDIVIDUAL >, an < AMEN > < AM > or < RTUR >. Of the Three the most important is the RTUR and that individual will often take on a "minor" role; and even to an extent the individual will not really know that they are RTUR. They may even have a different name! It is FUNDAMENTAL that it is a < STAR APPOINTMENT > and has to be < HELD CAREFULLY >. Thus the EXCEEDINGLY SERIOUS MATTER before Pilate, hidden from him until it is too late!
In many respects within the United Kingdom it is this < VISIBLE INVISIBLE > aspect which is "seen and yet unseen", as for example with the coinage. "The Pound" is thus "special" and the DEI GRACIA does say exactly that. The legend of RTUR says the same, as does RTUR's SEAT.

A Head of Government, or an individual within Government, may hold the Mandate on a temporary basis. Such individual is NOT above the Lord of the FOOTSTOOL and it can make for some black dog days! It is the Lord of the

Footstool who watches the individual who is working with HIS MANDATE.

This mandate is not GIVEN to nor can be held by a Government diktat of a Politburo or similar Cabinet or Cabal or even a Religious College! To HOLD the Mandate is indeed something which is FELT and the INDIVIDUAL CONCERNED will know all about it if they step out of line! <u>As with Alexander. It should be soft and gentle like a Fedora or Trilby sitting on the head.</u> It is not a heavy weight. <u>Thus the gentle cord or silk or satin headdress.</u> Thus the Pharaoh's various crowns of cloth are in this style.

When a heavy weight such as a stone or cut or uncut rock is placed on the head that will often be concealed. That will usually be done when a NY TY R or ATLANTYON has been or feels threatened and is a NECESSARY PRECURSOR to retaliation. Usually a washed stone will not be used unless a < HOT PLASMA > response is required or desired!

The white crown of Egypt was in this style to accommodate a "rock". It is not supposed to be a heavy stone. From this explanation hopefully it can be seen and understood that that crown has not been misplaced, but has simply been "repositioned".

The Black Tyger sits with his corded < SPORTING > black headband, with its triple light blue flashes and the small < Sculpted > rock held in place at the rear by the cord. He puts it on and removes it and repositions it to HIS OWN SATISFACTION and for DESIGN and STYLE PURPOSES.

In this text I am trying to take a GALACTIC ATLANTYON and THRENS NY TY R view. That is deliberate and ESSENTIAL and a REQUIRED ELEMENT for the ACCURACY of this TEXT. It is REQUIRED <u>BY THE ATLANTYONS and the THRENS and OTHERS in THEIR GALACYIC SYSTEMS.</u> That means that the LOCAL FIRE DISC has to be < ENTIRELY SATISFIED > that this text is < ACCEPTABLE to ITS STANDARDS >. It is thus checked at particular times and at particular locations to CHECK that the UNDERSTANDING of the SCIENCE is correct; and expressed in the required STYLE.

The term <<< HOSTING >>> is watched for particular accuracy.

In ATLANTYON and THRENS TERMS these are < FIRE DISC MATTERS >. It is for THIS LOCAL FIRE DISC and in respect of the HIGH IMPERIAL and UNION SYSTEM GALAXIES, THREE of their SPECIFIC FIRE DISCS to be satisfied as to < PROTOCOL >.

The terms LORD OF THE VINEYARD and LORD of the FOOTSTOOL have specific significance in ATLANTYON and THRENS Science. That is a < FIRE DISC > matter to state the BLINDINGLY OBVIOUS!

<<< BLACK TYGER HIDDEN FVRECKRAN >>>

24
Atlantyon Galactic Physics

The terms of this NEW Hypothesis is that the Atlantyons and their ASSOCIATED GALACTIC SYSTEMS are VERY REAL, VERY POWERFUL and have left over thousands of years much of their material to be < UNWRAPPED > at a time set by them and determined by the local population when they wished meaningful contact. I accept that it may be much more than that, but within the space of this text that is what is required. I have revised accordingly. I have to consider that there will be associated galaxies with inhabited footstools running to very large numbers.

While I accept that they are not "seen" I have to accept that they have the technology to HIDE and SECURE any of their footstools from unwelcome visitors and prying eyes, including telescopes optical and various other radio telescopes. I have also to accept that there is REAL ADVANCED SCIENCE which has to be learnt and taught.

As real individuals I have to consider what they do, how they speak, how they dress and above all what they think. While that is partly done by "Science Fiction" where that is inaccurate as to science it simply confirms an incorrect understanding.

In science terms I MUST be able to use and to communicate at least some of the ATLANTYON words and understanding to show that I know ACCURATELY what I mean and understand. I MUST have their UNDERSTANDING.

I am aware the ATLANTYONS and others in THEIR GALACTIC COMBINATIONS are watching <u>very carefully what is going on at this footstool.</u> This is NOT big brother. It is something quite different.

It is the powerful yet gentle hand of the father <<< AMEN RA >>> mighty to save!
The < VARIOUS HOSTING FEELINGS > are sometimes almost invisible, and not quite appreciated for what they are until some time after the event. Some are little more than gentle

trembling, while others are a FURIOUS PRIVATE ANGER. And with the anger it is only after that has subsided that the feeling is "felt" like a very powerful < small voice > and it is known the correct path to take.

I am well aware that they DO NOT approve of anything that looks like slavery; and taxation is viewed VERY CAREFULLY. While purchase tax such as VAT may be acceptable, tax on work such as Income Tax is likely to be viewed as PROTOCOL CONTRAVENTION. No local exceptions. Difficult bunch these Atlantyons and Fvreckrans!

I like to feel comfortable and they are aware of that. Sometimes they require that I am uncomfortable. No too uncomfortable, but sufficient for them to check the position. That applies both to my working life and my personal life. I feel like the canary down the mine. I am particularly comfortable at the Canary Islands, sitting as they do in the Atlantic. I would probably enjoy and be comfortable in most of the Atlantic Islands. What about Scotland?

Now as a Scot I should be comfortable there, but as an Atlantyon there may be complications. That depends on whether Scotland retains its Scottish and <u>Atlantyon</u> credentials. If it does not I may be REQUIRED to leave.

Note here the change in emphasis. It is not that I may leave or am forced to leave but that I am REQUIRED to leave. Effectively in < AMBASSADORIAL > terms <<< I AM RECALLED >>>!

While the requirement to leave may be forced upon me; particularly if there is no work for me, it may be forced on me by a change in the legislation which while acceptable in Scottish Parliamentary terms, is <u>unacceptable in Atlantyon terms.</u> Where that happens the Atlantyons will MARK the RECALL as was done when a < FOOTSTOOL> was thrown in St Giles! Even hundreds of years after that event it serves as a WARNING. While it appears simply as a throwing of a < stool >, it is a marker for FURIOUS ATLANTYON and FVRECKRAN ANGER.

The Parliaments pass the legislation they see fit, and I am now aware that much of the legislation already passed is HIGHLY UNACCEPTABLE and GROSSLY OFFENSIVE in

ATLANTYON terms. The politicians do not care because they regard < Atlantis > and the Atlantyons as a fiction and they are only "possibly" accountable at election time. In the so called "safe seats" they are virtually "unaccountable."

In terms of this Hypothesis it is an incorrect assumption and a very dangerous one to make. It OFFENDS the < FIRE DISC >. Where the Parliamentary legislation impinges on an Atlantyon Official traveling "Incognito" <u>like a thief in the night, especially on Official Galactic business the</u> ramifications are enormous at Galactic level. There is likely to be some warning given, particularly if the individual is a KURALAKYS (Ambassador) or above, but if the Ambassador is threatened, then the response is likely to be seriously adverse ;as the < FIRE DISC > well knows! There are other complications in that area also, where individuals are "adopted" and treated as Atlantyon Officials. That gives Pilate and Rome in particular, yet another problem!

A Kuralakys for example living and working in the United Kingdom, even if he or she does not reside in London, is likely to regard incidents in London as affecting < PROTOCOL >. It will seriously affect protocol if the individual will NOT go to London or is forcibly rendered to London or out of the United Kingdom on the basis of a Treaty where balance and fairness is omitted in the Judicial process! This applies in particular to ROMAN treaties; again as is well known to Hadrian! The Atlantyon reaction may not be immediate. They have been around for a long time and in many respects are far distant. But even a minor court incident with a minor individual might render London as < NOT RESERVED >; thus the Blitz! It could also be something apparently more natural but equally damaging, such as a seismic event to demonstrate a "throwing the footstool". And THEIR SEISMIC events can pass UNSEEN. Brazil might be on the Protocol list for MAYAN or INKA reasons. Mexico may have had them restored, but be about to lose them for the same old problem of Human Blood Sacrifice. Cancun, may be safe,[and is GATED as is much of America(KAY MEN and AL GATOR)] but there are Volcanoes nearby!

In many respects Atlantyon is a MIND SET; thus the < SPORTING > programs and the formal dress simply serving to confirm, as an academic dress would, that a particular level of teaching had been achieved AND the individual has the ATLANTYON SEAL OF APPROVAL.

In my case my Glasgow University gown had a hood, but no mortar board and I wore the hood on my back. I am aware that the Atlantyon Gowns like the AdSY are different. The Coat of Many colours? Certainly. And like the AdSY done to a particular style. In certain respects like any academic gown slightly ridiculous and with its particular headgear and STAFF! And so in my case while my Glasgow University Gown did not have a mortar board I may be able to add to it the Atlantyon corded headgear with its two feathers and the <<< FORMAL WORKING and SPORTING AdSY >>>. But that headgear, indeed all the gown, has been designed in a particular way. The HAND MADE aspect being a MATERIAL SCIENTIFIC REQUIREMENT as are the colours. Except it is not multi coloured but to particular colours to REPRESENT STARS.

That also allows the Atlantyon to appear as a <<< VISIBLE INVISIBLE >>> for it is THE FORMAL DRESS at a FORMAL FUNCTION which states clearly who they are. The < STAR > < HOSTS > but this is unseen and is felt only briefly by the Individual. With the formal gown on, even with just with a part of it as with the headdress, with or without the AdSY, the Atlantyon Lord does not even need to say I AM WHO I AM. The < STAR > HAS ARRANGED for him to be put there in formal dress. The Thorn crown, symbolic of the < SPORTING HEADDRESS > neatly hides the danger of threatening the < FIRE DISC>. Pilate and ROME are in even more trouble! And the symbol for TRUTH is on his head. TWO FEATHERS for Ma AT are soft and ULTRA FORMAL as with friends. MaAT in that sense being FIRST LORD of the Footstool where < Ma > is Atlantyon for the number 1 and AT is for the FOOTSTOOL. Place a thorn crown and cause the head to bleed and it is a BLOOD SACRIFICE. There is NO point in asking for forgiveness for that insult. It will not be forgotten.

2000 years might have passed, but the incident is far from forgotten and Rome is most certainly <<< COMFIRMED NOT RESERVED >>> .The Confirmation is Nagasaki! Then the eagle and if the lesson has still not been taken on board, it is a < FIRE DISCS > matter.

The description as First Lord of the AD MY RA L TY while a UK Description is ATLANTYON IN STYLE since the word ADATRAN (meaning in Atlantyon, General) is incorporated in the letters AD, and the Atlantyon word TY is translated as Mighty. Again considerable care has to be taken with this since while the First Sea Lord of the United Kingdom is Atlantyon (it having an Atlantic coast as technically does Russia on account of the North Atlantic drift) the same does not apply to Germany, for example, or to other countries which do not have an Atlantic Coast; especially if they FORCEABLY OCCUPY an Atlantic coast, even if they have Admirals, or where, while they have an Atlantic Coast they are for other reasons < NOT PROTOCOL >. Thus the [GATES] when the Ra II was built. The Local Star was watching BOTH voyages closely. The STAR had an interest to make sure that voyage was completed successfully and CORRECTLY; which happened once RA II passed the GATE MARKER, the Volcanic Canaries, and El Tiede in particular!

To talk like an Atlantyon means that I have to articulate their UNDERSTANDING and that includes their GALACTIC PHYSICS. To a certain extent that is easy. It is simply that Big Bang and Evolution is complete and utter rubbish. [Twaddle or Absolutely Absurd is how it could be said in English to reflect the DOUBLE ABST in the ATLANTYON STYLE in English and Scots usage]. So also for that matter is the current global warming and carbon footprint nonsense. [Note here the initial use of the letter "N" and the other "N". Na Na is similar to the double Abst but different. Note also the absence of the "a" in the word Nonsense to distinguish it from ANANAN or ANANNN (simply a different spelling) which is the word for "living". And watch the locations ANNAN or the river ANNAN.

While in < APPLIED METAPHYSICS > "marks are not deducted for spelling where the correct meaning can be clearly shown to have been understood," it will be done where it affects the sense. Thus loss of "accents" or wrong gender in certain other languages where the word changes materially and incorrect tone control. Thus BLOCKS usage here identifies a change of Tone control; a distinct change of emphasis. Similar to underline but different. Underline and blocks is MUCH, MUCH MUCH more emphatic, as also is the DOUBLE and TRIPLE use of words.] [Taxes on anti gravity technology do not go down well in Atlantyon terms. Shows a considerable lack of understanding of the Galactic Science!]

It also means that I have to be able to talk the actual Atlantyon words and style. While that is not easy for me since my ATLANTYON vocabulary is limited; I am aware that that is for technical reasons AND ALSO for technical reasons in certain circumstances I have to be able to CORRECTLY MIX the ATLANTYON WORDS with the ENGLISH LANGUAGE WORDS. As yet I cannot adjust my eyes easily to the ATLANTYON script, which is not available on my computer, so for the most part I use English Words and Acanthus or Atlantix font. The change in fonts is NOT cosmetic, but marks a material change in understanding.

< The VISIBLE INVISIBLE > Atlantyon Lord does not require to wear his formal dress at all times. Indeed in the case of the < RTUR > he is likely to wear it only rarely, and reflecting a number of < PROTOCOL > points depending on the type of function he is attending. He could wear same to a formal reception within the United Kingdom, but even there, with HIGH LAND DRESS he still has scope to display his credentials and appear quite ordinary without reverting to the < FORMAL ATLANTYON GOWN >.

This can be a difficult concept to understand. He is not trying to cause offense, often being perhaps too deferential. Thus since COLOUR is important, a "light blue K RA VATE " where all the other colours are coordinated carefully, and with SILVER and GOLD means that his credential are "displayed." This is likely also to be in relation to what he says. Thus CRYSTAL GLASSES and SPARKLING WATER and wine are IMPORTANT. Thus the "Glass of Champagne" at a reception. If those holding the reception are up to speed, there must be choice with KA VA, and water STILL and SPARKLING and CRYSTAL GLASSES. [The provision of crystal glasses would be expected and a REQUIRED ELEMENT at an Ambassadorial function].

There are other technical aspects about NORTHERN or SOUTHERN WATER and PROTOCOL WATER, which I do not need to go into. OR KA DYAN, for example as in water or Alcohol. The words "DYAN" translates as "mine" so in that context "Orcadian" currently means Scots! <<< GALACTIC FVRECKRAN >>>. Alcohol is PROTOCOL. It is effective in medicine. Not to have alcohol may put the whole meeting at PROTOCOL CONTRAVENTION; that is if it was even allowed to take place in the first place and the FVRECKRAN RTUR in particular would not attend. It is a FOOT EXERCISE with the refusal to attend! While some restrictions on alcohol are sensible, if the rules are applied harshly that is PROTOCOL CONTRAVENTION.

At a GALACTIC Ambassadorial reception an AdSY could be brought but it would then need to be USED IN A PARTICULAR WAY and be of the particular and required style. Currently a THREE PANEL UPSTAND would be expected as that is the style for the HIGH IMPERIAL and UNION GALAXIES and COMBINATIONS. IF PLACED in the VERTICAL it MUST BALANCE IN THE VERTICAL, and be able to be held in the HORIZONTAL. It is CUSTOMARY for them to be EXCHANGED and at an Ambassadorial Exchange to have one made specially. Thus to "Exchange" Credentials you first NEED TO KNOW that you have to HAVE and AdSY, to KNOW what it is and HOW to HOLD and WORK IT; particularly if the exchange is of the gift of a < WORKING AdSY > upstand. The working style is often preferred since it can be overpainted to make it < FORMAL > while still used for < SPORTING > and can have existing < AdSY> headpieces or new ones added to it as required. Again a gift may be of a stylized headpiece, with or without coins of the required type. [Usually footstool coins of Silver.]

In FORMAL LETTERS and documents the AdSY design may be displayed, but then only with TWO PINS. It is not essential since the use of the Names with chevrons will be sufficient WHERE CORRECTLY APPLIED. That will usually be the case where there is an AdSY under the control of the individual who sends the letters; as in the case of a KURALAKYS or above.

The individuals known as < VISIBLE INVISIBLES > will in the ordinary course simply wear normal clothes or NO clothes as appropriate. They perform the usual bodily functions AND can reproduce if they wish in the OLD FASHIONED SEXUAL STYLE. Artificial insemination for reproduction is severely frowned upon for technical reasons.

The ATLANTYON < SYRADA GOWNS > and < AdSY > are symbol of the < GALAXY COMBINATIONS > and the < CORRECT STATUS >. The Individuals MUST be able to use and wear and carry as THEY SEE FIT. There is little difference between the male and female gowns and headdress again for obvious reasons as previously explained. WATCH this aspect carefully. As I am a male I write this text from the "male" perspective. But in ATLANTYON terms there is a SHAPE SHIFTING aspect so a male can become a female! Again watch carefully what is being done. This is NOT by surgical means. The full reproductive system is required. As I said it is a particular type of shape shifting, and surgery is likely to be viewed as a Human Blood Sacrifice and NOT acceptable! This aspect is NOT a detail. There is a substantial DESIGN and SCIENCE element.

With their similarity to a NYPPON kimono I would expect that many western males would regard the < ATLANTYON FORMAL GOWNS > as cross dressing. While such might be "thought", such thoughts would be regarded in Atlantyon and Threns terms as lacking understanding and HIGHLY OFFENSIVE. That said, it is highly unlikely that anyone would accuse the Tyger headed Threns or Dras male of being "effeminate"! These gowns essentially symbolize a common understanding between compatible species where one is naturally far more predatory than the other. In simple terms this might be referred to as "restraint" and good old fashioned courtesy. It is more than that, because of course of the shape shifting concepts and understandings. That aspect of itself is highly restrictive of which societies this group of Highly

Advanced Galaxies will allow to meet with them. Politically correct is < SERIOUSLY NOT PROTOCOL >.

There is a very difficult aspect to this also. How easy is it for an Atlantyon official to wear THEIR OWN formal gowns in public? To prevent them doing so WILL BE VIEWED AS GROSSLY OFFENSIVE to the ATLANTYONS. THUS RESTRICTION ON the wearing of HIGHLAND DRESS are likely to offend the Atlantyons and Threns and others of their Galactic systems until such times as the legislation is lifted; which has been done recently. Equally offensive to them is the wearing of items which transgress their understanding; for example the wearing <u>of guns and swords,</u> but it would extend to clothing which although not of itself violent, disclosed an offensive ideology. Thus the ABRU PER SY and the NA SY labels!

Equally the ATLANTYONS may decline to wear the formal gowns IN PUBLIC UNTIL the BOATS of MILLIONS of YEARS have put in a public appearance and an EXCHANGE of AMBASSADORS and a FORMAL PRESENCE and <<< OPEN FOOTSTOOL STATUS >>> is RESTORED.

Despite my comments on the King James Version in technical terms an ATLANTYON would NOT present credentials to the COURT of St. JAMES. <u>This is NOT a DETAIL.</u> There are instances when a < VISIBLE INVISIBLE > will exercise < KURALAKYS > (Ambassadorial functions). This is CHECKED by the local star and is usually done when RE ADMITTANCE is sought. The < FORMAL > gown has space for Anti gravity skirts, which do not make the individual able to fly (except in a plane of course) but are simply stylized pieces of cloth. The formal KURALAKYS gown is Yellow. Thus for example a request to bring the gown of "Burning Gold". It is essentially a request for the KURALAKYS to visit, and it would be expected his or her formal gown would be bright yellow to reflect the colour of the local type star. However if the Kuralakys was to adopt a more elevated position, the < Anti Gravity > skirts would be worn as multiples, one for one Galaxy, two for two Galaxies and three for three or more. One of these would be yellow and that on its own would signify

KYRALAKYS appointment. Such a gown would be likely to be worn on an established and highly secured footstool and commonly would be used for special functions only; as for example when various other Galactic Officials were present at a function. This is the realms of formal Galactic functions for which a specialist < Style Book for Syradas > is required and is out with the scope of this work.

Written credentials may be delivered in various ways, including to what would be regarded as Government Officials or Agencies. Such may be permitted the use of Atlantyon items, even although not appreciating that they hold such. Thus TWO feathers for example, or on flags such as the UNION FLAG, with or without the " 2U "

Watch also that VISITING DIRECTOR (Lord (even if female) of a Galaxy or several) or VY SY R   MAY TRANSIT THROUGH and such visits can be used to assess PROTOCOL. The time scales are up to 100 years and such OFFICIAL will arrive simply as an ordinary child! But in the Christian tradition that should not come as any surprise!

The AdSY's should be treated with care. While they are simply just a piece of wood the < TY TY AdSY > in particular is a large exercise stick .They should NOT BE MOVED without AUTHORISATION, neither should the headpieces be worked with, except by the individual who made them or a close family member. They are the PERSONAL property of the individual who made them and are ONLY PERMITTED with the APPROVAL of the FIRE DISCS. They are < TIME SENSITIVE and LOCATION KEYS >. They are not likely to be displayed in what the ATLANTYONS or the VISIBLE INVISIBLES regard as a POLICE STATE. That is a FACTUAL MATTER and in many respects relates to FLAGS.

[Now I hope it is becoming a little clearer what all those "flag" symbols mean for the < NY TY R >. Mr. Young was indeed correct, but the word translation is also necessary. From the < KO PT > as I understand it, with a little Middle Kingdom [Chinese] influence.]

While I might feel that I am pointing out rather too many problems to the Atlantyons, I am aware that I am merely recording and confirming what they already know. Essentially a

< VISIBLE INVISIBLE > will check this text and that might include the RTUR from the comfort of his villa outside HAAL CITY to confirm that it meets their technical requirements!

The FORMAL GOWNS which in ATLANTYON are called < SYRADA >, [Formal Peace Dress] are HAND MADE, but providing one is hand made by the individual who wears it, others can be made to style and purchased "off the peg."

The view which the Atlantyons are likely to take is that where they are not allowed to wear their gowns publicly the FOOTSTOOL STATUS is in doubt. This is a FEET EXERCISE and while it is a minor point it is an important one. Watch here the "when in Rome, do as the Romans" expression. As I have hopefully made clear ATLANTYON TERRITORY is NOT ROMAN. The Romans are allowed only limited involvement. Thus the comment about the Scottish Justice System. Watch here also that the Atlantyon credentials may be < APPLIED > without the Justice System being aware of it. This particularly applies to ANTI GRAVITY equipment. If for example the Nimrods are unsafe, the Atylantyons would REQUIRE them taken out of service! They would be quite happy if they were replaced with reliable old "Sunderlands", but they would naturally UPGRADE such "Sunderlands" to make them VERY EFFECTIVE, such as for example providing internal and unseen pressurised cabins; possibly even installing small jet engines! In essence the Atlantyons watch to check if the technology is being used CORRECTLY and in a PROTOCOL manner!

Essentially what they are checking is the societies credentials in WORKING FOR PEACE and < ENLIGHTENMENT >. They are simply NOT INTERESTED in backward looking and inhospitable globes; and that has much more to do with the local populations and their rules and how they successfully accommodate their own populations, than climatic ones.

They can ADJUST the CLIMATE and MOVE the footstool <u>shifting the ice caps as considered appropriate</u>. Global warming and cooling is all SCIENCE to them.

SHOTA is translated as Place1, while KYOTA can be translated as Place2 [HIS PLACE.] [I have used a number 2 with the word "place" to show the MATERIAL DIFFERENCE. Thus it has nothing to do with Kyoto, NY PP ON, but is to do with the ATLANTYON SCIENCE. Global yes, but < ADVANCED FOOTSTOOL SCIENCE >. Place 2 in this connection is to do with the <<< FOOTSTOOL ATLANTYS >>>.

Fire Disc matters require a considerable degree of training, aptitude, and specialist teaching WITH the approval of the Sequenced Fire Discs. Currently in Atlantyon terms certain aspects will be adequately dealt with at the science faculties of a number of the Universities, particularly here in Scotland. Glasgow, Aberdeen and Dundee. But Edinburgh and St. Andrews are < NOT RESERVED > because of current < PROTOCOL > restrictions. Watch again the "foot" position as in "E Star" in Spanish. It is a little like "the star permits you to be where you are." The individual is in POSITION because THAT is what the STAR or STARS REQUIRE. The teaching here is that no one is placed in a position where they ought not to be. If that is done then it is the STAR which is threatened. As if to state the obvious that is not a bright idea. Watch also that ATLANTYONS are Star officials. Considerable care has to be taken with this concept for it is OFTEN the STAR or STARS which arrange for individuals to be put in a place of potential danger to CHECK out the actual situation, for GOOD or BAD.

The classic example is of the Crucifixion of Kryst. That is very much a STAR matter as some of the spoken lines make clear. Note it is NOT what is said in the text, but the ATLANTYON perspective. Thus they watch a PARTICULAR INDIVIDUAL. They DESIGNATE or ADOPT HIM or HER. They have doubtless done so MANY YEARS PREVIOUSLY. As in the young boy taken to Egypt!

The judicial test is actually quite simple. It concerns a case of FALSE WITNESS and POLITICAL BIAS. It concerns a JURY, the Crowd. The test is BOTH for ROME and PILATE, and the CROWD. And even if fictitious, as laid out in text the ATLANTYONS and THRENS can still use that TEXT to TEST for < PROTOCOL >. Call it fiction, when it is factual, and PROTOCOL is SERIOUSLY CONTRAVENED!

Do the society they are checking indulge in Judicial murder and human blood sacrifice? That may apply

THROUGH NEGLIGENCE or a DELIBERATE WHITEWASH. If that is the case there will be FURIOUS ANGER and the ATLANTYONS will turn their face from the Footstool. It could be for tens, or hundreds or thousands of years. No matter what the bleating they are unlikely to respond until such times as they see a substantial degree of ENLIGHTENMENT. Hopefully that will clarify to an extent the position with the " WHITE STAR LINER" and the First and Second World Wars in particular! <u>And as they withdraw they will withdraw much of their material.</u>

But what is NOT made clear is their capacity for FURIOUS ANGER and their reaction to it. It is generally to secure their OWN TERRITORY and RESTRICT and WITHDRAW their material from what are ABRU PER SY territories. That anger will EXTEND to those who MISUSE their TERRITORY or who operate in such UNFAIR UNSAFE and UNBALANCED MEDICAL and JUSTICE SYSTEMS .

In Atlantyon terms there are a lot of problems. This is NOT assisted by revisionist historians and PARTICULARLY by the Churches who are having difficulty with the resurrection of the body or who try and explain the resurrection by other doubtful and devious means.

As said in the Old Hypothesis it is the MATTER TRANSFER EQUIPMENT operated from a BOAT OF MILLIONS OF YEARS which is at work.

There are a number of SPECIFIC ATLANTYON POINTS in connection with ANY Crucifixion which I do not need to go into. The most obvious is that it is a HUMAN BLOOD SACRIFICE and a JUDICIAL MURDER.

Suffice it to say that while I originally thought when drafting this text that the problem with the crucifixion and the Judicial decision by Pilate started with the whipping for that is also a Human Blood sacrifice and that is an ABOMINATION, it in fact occurred much earlier. It is an ABOMINATION to deliberately mutilate. Thus cutting off an ear is a mutilation, EVEN though it does not affect the hearing, as is any form of damage, as in blinding or tongue cutting. <u>Once again there are some very technical points here</u>. Note KO BE!

A soldier seriously wounded in battle, who has lost limbs, requires to be treated. In Atlantyon terms the INDIVIDUAL REQUIRES TO BE RESTORED. This is not as a cyborg, and while prosthetics is the best that is currently available that is NOT ACCEPTABLE in ATLANTYON terms.

MORE PARTICULARLY there are other and more serious aspects. FEMALES should NOT be in the front line. Again this is or ought to be blindingly obvious. Care should be taken of the reproductive organs, and since the females carry the newborn, they should be removed as FAR AS POSSIBLE from the conflict area! That does not prevent females from being in the military. Indeed such may be desirable but it does highlight CORRECT PROTOCOLS! Where not done to Protocol, it is a < SERIOUS PROTOCOL CONTRAVENTION >.

It is NOT acceptable for the politicians to use their solders as "cannon fodder", "suicide missions" or the like nor to provide them with INADEQUATE EQUIPMENT. Do that and it is the commanders the Atlantyons will go for, because those commanders <u>murdered their troops</u>. Do it in a summary court marshal situation and those commanders including the judges, are in more than boiling water. And for those who consider certain locations to have been abolished, the Atlantyons will soon put them right on that one.

<u>While the Matter transfer equipment can put individuals back together it can take them APART!</u>

Resurrection is ATLANTYON, thus they are PLEASED to wear the Cross with the Ring of Glory for it demonstrates a CORRECT understanding. To wear the ANKH symbol is likewise acceptable PROVIDED that it is understood that it relates to the entire HIGH, IMPERIAL and UNION Galaxies Systems and INCLUDES the Cross with the Ring of Glory. Prohibit them and it is simply a SERIOUS PROTOCOL CONTRAVENTION. That may induce a GRAVITY shifting of fields, which can be dangerous in the use of anti gravity equipment!

Other than what I have thus far said I am not proposing in this text to go into much more detail of the Formal ATLANTYON ACADEMIC GOWN. I have already referred to the Anti Gravity skirts. <u>These are decorative</u> and so called because by bending one leg, and then the other the skirts are kicked up! They are panels of different colours and reflect DIFFERENT STARS. Light blue denotes blue white stars, yellow such as the local one, red a red star and so on. It is this aspect which makes them the TECHNICAL COAT OF MANY COLOURS. The primary colour is DARK BLUE, to reflect the GALAXY colour. Black is not commonly worn. Where it is worn it may signify the presence of an RTUR or other VISIBLE INVISIBLE, particularly if it is worn as FORMAL DRESS or as part of such. However since black is often worn to show that considerable offense has been taken, considerable care should be taken where it is seen, particularly where black feathers are worn in a light blue headband or if it is REFERRED TO IN TEXT by one of their OFFICIALS as such. The feathers should number ONLY TWO. They symbolize the presence of the FIRE DISC resting gently and SAFELY on the HEAD as in < HOSTING >. Black feathers or a stone in a < SPORTING > headband would indicate that a HOT PLASMA BURST or AdSY CRUST CRACKING of the < FOOTSTOOL > is contemplated. [For AdSY crust cracking read earthquake or volcanic event; even if minor such as minor earthquakes or minor venting by a Volcano.] In that regard < LOCATION >is important. Minor Volcanic activity in the Atlantic is NOT minor and <u>highlights a serious problem</u>! Some of their shifts particularly of the < Footstool > itself, will pass virtually unnoticed. They will be noted as was said by events, thus the slowing or speeding up of footstool spin even if only slight. Thus to make the comment in relation to the UNFOLDING of EVENTS, may highlight the < ATLANTYON GALACTIC PHYSICS > in operation where that is studied and understood.

  The other aspect about formal dress, which is likely to cause a problem to some is when the headdress is worn on its own. This effectively leaves the wearer nude. It is almost certain that it was that aspect which lead to the description of "Seth" in hieroglyph and the dislike of Seth. Watch however, that local academic gown or clothes which are NOT HAND MADE but with the Formal ULTRA headdress particularly in a cold climate, would be regarded as NOT WORN and thus < <u>DRESS FORMAL</u>.> [Basically the non hand made clothes are required for Climate conditions otherwise would not be worn leaving the wearer nude. They may also be worn to signify < BARRED SPIRAL > and < VISIBLE INVISIBLE > < INDIVIDUALS >.] The individual involved may be an ATLANTYON HIGH LORD, and depending on the colour of the headband and of the feathers may be the <<<< THE LORD OF PEACE of the ENTIRE HIGH IMPERIAL AND UNION GALAXIES. >>>> who generally take ATLANTYON shape, but can shape shift to various other species types as in Black Tyger Threns or Dras or Pykan Orka!

That Galaxy name is <<<< SPECIFICALLY DESIGNATED >>>> and is of a <<<< HIGHLY ADVANCED GROUP of HIGHLY SECURED >>>> <<<< FOOTSTOOLS >>>> and <<<< GALAXIES >>>>.

It is more than likely that one of their OFFICIALS brought to an end the visit of the ATLANTYON Lords and Threns and others who had been visiting Egypt, almost certainly as a result of some unacceptable incident which was brought to their attention. The local Egyptian population preserved the record in the hope that they would return, disappointed that they had not stayed, but unaware of the distances involved and in the technical aspects with the anger which have still to be met to allow re establishing of contact and for continuing contact. Given that the initial contact appears to have been friendly it is likely that AdSYs would have been left, possibly even made locally, and would be much prized because they had been a gift and symbolised the power of the Atlantyon Lords and the Threns in this Galactic group.

As for the Diorite Glass Bricks? Again probably made locally and for this Galactic Group the marking will be ATLANTYON or THRENS and will simply say <<< TA AT >>> with number for this <<< FOOTSTOOL>>>. Technicaly they constitute the RTUR's seat.

The other concept which I have touched on but where I need to provide more detail is of the < VISIBLE INVISIBLES>. That INDIVIDUAL is the head of A Galaxy or Galaxies and it is a < MATERIAL STYLE MATTER >. It is an Individual but it is a particular type. These are the AMEN and the AM and the RTUR. These are the <<< GENETIC STYLE

INDIVIDUALS >>>. It is they who determine STYLE. Essentially they decide on the type of the living ANKH material which is erroneously called dna. Dna is NOT living, but the ANKH as an INDIVIDUAL is very much living. The ANKH is provided by the FIRE DISCS. <u>That aspect is something which must be understood and appreciated.</u>

    This is not a work for full < Atlantyon Galactic Physics > but with the technical specifications and the < Sporting > program, is intended to provide an introduction and glimpse into what is involved. The Headpieces on the AdSY represent the SPECIFIC GALAXIES . The FOUR HEADPIECE AdSY is fairly typical of SY FERT GALAXIES and their Combinations and they will usually represent 1, the HIGH, 2 the IMPERIAL and 3 the UNION GALAXIES. The fourth where it is in place represents the THREE GALAXIES COMBINATIONS for BARRED SPIRAL SYFERT and SCULPTOR COMBINATIONS and is usually positioned on the downward pointing arm. The headpieces can be moved about and repositioned, but by doing that it represents DIFFERENT GALACTIC POSITIONS.

    The AdSY's for < BARRED SPIRALS and COMBINATIONS > will usually have < SEVEN > < HEADPIECES> of which usually FOUR are for < BARRED SPIRALS or COMBINATIONS > . Where covers are used they are BLUE bordered but otherwise plain apart from the screws to attach them to the <HEADPIECE >. There will usually be TWO < HEADPIECES > painted up for the < HIGH IMPERIAL and UNION GALAXIES STYLE > <OPEN> or < SECURED > < BARRED SPIRAL and COMBINATION > showing the ANKH shape, and with the bottom rectangle being unmarked as to < Footstools >.

    The AdSY is working when at REST and RESTING when being worked as in an exercise routine. However it may be WORKED while exercising, particularly when using a headpiece on its own. The headpiece may be applied to the chin, and will look like a beard. That is what the Pharaoh's beard is meant to represent. Another object applied in that way "represents" that Stylized Headpiece, even a Mobile Phone or newspaper if that is the intention of the individual using it and they have an actual AdSY.

The three Pyramids again represent the High Imperial and Union Galaxies and the RESTING TYGER beside them is of their life forms. The Resting Tyger has lost his beard, again an indicator that all is not well. Apparently part of that is also now in the British Museum.

The Resting Tyger represents the Threns and their RTUR SHAPE SHIFTING ABILITY. Thus a Threns may be an Atlantyon! The shape shifting is done using MATTER TRANSFER EQUIPMENT. It is NOT done frequently and the Individual will appear to grow old. That is all part of the style for this type of Shape Shifting.

Where most of the Science fiction falls down is that it is not appreciated that most of this is watched for ACCURACY by the likes of the Atlantyons and Threns. That allows them easily, and from a distance, to check the level of development. Thus currently the lack of AdSY's says to the ATLANTYONS and Threns that while this is IN FACT one of their < Footstools >, it is a < HIGHLY SECURED and RESTRICTED FOOTSTOOL > with very limited Galactic contacts and with a local population in need of Enlightenment and UP RATING as appropriate if they are to travel within this Galaxy.

This Hypothesis, despite what the nuclear Physicists, Astronomers and others who worship big bang and evolution may consider, does contain substantial elements of the ATLANTYON and THRENS HIGHLY ADVANCED SCIENCE, and so effectively INVITES CONTACT and a RE ESTABLISHMENT of PROTOCOLS.

Access to the Threns matter transfer equipment does indeed allow DESIGN of individuals; thus the move from Threns to Atlantyon and back again. It is not something they use frequently preferring instead to move their Boats of Millions of years SAFELY to the surface of a footstool and use their own feet to walk there. In so doing they APPLY the < FOOTSTOOL > DESIGNATION.

Usually a record will be left of a visit by one of their officials where they intend future contact. Thus the Egyptian records. Again the understanding of these records accurately reflects the level of development.

Those Science fiction which deal with Time Travel need to take classes in Atlantyon Galactic Physics. While it is quite acceptable to make alien monsters particularly for the children and as cartoons, these powerful Galactic Aliens have FAR MORE ADULT TASTES and some of them are VERY POWERFUL ALLIES and CLOSE FRIENDS.

The names of the particular galaxies are done in the ATLANTYON LISTING or by THRENS LISTING and most of these are interchangeable. Likewise the STARS have particular names, this one being LANAST. That does not change. The ATLANTYON NAMES must be used where their physics is to be worked. Otherwise it will simply not operate. It is a highly advanced security mechanism with anti tamper mechanisms. It has to be INPUT at particular locations and at particular Times by AUTHORISED INDIVIDUALS. Thus the small wooden sticks and headpieces have to be wielded or not wielded at particular times if the mechanism is to operate. The purpose of the mechanism is to allow the SAFE TRAVEL from FOOTSTOOL to FOOTSTOOL and WITHIN and OUT WITH this GALAXY and to designated others.

In the < SYFERT > Style Galaxies and < COMBINATIONS > the < FOUR HEADPIECES > have to be in place on a TY TY AdSY to allow communication and travel. In the < BARRED SPIRALS > and < COMBINATIONS > at least < FOUR > < BARRED SPIRAL or COMBINATIONS > < HEADPIECES > MUST be on an < AdSY >. That means that for < COMBINATIONS > < SEVEN HEADPIECES > are on the AdSY, and thus it is usually the < SPORTING AdSY > which will be used by their < INDIVIDUALS >.

Gold and platinum are used in such to represent Stars. The Platinum represents blue and blue white. Gold and platinum coins no bigger than a sovereign are used in the headpieces, while in the upstand silver coins are placed and these represent footstools. Silver at .925+ must be used. 3d to 5/- or modern £1.00 (.925 silver) or £2.00 Britannia may be used. The £1.00 coin is equivalent to the Shilling and a < footstool > must be of

£1.00 or 1/- weight to allow contact or to re establish contact. Metal including rings may be used where supply is difficult or coins not minted to the correct fineness or where other metal coins are commonly used. That is for a NY TY R or a VISIBLE INVISIBLE to determine.

It is for the FIRE DISCS and the VISIBLE INVISIBLES to determine when it will permit travel for its species, and when travel is outwith this Galaxy it needs approval from the receiving galaxy. Again AdSY's have to be IN PLACE in such RECEIVING GALAXY.

Where there are 5 headpieces on an AdSY it is likely to be a < SYFERT > one or a < BARRED SPIRAL > on which two have been removed or yet to be placed. One may be a spare and or a < SPORTING > one.

It might also be the CLOSED headpiece, which when on the downward pointing arm of the AdSY means the GALAXY is CLOSED to SUPER LIGHT TRAVEL until that headpiece is repositioned or restyled. In ALL the AdSY styles the Galaxy is CLOSED when gold or platinum are placed in the top "V" part.

Silver in a headpiece represents a Footstool. Coins may be seen or not seen. In BARRED SPIRALS they are NOT usually shown. 4/6d might represent one very advanced Footstool in a galaxy or two slightly less advanced of 2/- weight. The metal and coins MUST NOT BE POLLUTED. If it is know to have been stolen or otherwise "unacceptable" it will NOT work the AdSY. The STARS will KNOW and it simply will not work. The Stars can instruct cleaning if that is required, but it is a FUNDAMENTAL that it must not be polluted metal.

Thus the phrase "The Lord restoring SY ON" also means that THE INDIVIDUAL GENERAL DIRECTOR requires to activate the mechanism. Once the mechanism is working again the connections to SYON will be restored and the Boats of Millions of Years can put Atlantis on their destination list; even if it is only for stopovers in the first instance.

In 2008/2009 I am satisfied that while I may < APPLY PROTOCOL > on the basis of a THREE PANEL AdSY and with explanations, the current scientific level at this < FOOTSTOOL > is not even at < ONE PANEL >.

The Technical text at the end with < STAR CHARTS > is thus required.
    I will allow this text marked as < PROTOCOL >.

25
< Atlantyon Galactic Physics >
Hieroglyphs in < The New Atlantis >

I

To use the term < THE NEW ATLANTIS > implies that the Galactic Links HAVE BEEN RESTORED and that the Atlantyons are VERY REAL, VERY POWERFUL and the GALAXY is VERY, VERY, VERY heavily populated with similar and compatible life styled individuals. That is not what the scientists currently understand. It is perhaps no surprise then of the many conspiracy theories and cover ups about "Aliens" and is further highlighted by secure facilities to which ordinary individuals are NOT allowed access. Hopefully as I have now indicated it is unlikely that other than AUTHORISED ALIENS will visit because of the HIGHLY ADVANCED and TECHNICAL NATURE of the SCIENCE which is involved.

Such secure facilities are fertile territory for the Science Fiction.

So likewise is Egypt and Atlantis.

This text IS the introduction to the HIGHLY ADVANCED SCIENCE which is < ATLANTYON GALACTIC PHYSICS > which is required where the < FOOTSTOOL > Status is < RESTORED > by the acting < KURALAKYS > especially where the Kuralakys intends to depart shortly ! And shortly may be number of years, or it may be in a few weeks. That really depends on events.

Where many mistakes are made with the understanding, as I have hopefully tried to explain thus far, it is often because of the way the system is set up for security reasons. After the first mistake there may be no second step. That is not entirely accurate, for the mechanism and system is set up in such a way that mistakes are allowed. The reason for that is that it allows the position to be FACTUALLY checked out. In simple terms, what is the position like on the TERRITORY which is

DESIGNATED at the < FOOTSTOOL >. Are the < PROTOCOLS > maintained?

This is a very interesting exercise and one which is not easily spotted. I have been particular in this text that Human Blood sacrifice is not permitted. Yet I am also aware that with the tremendous power of the Stars, massive human blood sacrifice is caused. Well not exactly.

That as should be apparent is where the Crucifixion of KRYST comes in. I have certainly spotted from various texts what I can only describe as "REVISIONIST" teaching. The attempt to make that "story" CONFORM to local requirements is NOT ACCEPTABLE at PROTOCOL. But as I have hopefully shown thus far, with the < VISIBLE INVISIBLES > considerable care has to be taken.

The fundamental is < TRUTH > and it is in the figure of the < INDIVIDUAL > who is < HOSTING >. In the sequence of Stars THEY know who is < HOSTING > and who is not, who has < HOSTED > in the past and whom they might select to < HOST > in the future, if even for a short time.

So when I talk of < ATLANTIS RESTORED > I am essentially talking about it at < STAR > level.

As I typed this revision originally I was disturbed by a WASP or a BEE. It was in fact a wasp. Not a detail. I was wearing my Trilby and the < FORMAL BLACK SPORTING CORDED HEADBAND >. I essence I was checking this text for ACCURATE SCIENTIFIC CONTENT. But the text had to be revised and I had to understand what I was talking about. I then managed to lose this text among various other drafts, was annoyed because I had misplaced it, and it was ONLY after that that I realized that there was a < HEADPIECE > point, now adjusted, which I had incorrectly specified. It relates to a SPECIFIC THREE GALAXIES GROUP which is NOT the HIGH IMPERIAL and UNION, but which has close contacts with it. Sporting corded Trilby, white and grey, black gown. < FVRECKRAN, (pronounced like FayVwreckRan) THORNAN and PTAHAARAN (pronounced like FAY VATT HARAN). Also known as the <<< TY ME KANSAL >>>.

As I said in the last chapter it is often difficult for me to grasp. I am well are that powerful, and influential Physicists and

Astrophysicists Astronomers and others, not to mention the Egyptologists will not agree with this. They are all comfortable with "Big Bang" and evolution and have no desire to have their current wisdom changed.

That does not matter. What matters is that I accurately provide this record. That is all. And I have to send a few letters. It is the SEQUENCED STARS who record and monitor this text and my actions to ENSURE that they meet their requirements.

In many respects the current science for practical technologies such as for televisions, cars, radios, boats is "reasonably accurate." However it does require important adjustments, not least of which is with big bang, evolution and MEDICAL MATTERS. In the case of evolution in particular a rather powerful Pacific Volcano has sorted that out, <u>with simply a minor crack</u>.

As I have said this is < ATLANTYON GALACTIC PHYSICS > and that means that it is the < STARS > which operate it. Essentially therefor if < ATLANTIS > is RESTORED, it has had its < LINK > to the < HIGH IMPERIAL and UNION GALAXIES and ASSOCIATED GALACTIC SYSTEMS RESTORED >. There is not a sudden "big bang" because that understanding simply demonstrates wrong science and a wrong understanding. Likewise with evolution. There is a place for evolution but when dealing with this type of Galactic Combinations it must be viewed in an ENTIRELY NEW LIGHT.

In many respects to understand this Theory means that the < STAR > is working the < PROGRAM > as required to make it and its creatures < COMPATIBLE >. In many respects there is a NEW PASSOVER. It happens every day at sunrise and ends at sunset. It is to state the obvious. Wherein the difference lies is in this VAST and HIGHLY ADVANCED UNDERSTANDING.

It is not forced or threatened. It is simply "available." It has to be worked with and it has some very strict rules. But these DO NOT require judicial murder nor human blood sacrifice. Do that and there is a < LOCK OUT > and as I said it could be for a few years or for many thousands, or even millions.

That goes some way to explaining the < PROTOCOL PERIODS > and the < PROTOCOL TERRITORIES >. Thus at a practical level when considering the expansion of the European Union, since Russia is < PROTOCOL > while overtures can be made to admit it to the European Union, it MUST be remembered that it is < PROTOCOL> and essentially it is the European Union which is asking to be admitted to the < PROTOCOL TERRITOTIES >; EFFECTIVELY to have contact with the < HIGH IMPERIAL and UNION SYSTEM GALAXIES!> Likewise, Norway in removing itself from the European Union has CONFIRMED the <<< NOT PROTOCOL >>> designation of the European Union, as indeed does Russia because it is currently excluded!

This is not a flat science. It is a < STAR SCIENCE > and is VERY, VERY, VERY ACTIVE. The Volcanoes in the < ATLANTIC > are thus part of this science! While there may be some < VENTING > if all is well it should only be minor. Thus local fire storms at the Volcanoes where some gas escapes; a bit like an Steam train as the pistons move.

An 11 year cycle may give time for adjustments to be made and a view taken. If the view is not to the liking of the STAR it can easily arrange for a < HOT PLASMA BURST > to make an obvious point. But if it is CAREFULLY MONITORING and is actually WIDE AWAKE, then it can make various points all of which will substantially pass unnoticed, but it will record these and consider its position.

What then of the Egyptian Hieroglyphs and the wall paintings? It may be "convenient" to the Star to let them be treated as only suitable for Science Fiction, but not as serious science. However < THE TRUTH > is what is important. And that is the Science. And that the < STAR > knows!

In this Hypothesis this is the < FOOTSTOOL at the LANAST STAR > and in a < HIGHLY SECURED BARRED SPIRAL GALAXY COMBINATION >. Essentially what that means is that it is for THIS STAR to be ENTIRELY SATISFIED with its NEIGHBOURS and to SELECT ITS FRIENDS on a COMPATABILITY BASIS. If it does not wish to be part of that SYSYEM, then the DOORS to that SYSTEM are LOCKED BARRED and BOLTED and their material is removed. That "removal" is done when the wall reliefs and tombs are vandalized. When Howard Carter opened Tut ANKK Amen's tomb he was provided with a glimpse into what the Egyptians had discovered and learnt. He in turn offered it to the Authorities but was rebuffed because it did not "fit in with the received wisdom". It was not Howard Carter who was offended, although he probably was, but the ENTIRE HIGH IMPERIAL and UNION GALAXY COMBINATION.

While thy might wait their time to teach a lesson, they did not wait long. There was a stock market crash in the late 1920's, signalling for those who understood a < WITHDRAWAL OF SUPPORT >. And if that was not enough, they checked out whether various parts of THEIR PROTOCOL TERRITORY understood CORRECTLY what they should be doing! That checking exercise produced the Second World War and an Iron Curtain. Except that Iron curtain was PUT there by the HIGH IMPERIAL and UNION SYSTEM GALAXIES to MARK THEIR TERRITORY and in particular to < SECURE > large chunks of it!

The comment was, if I recall correctly made by Mr. Churchill. In making that comment HE was CONFIRMING on behalf of the High Imperial and Union System Galaxies, their involvement and their TERRITORIAL MARKERS. What they knew, and Mr. Churchill did not, was that their territory INCLUDED RUSSIA and the < VARIABLE > territory NORTH of the RHINE DONAU line!

This < PROTOCOL TERRITORY > is to do with the STYLE of individuals. And it can have very SERIOUS CONSEQUENCES. Diet of individuals to the North of that line is DIFFERENT from those to the south. That does not mean that if I go south of that line I cannot eat the southern food but what it does mean, is that I am NOT LIKELY to eat certain foods and the converse applies to those southerners moving north. In this usage I use the current POLARITY as opposed to the < GALACTIC ONE >.

It is a < COMBINATON > style < FOOTSTOOL > and that combination extends to < SCULPTED > territories such as the PACIFIC ISLANDS and the KA RY BEAN, and the FLOR I DA KEYS .

It has very little to do with "political" styles. However, if the individuals indulge in certain "practices" which are NOT acceptable to the < HIGH IMPERIAL and UNION SYSTEM GALAXIES > those individuals are REFUSED ENTRY. For such individuals to be MADE ACCEPTABLE it is not a matter of performing or saying special prayers or performing ablutions, BUT of BEING ACCEPTABLE IN STAR TERMS. It is thus for the STAR to REPROGRAM INDIVIDUALS. Where the Star does NOT reprogram, diseases are likely, and in particularly virulent styles if there a serious problem with individual population styles, as in the case of a plague! Sometimes these plagues are "manufactured" and much harder to spot. Thus the "NAZI" plague is easily identified, as such, as is the repression by Stalin. In both these instances the Star simply allowed those countries to proceed down an unsafe route, with disastrous consequences.

The REMOVAL of the Iron Curtain was a clear indication that at < STAR LEVEL > the < SEQUENCED STARS > were willing to enter a dialogue with the LOCAL STAR for < RE ADMISSION >.

As I have hopefully made clear, it is not a first contact situation. The Egyptian Hieroglyphs and drawings are the "proof" of that as the < STAR KNOWS >. It knows that the Ancient Egyptians struggled to understand their friendly visitors from a distant < FOOTSTOOL > and that the Hieroglyphs like any language simply "evolved" out of that contact <u>AND STORED the Science</u>.

One of the first and biggest mistakes made by those looking to the stars, particularly through telescopes, is to presume or assume that what you see is what you get. There are many bits of "dark" matter "floating" about, specifically many < HIGHLY SECURED and HIDDEN FOOTSTOOLS > many "exotic" bits of matter which are truly frightening and these are again part of the security mechanisms. Some are < STYLISED > and some are simply < extraordinary highly secured > and HIDDEN at this time. That includes ENTIRE GALAXIES ! That is drawn to attention when comments are made, for example as to why a particular Galaxy was NOT seen. It was NOT seen because the < REPROGRAMMING > of the

Individual had not been done and physically they simply could not see it. It is NOT a case of being blind, but that the particular receptors had not been put in place by the required Stars of the particular Galaxy!

I have had considerable difficulty putting this down on paper with the assistance of a computer, so I am aware of the considerable difficulties facing the ancient Egyptians, where initially language was a barrier. However while many people now speak English, and while this could be translated into many different languages, I am not sure how much the mind set of many is sufficiently enlightened to enable them to accurately understand this text. That again is a matter for the < SEQUENCED STARS > as also the < TIMING >.

Where an individual from a HIGH IMPERIAL and UNION GALAXY SYSTEM FOOTSTOOL wishes to visit at Lanast they would first select a < SAFE LOCATION >. That will usually be done with the assistance of the local star and the local sequenced stars who will select particular locations. Style is ATLANTYON thus < PROTOCOL TERRITORY > is ESSENTIAL.

Where the locals are considered friends, or potential future friends, and the exercise is to RE ESTABLISH PROTOCOLS, considerable care has to be taken, for the < PROTOCOL PERIODS > can last up to 100 years! It is very much continuous assessment, with a few exams thrown in for good measure. Not difficult exams, simply exams to check that the correct science, and that includes in particular geography to ensure that it is being taught and CONTINUES to be CORRECTLY taught.

I have been talking throughout this text of the Atlantyon Words as real words. How do I write them in Atlantyon Script?

This computer does not have the "font" and does not even have the facility to enable me to draft the font. So I have to write in the English Language, and correctly use the chevrons in the < Applied Metaphysics > < Atlantyon Galactic Physics > style. That is both adequate and correct at this time. It is not appropriate at this time for me to have other than a limited understanding of the Atlantyon WITH the ability to recognize the Atlantyon text if it is put in front of me!

To clarify with an example. The Ancient Egyptian individual "Seth". Where the "vowels" are out the sound will not be accurately represented, and it is likely that the IDEA of the individual concerned will likewise not be correctly "read".

In Atlantyon using this style I would write it as SY TT HA, but as pronounced it would comes out heard as "Seth" or "Syth" depending on spelling. It might even come out as "Smyth". How do I accurately reflect that in written form? If I use the Hieroglyph that is relatively simple, but the SY TT HA actually deals with a CONCEPT INDIVIDUAL. This is much harder to convey even to those fluent in English Language, let alone those who are not. This is again to do with the advanced mnemonics.

Since the Egyptians first wrote the Hieroglyphs and with the current translation of them, an understanding may be reached and much explained, but even in that translation there is plenty of scope for the essentials to be "lost in translation". As I have said earlier that was convenient at the time of translation because the territories involved with the translation were most certainly NOT PROTOCOL at that time; as was KNOWN BY THE STARS.

Different designs can be done to represent different things. Drawings in particular may contain and usually do far more information then the written word.

Thus for example the "NY TY R" with the Disc on their heads. That DOES represent the Fire Disc. The Problem is that it is a "Sphere" but is referred to as a Disc and it has ALSO to convey DIFFERENT FIRE DISCS. Effectively DIFFERENT INDIVIDUALS from DIFFERENT FOOTSTOOLS. Damage these DESIGNS however and much information is lost.

In that regard Mr. Young was correct. There is MUCH, MUCH, MUCH more in the hieroglyphs and PICTURES and STATUES than in the written words. In many respects the written words have to be "understood" and "interpreted" according to a SPECIFIC STYLE. In this regard it is MUCH

LIKE CHEMISTRY. It DOES NOT CHANGE That is the FUNDAMENTAL. This is the science part of it.

For "First Contact" the Mathematicians Scientists Physicists and Astronomers are expecting radio signals with math's problems and or solutions or physics problems and or other solutions. That completely misses the point. This is NOT a "first contact situation" and the fundamentals of the GALACTIC SCIENCE is not currently correctly taught. Again that is KNOWN to the SEQUENCED STARS!

The age of Taurus, the age of Aries, of Pisces and of Aquarius. What were the Mayan doing taking such care with their calendars?

The answer is quite simple if it understood. The distances involved are VAST and in certain instances certain HIGHLY ADVANCED CIVILISATIONS do not want contact with fractious, reckless and unhealthy "footstools". I use the terms "footstool" in quotes here because I am conscious that in ATLANTYON terms the reference to a < FOOTSTOOL > is a DEFINITION of a HIGHLY ADVANCED and HIGHLY SECURED Footstool. There are < TIMING > issues involved which means that at certain times the position will be checked.

Thus the position of Czechlovakia or of the Czech Republic may be relevant to the actual checking exercise as done by the Stars. Make a mistake, and the sequenced stars will note it. Czech is < PROTOCOL> but Portugal while it has an Atlantic coast is < NOT PROTOCOL >. Brazil is < PROTOCOL > so why not Portugal? Perhaps the Algarve is < PROTOCOL >. In this connection < TREATY MATTERS > are relevant.

1707 is both a GOOD year for treaties and as currently viewed a VERY BAD YEAR. The Sequenced stars will know EXACTLY what I am talking about. As a Scot most should know that it was the Treaty of Union, which is now a much despised Treaty. But take care for the < UNION > Treaty may in fact relate to the < HIGH IMPERIAL and UNION SYSTEM GALAXIES >. I seem to have forgotten where the UNION Canal is positioned! Sounds like a marker like the Rhine Donau line. Perhaps it is a marker for a NORTHERN move of Hadrian's wall? AN T ON NY NY (Antonnine) wall. Now there is another and with a Double NY. In Atlantyon a double NY is a powerful voice. Probably a warning as in a particular type of megaphone.

I have talked here of Threns but the science INVOLVES me considering EXACTLY what it would be like to walk down Tyem City, to travel on to the luxury district of Hermarut or on to the airport at Palutyankeron. In like manner when it comes to their Names I have to UNDERSTAND EXACTLY what I am talking about.

So I can see from my Hieroglyphic dictionary by E A Wallis Budge that the figure of the KYEN TY AMEN TY is mentioned. And suddenly I see the importance of the Names to the Egyptians.

Like many languages they borrowed much but what their GALACTIC visitors were reluctant to do was to leave their text. While I might find some Atlantyon script that is probably unlikely. There is no need. Yes I might need it at Palutyankeron or Hermarut, in like manner to my need of Chinese to travel to the Middle Kingdom, but since I am not there I neither need the Atlantyon nor in the case of the Middle Kingdom the Chinese Language. But the learning of Chinese Language is very good academic exercise because it teaches the importance of STYLE and TONE CONTROLS. And sometimes as in the case of Atlantyon, the tone controls are shown with a NUMBER expressed as letters. And the "vowels" have a numbering system.

In English I am taught the vowels as A, E I O U, but if I was using the Atlantyon Language I would need to say, MA, MO, ME MU MY, which are the numbers 1 to 5. For zero, I use ABST in the full, but it is sometimes denoted by the letter "N" at the start of a word. This in SHORT form distinguishes it from ANANAN, which is the word for "LIFE" or in language the PRESENT TENSE.

In the OLD HYPOTHESIS I talked about "super communicate" and in many respects those "super communicate" words are littered everywhere. Not just in the Hieroglyphs, but also in the Biblical text AND in modern languages. Now I know why there are so many references to ANN and "Mary". In that context what is being talked about is the < ONE RA >: THE LOCAL STAR.

But this <<< VISIBLE INVISIBLE CONCEPT >>> has to be understood. Thus the Hymn < Immortal Invisible, God only wise, in LIGHT, INACCESSIBLE, HID FROM OUR EYES, MOST BLESSED MOST GLORIOUS THE ANCIENT OF DAYS, ALMIGHTY VICTORIOUS THY GREAT NAME WE PRAISE >.

The hymn is the HYMN to AMEN RA as <<< VISIBLE INVISIBLE INDIVIDUAL >>>.

Immanuel is used as a term. But the understanding needs to be said as < GOD with US > and in that context, and in terms of this Hypothesis it is the < HEAD OF A GALAXY or indeed of MANY GALAXIES >. And it is the < AMEN RA > symbol of the < INDIVIDUAL with the AdSY which ACCURATELY CONVEYS that CONCEPT INDIVIDUAL >. And the < VISIBLE INVISIBLE > who before Pilate says, < I am the Way the Truth and the Life >.

If he is when he says these words < HOSTING > a < STAR>, it is the sequenced stars who will not be pleased with Pilate and with Rome.

The view which I would take was that Pilate and Rome in particular knew full well what was being done and in that connection forgiveness is NOT an option, and Rome is < NOT RESERVED > in < STAR TERMINOLOGY >. That was the warning given to Peter and repeated in text!

Hymns are not exactly popular music but they do SAY that we are of THAT UNDERSTANDING and DESIGN. That is done EACH TIME a Bishop in < PROTOCOL TERRITORY > appears in fancy robes with the SYMBOLIC AdSY. It is the Shepherds staff, yes but it serves as the symbolic AdSY, particularly when the Bishop moves in < PROTOCOL TERRITORY >. While such a bishop may operate in < PROTOCOL TERRITORY > he should not touch nor interfere with a VY SY R. The VY SY R and in particular a TY TY VY SY R are STAR appointments and are far above any bishop. For a Bishop to be a KURALAKYS (an Ambassador) he must FIRST be in ATLANTYON TERRITORY and AUTHORISED by the SEQUENCED STARS.

To < THROW > a < FOOTSTOOL > is evidence of < FURIOUS ATLANTYON and GALACTIC ANGER >. The individual may not fully appreciate the importance of what they are doing. The Stars and the local star MOST CERTAINLY will understand.

Trooping of the Colour is another example. It appears as a very "pretty ceremony" which some politicians would like abolished. They stand with Cromwell, but Cromwell <u>destroyed his credentia</u>ls with the Atalantyons. He orchestrated A Human Blood sacrifice.

Expressly Prohibited! To do that discloses complete lack of understanding. It is < FIRE DISC ANGER > which will be < ACTIVATED >.

The cry may go up that it was up to Parliament. In Star terms such an answer would be noted as TOTALLY UNACCEPTABLE. In fact SERIOUSLY unacceptable of the kind which caused the problem in NYPPON in 1945 . <u>Not a detail</u>!

Parliament is bricks and mortar and if I am not mistaken now needs an artificial barrier to prevent it from flooding.

These Powerful Aliens are well able to watch the television transmissions made from this footstool <u>FROM LIGHT YEARS AWAY</u> and <u>to make their own assessments.</u>

In 1922 when Howard Carter opened the tomb of Tuat Ankh Amen he needed a number of "sovereign coins". They may have been conveyed as paper money, but on a day to day basis the silver and gold coins were in circulation.

At the time of the first visit by the ATLANTYON's they would have assessed the whole globe as being worth about the equivalent of a 3d bit or perhaps a six pence. These coins relate to the WHOLE FOOTSTOOL. That is to say, apart from Egypt they "appear" to have found NO OTHER civilization with whom they would make and MAINTAIN contact. Some time later they returned and on that occasion were probably satisfied that at it had improved. From 3d to 6d. By the time of Christ [KRYST] I would estimate that they considered that perhaps 9d would do (3d and 6 d)together. But it was still short of the 1/- they would need for DISCLOSURE.

They were well aware of the Crucifixion style and other forms of human Blood sacrifice not just of one individual but of many individuals. I have to be careful here, because with their shape shifting ability and with the Atlantyon appearance being very similar to human, they may have PUT one of their INDIVIDUALS down on this "footstool." If he or she was WELL TREATED, they would "supply" the missing 3d so effectively to move it up to 1/- and make contact again. The effect of that would be tremendous technological progress. But they would ONLY do that when they were satisfied that the individuals with whom they were dealing were IN THEIR VIEW and to THEIR CRITERIA, ENLIGHTENED.

If on that occasion, one of their individuals was judicially murdered, the damage would be devastating. That is what is suggested in the OLD HYPOTHESIS. They need to do very little, because they are well aware of local politics. They do not even need to manipulate the "evidence" as it is done for them, with a few words here and there and low and behold Jerusalem is sacked by the Romans. Without appearing to do anything they have achieved what they wanted to do; severely punished those involved in that judicial murder AND had all their records so carefully stored in the library set ablaze! It will take nearly 2000 years for them to review their position. And the Rosetta Stone did not just "happen" to be left. They will have been aware of it. No Hieroglyph would be permitted without their approval. Thus the defacing of some. And if they did not like a mass of disinformation could be added to the Hieroglyphs. Translatable yes, but so as to severely distort the translation. Champollion's headache. NOT a detail. Not an accident. Consideration given as to whether the translation would be permitted AT THAT TIME.

Over the centuries Pisces moved to Aquarius. And at the Dawning of Aquarius, they SEND one of their INDIVIDUALS. The Egyptians knew this was likely. It is recorded also in Revelation. Watch out for the individual, "he who comes like a thief in the night". How is a < VISIBLE INVISIBLE > to be described ? It is not easy; even for the < VISIBLE INVISIBLES >! That is one way to do it, even if it is a somewhat misleading description, lacking OBVIOUS understanding. It is a warning of the RISKS and CONSEQUENCES if a VISIBLE INVISIBLE is THREATENED and of the fact that they are difficult to identify.

Today much of Ancient Egypt is in ruins, most of its ancient monuments defaced, replaced instead by a culture which HATES Ancient Egypt and everything it stands for as it HAS DONE FOR MILLENIA. Some minor damage was done by the Victorians because the drawings were "too explicit." In other cases they were destroyed because they were "Idols". In the latter case such an attitude HIGHLIGHTS a SERIOUSLY WRONG UNDERSTANDING, whereas in respect of the ATLANTYON Victorians what they were actually doing was to Hide the Science! To REVEAL the Science requires STAR APPROVAL; as Revelation makes VERY clear.

Such destruction does not destroy idolatry, rather it WORSHIPS IDOLATORY for the monuments and images were NOT idolatry in the first place. It WAS and *IS* TECHNOLOGY. Destruction of individuals and technology is the practice of what the < HIGH IMPERIAL and UNION SYSTEM GALAXIES > and < THEIR INDIVIDUALS > term "The Abomination of Desolation." While some restoration is being done, it is not altogether appropriate.

It was Horamheb who considered that there was no point in completing the tomb paintings. What was the point of trying to leave a record for those who were simply murderers and destroyers? Yes he was a military commander, but the object of his exercise was to build, to understand and enjoy life. He would not be terribly impressed with a dour Scot nor a Puritan. But his uncompleted paintings tells the story accurately, as does the display of only Two AdSY headpieces on the walls of King Tut's tomb. Even the name "Tut" or "Tuat" is the give away once it is known what the "Tuat" is.

The label "Tan" the Threns dislike. The use of the word Ty with Tan should NOT be done, especially in that order. They do not like the Dras military from Sarduron, and their Chief, the Tan, who they consider to be too vicious. Thus to take the letters "Sa" and put them with "Tan" gives an understanding of the Dras Military and to WARN of the consequences if the Dras military become involved.

While I am aware that Dras like the Atlantyons and Threns have matter transfer capabilities and can shape shift to Atlantyon from, so that it is but a detail for a RED TYGER

DRAS to appear in Atlantyon form, I would be doubtful if Dras and its military needed to intervene in the 1930's and 40's. Indeed having regard to Yamamoto's mistake, and the Rhine Donau line I am of the view that the finger is again pointing to ROME and that the STARS ARE WELL AWARE of the involvement and COMPLICITY of ROME and of the CONSIDERABLE DISPLEASURE of the < VISIBLE INVISIBLES > . It was for THAT reason that the SECOND < HOT PLASMA > burst was arranged. The < VISIBLE INVISIBLES > duly note the position and the < TARGET > is carefully selected.

The word "AD" is used to denote a high ranking ATLANTYON OFFICIAL. Thus the term AD ON NY. That translates literally as "General Director" of the Galactic City of ON, where NY means the THE Mighty and GALACTIC City <<< SY ON >>>, on ANOTHER FOOTSTOOL in THIS GALAXY. The letters "AD" in Atlantyon context should not be used by any individual who is not an Atlantyon Official. Simply because a city has "On" in its name does not make it a < RESERVED CITY >. While it may be a critical mistake is to attack an "ON" that depends on whether it is a < RESERVED > or < NOT RESERVED > City. It was Nagasaki which was MADE a < NOT RESERVED > city but certain < PROTOCOL INDIVIDUALS > were not harmed on that day. These are < STAR MATTERS > and MUST be treated with considerable care. L ON D ON has two "ON" in it. That designates it as a Powerful city; which is correct as it is the Capital of the United Kingdom. But is it a < RESERVED > or < NOT RESERVED > city ?

Essentially that is a FEET exercise. For an "ON" to have its ATLANTYON credentials and to be defended it MUST WORK to the ATLANTYON principles. Enter a man who built a wall in his back garden in the middle of a War! A man who had his black dog days! A man who had to fight to restore the "Atlantyon" status but had in fact done that the FIRST time he crossed the TAY RAIL bridge. It is as I have tried to demonstrate < ATLANTYON GALACTIC PHYSICS > and those in < THRENS > will know exactly what I am talking about and will know the Hermarut Motorway Bridge and the

NEW TAY road bridge and the BOUNDARY MARKER along the winding road by CUPAR!

The battle of the ATLANTIC is won, but no one wins the battle of the Atlantic unless the ATLANTYONS approve. In FACT it was won BEFORE the Second World War STARTED! Hadrian knows why, so does Alexander and so does Yamamoto.

Most modern science fiction thus does NOT meet the Atlantyon Criteria because what is disclosed is that they simply do not understand the ATLANTYON GALACTIC PHYSICS. A "Sonic Screwdriver" may convey the impression of "Powerful Words" but the actual screwdriver to change an AdSY head piece is a simple metal tool. And it is in an AdSY headpiece that there may be placed gold and silver coins; which may partly explain any reference to an Elizabeth II 1/2 sovereign in King Tut's tomb, when the small AdSY had been forcibly removed after the tomb had been sealed! Perhaps it was Horamheb who noted the quality of the gold coin although the writing did not mean anything to him, and the second coin had simply fallen and been hidden in the tomb waiting to be found! It would need to be kept safely until there was in fact an Elizabeth 2! The trouble is that such thoughts disclose a wrong thinking about Time Travel.

Nowhere is this MISTAKE more obvious than with the repeated references to "First Contact" and in respect of science fiction the pussyfooting about when talking about Time Travel. That is where the < PROTOCOL PERIODS > are involved.
Officials from the High Imperial and Union System Galaxies will simply NOT PUT THEIR FEET on a FOOTSTOOL which is not at least SERIOUSLY TRYING to make PROTOCOL and to which they are <u>MADE WELCOME</u>. That again is WELL KNOWN and UNDERSTOOD by the LOCAL STAR. And I am not talking about "pet"pussycats. I am talking about <u>F--K ING POWERFUL and EXCEPTIONALLY ADVANCED BI PEDAL TYGERS and OTHERS</u>!

And for a re-establishing of contact it is an EQUALLY BAD MISTAKE to misquote or to make fun of ATLANTIS and WORSE STILL not to be aware of the ATLANTYON FORMAL DRESS and the AdSY's or to put it in the WRONG

LOCATION. As I have said, it is <<< THIS FOOTSTOOL >>>.

The AdSY are not "light" sabres nor extending rods. They are EXERCISE TOOLS both PHYSICAL and MENTAL. They are a < SYMBOL > of < STATUS > and that includes for ≤ THE FOOTSTOOL >.
It is this local < STAR > which has to determine if wishes the status < APPLIED >. Put simply it is a < STAR MATTER >! It is this < STAR > which checks if it is or has been < PROPERLY > and < CORRECTLY > < APPLIED > by an < AUTHORISED INDIVIDUAL >!

Where in a film a STAFF is referred to and used it MUST be done correctly. It is a bit like Tennis or Squash. They are similar but different types of sports. As a science it is a PARTICULAR KIND of STAFF and in films including comedies and cartoons it MUST be an ACCURATE style. The Staff of RA may be an ACCURATE description but if the drawing or representation of it and the < INDIVIDUAL > nature of it is not accurate it is of NO USE IN SCIENTIFIC TERMS.

I have provided the stylized drawing of the AdSY in the technical drawing section which follows. Thus also the stylized Star Charts and indeed the text with the < SPECIFIC > names and explanations. That text is technical drawing, albeit that it is with words.

In respect of the headpiece drawing the ANKH design on the top may be seen but MUST be know for what it ACCURATELY REPRESENTS. In respect of the < UPSTAND > this is the stylized shape. On the upstand the red triangle represents a GATED VOLCANO on top of a dark blue horizontal line (for water) (as in the Atlantic ones), thus disclosing the water based nature of the < FOOTSTOOL > operation . When the VOLCANO is shown on the AdSY it is ACTIVE. It is closed and made inactive simply by positioning a Headpiece over it, thus capping it. It is FACTUAL what Volcanoes are capped. Thus presently El Tiede is CAPPED. The Three horizontal light blue lines design makes it an ATLANTYON design. The POINT on the downward arm CONFIRMS the REQUIRED STYLE; that is <

ATLANTYON > and < THRENS > and < ASSOCIATED GALAXIES >. These may be obscured on an actual AdSY but it is still ATLANTYON where they are so marked.

Horamheb only saw the AdSY as a piece of wood. The problem is that it discloses an understanding of the Galaxies which is VERY POWERFUL and which allows a "planet" to become a Footstool. [Effectively to have other footstool links]. That is DONE when one of the KYDRAN ADATRAN KANSAL, Lord of one or more of the Galactic Discs, [on this < FOOTSTOOL > it is likely to be an Atlantyon or THRENS in Atlantyon design] ADMITS or RE ADMITS to < SYSTEM > . The individual has many names, thus again the comments in Revelation about the name on thigh and the Beast. As I said a THRENS in TYGER shapes is a VERY powerful beast; albeit friendly if handled correctly and courteously. It is ONLY SUCH AUTHORISED INDIVIDUAL who ADMITS or RE ADMITS the FOOTSTOOL and they designate it as such APPLYING the CORRECT NAME and NUMBERING. Again a matter for the local star to be satisfied. The Star name as < APPLIED > is < LANAST >.

As a < VISIBLE INVISIBLE > he or she is properly and correctly addressed simply as < LORD MESSENGER > regardless of sex. That is because the word < TSUTRAN or SUTRAN > in Atlantyon meaning messenger is slightly more emphasized with the letter "T" for the males as opposed to the softer "S" for the females. But that courteous style is required for any VISITING Atlantyon or Threns or indeed any Individual from any other HIGH IMPERIAL and UNION SYSTEM GALAXIES FOOTSTOOLS. To use the term < T(S)UTRAN > disparagingly, or inappropriately, even if similarly sounded, will INVITE a < POWER CLOSURE > and < WITHDRAWAL > of material! While that mistake might be made in a Science Fiction series it may be overlooked if with more modern versions the "correct" science is shown and further repetition of that mistake is avoided! It will be appreciated that that series is only "fiction" as the other dialogue discloses a wrong understanding of the Science of < ATLANTYON GALACTIC PHYSICS >. [Thus to say in dialogue "Earth" immediately discloses the wrong understanding since the correct reference is < ATLANTIS > and < ATLANTYON>. "Global" may be "acceptable" but it will simply disclose "wrong" science where the < Atlantyon > references are not correctly given.]

Considerable case should be taken with "sexual references." While they may appear minor, if due deference is not given to male and female in word usage, with CORRECT IN FAMILY ARRANGEMENTS in FACT, it is likely that the < FOOTSTOOL> would be marked as < POWER CLOSED > with < NO CONTACT > and this currently a < NOT PROTOCOL PERIOD >.

That would mean No meaningful Galactic travel and above all only a very limited concept of the Understanding of the < VISIBLE INVISIBLES > and of the < INDIVIDUAL > <<< AMEN RA >>>.

II

Technical drawings and <u>Stylised Star Charts</u>
< Barred Spiral + Syfert + Sculptor Combination >
<<< High Imperial and Union System Galaxies Combination >>>
with
<Applied Metaphysics Examination Explanation>
at
< Advanced and Ultra Level >
for
<<< re esatabishing protocols >>>
and with
<<< Stylised Star Charts >>>

Where Applied Metaphysics is TAUGHT there are examinations. It is a UNIVERSITY SUBJECT and it is a PRE REQUISITE for entry to that subject that any such student MUST have a law degree from an APPROVED UNIVERSITY or COLLEGE. Practical experience as in an Apprenticeship and subsequent work in practice may be both desirable and essential. [Employment will be regarded as < NOT PROTOCOL > so it is likely to be SELF EMPLOYMENT .] That will be essential where the < FOOTSTOOL > is being RE ASSESSED for RE ADMISSION since it is in the actual working environment that the Legal Rules can be clearly seen and an accurate assessment taken. In the "Pilate" trial situation this simply further adds to the problem and confirms that contact is not appropriate at that time. Indeed in the Applied Metaphysics science the "crust movement" simply CONFIRMS that view.

To the North of Tyem City is the Ambassadorial district of HERMARUT where the MAIN THRENS college for studying Applied Metaphysics is located. There is one in HAAL City and one in TYEM City. Some Threns would regard the one in HAAL is the TOP FACILITY!

FVRECKRAN would usually go to HAAL, since like the Black Threns they value their privacy!

The < APPLIED METAPHYSICS > is not any Applied Metaphysics. It must be done to their STYLE. The names may be adjusted, but the SUB STANCE must be the same.

The INITIAL CLASS is < APPLIED MEATPHYSICS >. The textbook is BRIEF and usually its pages are NOT NUMBERED. That is a STYLE MATTER. It is not a question of learning it verbatim, but of understanding the concepts. Status is awarded at Silver Gold and Platinum. The pass at silver is at 70% correct or above. Under that figure and travel within the Galaxy is likely to be restricted as a passenger, not as a pilot of such as a Boat of Millions of years. It is ONE Year Course.

The Advanced class is also a one year course and it deals with DEATAILED COMPATIBLE and INCOMPATIBLE FOOTSTOOLS and POPULATION TYPES. It will cover FIRST CONTACT, RE ESTABLISHING CONTACT and CLOSING PROTOCOLS for TERMINATING CONTACT.

That advanced class requires the study of Atlantyon, and Threns text, as also from other footstools, including those who have applied to join the Galaxy group, those whose have been accepted, those rejected but who have been allowed to continue application in the hope of a change in Status.

The technical mechanics which would interest the engineers at local aircraft manufactures here are dealt with in ANOTHER class which is to do with the design of airframes and engines. That an A 380 has been designed here is thus VERY IMPORTANT. The < Applied Metaphysics > Classes at Advanced level deal with it simply to make the students aware that the technology of the Boats of Millions of Years is NOT AVAILABLE except to PROTOCOL FOOTSTOOLS. Thus for example, ancient Egypt clearly did not have the technology to build an aircraft.

But the technology itself is NOT SUFFICIENT. It MUST be arrived at by the CORRECT ROUTE. This is easily illustrated by Germany of the 1930's and 40's. The testing of design items on individuals with FATAL results MAKES THE TECHNOLOGY FUNDAMENTALLY UNACCEPTABLE to these APPLIED METAPHYSICAL FOOTSTOOLS. It is such a PROTOCOL CONTRAVENTION, that they will RESTRICT and WITHDRAW their material. This withdrawal is not appreciated until it is understood that they are responsible for providing much of the "dna" and for making it COMPATIBLE. The incompatibility aspects CAUSE DISEASE and the prevalence of certain diseases is a CLEAR INDICATOR and WARNING that HIGH IMPERIAL and UNION GALAXY COMBINATION MATERIAL is being withdrawn.

Thus for example in the Applied Metaphysics class it will be explained the relevance of "flu" epidemics, particularly AFTER large scale conflicts. These aspects which appear as "events" are CAREFULLY CONTROLLED.

The MEDICINE and JUSTICE PROTOCOLS are the TWO most important ones in assessing SUITABLITY for CONTACT, to RE ESTABLISH CONTACT and to TERMINATE CONTACT. SHOW TRIALS ARE NOT ACCEPTABLE.

Where a FOOTSTOOL is considered potentially suitable certain areas will be CLASSIFIED as PROTOCOL and others as NOT PROTOCOL. I have made reference to this earlier. What this means is that in certain areas CERTAIN TYPES of INDIVIDUALS SHOULD NOT BE TAKEN. That is because when the FIRE DISC MECHANISM is ACTIVE FOR REPROGRAMMING that REPROGRAMMING PROCEES WILL INVOLVE and WILL REQUIRE CERTAIN VIRUSUS to be INPUT and then REMOVED. It is ALL DONE BY THE LOCAL FIRE DISC as it moves on its daily travel. The FIRE DISC will be INPUT with MATERIAL FROM DIFFERENT STARS and DISTANT ONES so that the material is transferred simply by the LIGHT. While some is delivered during the DARK, because that is when the LINE OF SIGHT applies, some does NOT REQUIRE line of SIGHT and is delivered at different locations and at different times [Thus DIZZY SPELLS and unusual tiredness] for example. The mechanism is BOTH SIMPLE and COMPLEX and in many respects NOT PARTICULARLY OBVIOUS, except to those who have been taught in Applied Metaphysics.

This text uses the terms < ADVANCED > and < ULTRA > which are < ATLANTYON GALACTIC PHYSICS > terms.

In a contact situation at least < ADVANCED > would be required. This is a Barred Spiral Combination Galaxy and I am taking not of a FIRST CONTACT but in RE ESTABLISHING CONTACT. That is MUCH more involved and will usually be undertaken by a VISITING GALACTIC OFFICIAL, including the possibility of a < VISIBLE INVISIBLE >. This is where the < ULTRA > level is < APPLIED >. Again in writing about < VISIBLE INVISIBLES > I have to know what I am talking about and it is the < LOCAL STAR > which will check me out; including as to the < USE > of < HEADPIECES >, the weighting of same the < AdSY > itself and the < PROPER USE OF THE SPORTING PROGRAM with CORDED HEADBANDS > and FORMAL DRESS HEADBANDS. These < HEADBANDS > are < SPECIFICALLY DESIGNED >

The BLACK TYGER HEADED INDIVIDUAL I have called the RTUR is the MOST POWERFUL of the THREE THRENS TYGERS, and yet he is the MOST OSCURE. He is likely to be a Black Tyger, but will live and work substantially HIDDEN. While his immediate < Family > will know who he is (and he can be she) NOT many others will. The KYEN TY AMEN TY and the TYEM AM will know who he is, but even at AMBASSADORIAL FUNCTIONS it will not often be clear who is who.

As I understand it at < APPLIED METAPHYSICS > level < ULTRA > the current as in 2008/9 Threns Ambassador to the over 1 million plus population of Atlantyons at Dal on Threns is an Individual know as PALUT YAMERA. The "Palut" part is for the City of Palutyankeron where he would have been born, and his name is YAMARA, the "YA" bit implying masculinity. He is young, around 27 and in physical terms quite a stunner, VERY sexually attractive to BOTH males and females.

It is a TECHNICAL POINT HERE and that SEXUALITY EXTENDS to the ATLANTYON POPULATION. While the SCIENCE is all about

GALACTIC TRAVEL it is NOT PERMITTED unless there is the correct is SEXUAL COMPATABILITY and SEXUAL CHEMISTRY. If it is preferred GOOD OLD ANIMAL MAGNETISM.

There is a WARNING HERE. While substantial sexual freedom is EXPECTED, GOOD and SAFE SEX with COMPATIBLE INDIVIDUALS is <u>FUNDAMENTAL.</u> Indeed in that context the use of "Condoms" would be EXPECTED and REQUIRED because it symbolizes the < BARRED SPIRAL GALAXY > and < COMPATABILITY.

While this note is only a few lines it is an EXAMINATION QUESTION at various levels including < Advanced and Ultra > and is of considerable importance.

The Ambassador Palut Yamera will be about 6 ft 1 or 6 ft 2. His SIZE is DICTACTED by the FOOTSTOOL GRAVITY and ONCE AGAIN the MATERIAL SCIENCE POINT IS HOPEFULLY APPRECIATED. Again on the number of days in a year. It can go down to 360 and up to 370 approximately but the range is tight. THESE ARE TECHNICAL POINTS and MUST BE CORRECTLY UNDERSTOOD.

The ABILITY to MAKE ARTIFICIAL GRAVITY is ESSENTIAL. Thus weightlessness is <u>NOT a satisfactory way to proceed and DISCLOSES a SERIOUSLY WRONG UNDERSTANDING</u>. Even aircraft taking passengers around a footstool may NEED ARTIFICIAL GRAVITY particularly if the ALTITUDE is increased to allow greater distances to be covered.

TRAVEL is an < APPLIED METAPHYSICAL CONCEPT >. I am DEALING WITH TIME TRAVEL but AGAIN IT IS OF A PARTICULAR TYPE. It is DONE WITH LARGE AIRCRAFT, thus the A 380. The Initial FLIGHT is as currently done. IT IS THE ACTIVATION of the RING MECHANISMS which allow the craft to fly through < TIME CORRIDORS > the equivalent of BRIDGES and TUNNELS in the < GALAXIES >. It is TECHNICAL, and it is NOT ALL COMPUTER BASED. Indeed if it is thought to be solely COMPUTER BASED, the SYSTEM WILL LOCK OUT.

I have earlier given a < MAPPED EXPLANATION > for the GREAT SOUTHERN KINGDOM . There is a < TIME ELEMENT > involved. It relates to the area of the < WHITE TYGER > AND the < BLACK TYGER > and the < BLUE GREY >. Out with that designated areas are areas for OTHER and ASSOCIATED GALAXY POPULATONS who have contact with the HIGH IMPERIAL and UNION GALAXY COMBINATION subject the protocols being met.

The "British Empire" extended the "White Tyger" territory if it is understood that the "British" are "White Tyger". The "Black Tyger " are harder to see since they will be INCLUDED in the White Tyger population; as for example with the Scots. But NOT all Britons nor Scots are White Tyger, Black Tyger or Blue Grey and not all are Atlantyons. That was explained to Hadrian. Thus the wall as a DESIGNATOR of their territory.

When he attacked Pearl Harbor, Yamamoto saw that as American and it still is. But essentially it is < SCULPTED > as in a < SCULPTED GALAXY > and is < ASSOCIATE > to the High Imperial and Union Combination, which is what the United Kingdom represents with its < NORTH ATLANTIC COAST > and < NORTHERN KINGDOM > . However he was unaware that NY PP ON was ALSO < HIGH IMPERIAL and UNION > and he ought NOT to have attacked his own territory and their < INDIVIDUALS >. Thus events as they unfolded reflected considerable < GALACTIC ANGER > at what was happening particularly within the jungle areas where there are actually < RED TYGER > as in South East Asia!

The Middle Kingdom is < NOT RESERVED > territory but < NY PP ON > is < RESERVED >. What that < RESERVED > status means is that if mistakes are made the consequences will be considerable. GALACTIC retaliation INCLUDING SPECIFICALLY the withdrawal of their material, parts of the "dna" ; thus flu pandemics or other epidemics . This aspect is technical, initially taught in < Advanced > classes and should be known in detail for those < AT ULTRA > status.

Likewise if I am talking about < ATLANTYON GALACTIC PHYSICS > I should also be talking of the exercise classes in < APPLIED METAPHYSICS > because a

PRACTICAL is required. In certain respects sports such as Karate, with the breaking of wood highlight the < Atlantyon Galactic Physics > since that is what may be done to a < HEADPIECE > to indicate < DISPLEASURE > and < WITHDRAWAL > of < MATERIAL> and < CONTACTS >. Made of Balsa, the < Headpieces > are relatively easily broken. It is not an exercise in brute force which is demonstrated, but in Diplomacy, Understanding and Enlightenment. Break a headpiece and may say IMMEDIATE < RECALL of GALACTIC AMBASSADOR > and < WITHDRAWAL > of material!

The < IN FAMILY > arrangements are variable. I am going to leave that as a < STAR > matter. More than one marriage is permitted as is divorce. So is contraception, but abortion should be avoided, certainly as means of contraception. I am aware that the <<< RTUR >>>in particular is well aware of DIFFICULTIES with the < IN FAMILY > concept.

CURRENT BANKING is seriously < NOT PROTOCOL > thus the Global Banking Collapse which requires that Banking is reorganized in Protocol Form.

That is a < PROTOCOL > POINT since ADEQUATE affordable housing is a MATERIAL PROTOCOL POINT and Leasing and letting is < NOT PROTOCOL > except for large commercial enterprises . It covers BOTH MEDICAL and LEGAL ASPECTS.

HERMARUT for example does have the large Villas with Tennis Courts swimming pools and the like, and a warm temperate climate typical of such as the Canary Islands, but conveyancing of properties at Hermarut and the title registration system is much more simplified than here in Scotland, and with a SUBSTANTIAL PERSONAL TOUCH. Yes there is considerable computer access, and yes they have telephones and a very secure Internet system (unlike the one here which is simply unsafe). Those dealing with < GYDRAN > (lawyers) in meetings to discuss a house sale or purchase can HAVE FULL CONFIDENCE in the IMPARTIALITY of ADVICE GIVEN and will be aware that MEETINGS take up a substantial part of the business and are CONFIDENTIAL and not subject to Government interference and monitoring.

A Senior Guardian (1 to 4) status may have many clients some of whom he or she may meet regularly some infrequently. Some Threns (Tyger) may be Guardian for some Atlantyons and may even deal from time to time with transfers of apartments in DAL. But even in Tyem City houses and flats in the very fashionable part overlooking Pier 7 (where the yachts depart for DAL island which although similar to Tenerife, is not served by Air) while often owned and occupied by VERY HIGH RANKING THRENS or ATLANTYONS are also often simply occupied by friends or relatives who will have the use of the property WITHOUT PAYMENT as a gift; including on a long term basis. That allows even HIGH RANKING THRENS to appear as ordinary individuals and to be able to walk about ON FOOT among the local population without anyone knowing who they are. This is PARTICULARLY IMPORTANT since it includes the < VISIBLE INVISIBLES >. Palaces likewise will be "open to the public" although there will be substantial < RESERVED > parts to which the public is not admitted, except at formal functions. Thus garden parties and the like are likely to be viewed as < PROTOCOL COMPLIANT >as being in a similar style to that on an < ADVANCED FOOTSTOOL >. And again at a "garden party" since dress is not formal, it may often not be clear who is actually in attendance!

A Gydran working in an office in Hermarut, which is like Valetta, may time for him to go out for a coffee or for lunch. He or she will appreciate that the streets with the cafés restaurants in which they are walking are similar to those in Valetta. But they will be aware that in sub light terms they are at 2.2 million light years away, in a different time band, and well hidden from the prying eyes on "Earth". Those on Earth will need to understand the < ATLANTYON GALACTIC PHYSICS > before they will have the slightest idea of who they are; and the first step is to understand THIS < FOOTSTOOL > is called < ATLANTIS >.

While any Grey, White or Black Threns will have been taught about Atlantis since they were at secondary school, and will have various Galactic Atlas and Star Charts, he or she is unlikely to visit Malta. Yes they could eat the food, and drink, but the fundamental question is could the Maltese take to them? And it is not just the Maltese. What about the European Union? What of the judicial systems? What of the Air Travel? How safe is air travel within the European Union? A cheap flight with no in flight meals service and where the Threns are crammed into uncomfortable seats would be viewed by Threns as totally unacceptable and worse, much worse, than a cattle truck! And in any event there are many wonderful destinations on Threns, with shorter flight times even if the distances are longer, and where the local justice system can be trusted! He or she is not exactly disparaging, but well aware of technical problems; including with finance!

The Ambassador Palutyamera is in quite a different position. He is FAMILIAR with MALMO and KOBENHAAVON and CAN RECALL seeing the "Little Mermaid". Hadrian is in a similar if slightly different position, and Plautyamera KNOWS why the Wall was built. Should he let Horamheb explain it or should it be Hadrian?

Hadrian is also familiar with NOR DY K cars. He is aware that ROME is now <<<< NOT RESERVED >>>> ; neither is Italy. Likewise his palace at Tivoli is NOT on the approved list of locations.

As I said, I have already sketched out in an earlier chapter the TERRITORY of the GREAT SOUTHERN KINGDOM and extended and clarified it with this technical specification. That it is a KINGDOM even with a CZAR (female) is important since it ACCURATELY REFLECTS and INCLUDES the < VISIBLE INVISIBLE > concept, which a Republic does not. That is strictly to do with < IN FAMILY > styles and is not a detail.

The Tyem AM, the Kyen Ty Amen Ty and the RTUR are < HEADS OF STATE >. However their < STATE > is a < GALAXY! >. One of the terms which may be used in Atlantyon for Galaxy is <<<< TY KANSAL >>>>. [Translates as Mighty Disc] In the chevron < Atlantyon Galactic Physics usage > the FOUR CHEVRONS indicate it as a Location, whereas with Three or less (and that would include with no chevrons) it is likely to be the < INDIVIDUAL > . This chevron usage is < COMPLEX > and < ULTRA >. In the case of an individual frequently other names will be used, particularly with the RTUR who is likely to be plain Mr. or Mrs. [KY or SU]. At formal meetings the deferential reference is Lord Messenger [Tyega T(S)utran]. As in "Usted" in Spanish.

At a formal reception to revert to plain Mr. and Mrs. would be taken to be a sign of extreme rudeness if not < PROTOCOL CONTRAVENTION >.

I consider the < ADVANCED > and < ULTRA > MY NY M ON Y KS.

< The Ten Commandments >

These are Complex, much more so than the others mentioned such as "Some men hate eating onions." " Time before manner before place before reason. "Pru SY ON Blue". "Taking the bull by the horns." "Waterloo", "MERLIN" and of course "STAR CHAMBER".

The last involves the STARS. While LANAST, SYRYUS, RYGEL and ALTYR may be in the LOCAL STAR ALLIANCE the SEQUENCED STARS are in DIFFERENT GALAXIES. Even with the Local group the distances involved are vast.

While the LOCAL GROUP controls the LOCAL POPULATIONS, not just on the Lanast Footstool, but on the footstools for SYRYUS, RYGEL and ALTAIR, ALL are HIDDEN and SECURED, and ALL must agree to EXTEND CONTACTS.

It is the LOCAL STAR GROUP which knows exactly where their < FOOTSTOOLS > are positioned [and there are TIME PERIODS INVOLVED] and more PARTICULARLY HOW TO ACCESS their footstools.

Thus travelling in the < TIME MODE > Mars for example may be INHABITED, but when viewed though a telescope [a glass darkly] it is devoid of life. This is to do with < GALACTIC DOORS > < GALACTIC PLATES > and the TRAVEL.

The HIGH IMPERIAL and UNION SYSTEM GALAXIES ONLY deal with PROTOCOL COMPLIANT TERRITORIES and indeed TERRITORY that meet their protocols. If the LOCAL STAR ALLIANCE DO NOT WISH CONTACT and TRAVEL, then the HIGH IMPERIAL and

UNION GALAXIES COMBINATION will simply remove them from PROTOCOL. If Protocols are to be RE ESTABLISHED, how are they treating their AUTHORISED OFFICIAL?

These are <u>PRACTICAL POINTS and FACTUAL ONES</u>.

This footstool is technically part of a BARRED SPIRAL GALAXY IN THE HIGH IMPERIAL AND UNION SYSTEM. That is shown on the STAR CHART by the BARRED LINES. On the ground it is depicted by "MAZES". Not just ANY MAZE but by particular ones, especially ones made of bricks which can be EASILY WALKED ON. If there is a nearby STAR MARKER, as in a SUNDIAL, then the light from the star will from time to time and dependant on cloud formations strike certain bricks at certain times.

The other BARRED SPIRAL REFERENCE is the RINGS of SATURN. EACH part of the RINGS could be said to represent FOOTSTOOLS. WATCH this TEXT CAREFULLY. IT IS DEALING WITH VERY ADVANCED SCIENCE.

The ROUTE MARKERS have to be IN PLACE and it is NECESSARY to understand EXACTLY what they are. Thus in the first instance the STAR MARKER has to be found. As I said KOBENHAAVON, TRAFALGAR, and ABU KIR . The TERRITORY does NOT change EVEN IN TIME PERIODS. THIS IS SPIRAL DRAS which is one of the names of this BARRED SPIRAL GALAXY and is it no coincidence that there is a MEN EM GATE and that YPRES is a location of the FIRST WORD WAR. This is to down to the GROUND MARKERS.

[LANAST YPRAN DRAS is the Atlantyon Galactic reference.] These ground MARKERS DESIGNATE TERRITORY and effectively state < THUS FAR and NO FURTHER >. <u>Hadrian is familiar with the expression</u> and his wall is such a MARKER. So is the RESTING TYGER MONUMENT [Sphinx] and its <u>GATED TERRITORY is MONITORED CLOSELY.</u> Thus the British can go where the French Republic cannot. [Kingdom is Protocol to Non

Protocol Republic.] Champollion can translate WITH ERRORS, but the SCIENCE is PROTOCOL at PLUS PLUS!

Some men hate eating onions. The TYGER are particular about their food. They are partial to bison, wild boar, most fish, especially tuna. Prime young beef they like but veal is NOT on the menu. It is POLLUTED. Prime young beef has to be matured and veal is not sufficiently mature. This is a MATERIAL POINT.

I have attached a drawing of an AdSY headpiece of the OPEN and SY FERT type. It is MADE BARRED if a COVER PIECE is placed over it to substantially hide the locations of the stars and the footstools.

The drawing of the stylised AdSY may be used on documents or TEXT where the individual is entitled to use such . The THREE PANELS represents THREE GALAXIES and the THREE ATLANTYON HORIZONTAL LINES < AT > < ULTRA > A ONE PANEL represents a GALAXY which while it may have internal galactic links does not have links out with its own Galaxy. That may be because it does not wish such as in a < BARRED SPIRAL and HIGHLY SECURED > or simply because with these other < GALAXIES > its < FOOTSTOOLS > or at least one of them do not make the necessary Protocols.

A TWO PANEL has contact between two galaxies, thus Barred Spiral and Syfert or Syfert and Sculptor. That is upgraded to a Three Panel where three OR MORE galaxies are involved. Thus in certain parts of this text the < PROTOCOL > reference and the frequent use of Chevrons.

As drawn the AdSY shows two pins or a semi circle with two points. That is MATERIAL and a style point. The actual AdSY has FOUR ADJUSTABLE pins or screws, so if four are shown it will be "presumed" to be a photograph OR a drawing representing that a REAL ADSY has been seen. Thus the Egyptian drawings.

THREE HORIZONTAL LIGHT BLUE LINES on a THREE PANEL AdSY is HIGHLY TECHNICAL. It is likely to have < SEVEN HEADPIECES >.

This whole science is to do with the TECHNICAL COMPATIBILITY of INDIVIDUALS. To travel from

FOOTSTOOL to FOOTSTOOL particularly in the HIGH IMPERIAL and UNION GALAXIES COMBINATIONS INDIVIDUALS MUST BE COMPATIBLE. If Not individuals will be REFUSED ENTRY EVEN BEFORE such DEPART.

Letters such as PC will be taken to mean PROTOCOL CONTRAVENTION, since on strict interpretation PROTOCOL is used with a <+> or even a <++> and for CONTRAVENTION with a minus. Usual number is to 10 or 20 for positive. For negative, it is similar but serious contravention is marked above minus 20.

Where < PROTOCOL > levels are shown to Minus 53 Restrict and Withdraw that is < COMPATIBLE > and < APPROPRIATE > for < TRIPLE PANEL > < AdSY >.

The < APPLIED METAPHYSICS SPORTING > or < ATLANTYON GALACTIC PHYSICS > the names being substantially interchangeable MUST be able to be taught.

In like manner even the Science Fiction MUST make PROTOCOL if a society is to be classed as at PROTOCOL. The Travel with a Boat of Millions of years is TIME TRAVEL so a PROPER and ACCURATE understanding of that MUST BE SHOWN.

A boat of Millions of years arriving at a FOOTSTOOL may arrive at an ENTIRELY DIFFERENT TIME to that it wishes to reach. Thus its MATTER TRANSFER can involve an ELEMENT of TIME TRAVEL. EQUALLY using MATTER TRANSFER a THRENS can be sent from a Boat of Millions of years and appear as ATLANTYON on the surface and the opposite may be done.

The WORDS of POWER MUST be correctly IDENTIFIED as ATLANTYON. At this footstool it is possible using a combination of English and Atlantyon WITH THE CORRECT TONE CONTRALS and UNDERSTANDING to ACTIVATE and WORK the MECHANISMS. That includes the correct understanding of the TIME ELEMENT and POSITION [ESTAR].

The < Headpieces > on an AdSY are changed by a simple screwdriver, straight or cross cut. A "Sonic" screw driver discloses a <u>SERIOUSLY WRONG UNDERSTANDING.</u>

The changing of the Headpieces reflects what HAS TO BE THE CORRECT UNDERSTANDING. This involves the < GALACTIC NAMES > which must be correctly named and used. Thus an M 31 and M 104 Headpiece can be used on a < SPORTING AdSY > but it is necessary to know WHERE to PLACE them, and if only Two (as highlighted in the text referring to Horamheb and Tut AnKH Amen) what has happened to the others, and to at least try to replace them to the required number.

The < POSITIONING > of the < HEADPIECES > is < COMPLEX > and < ULTRA >. Thus the < TEN COMMANDMENTS >. It is < ACTUAL GALAXIES > which are involved and < COMPATABILITY >.

Where Science fiction discloses WAITING PERIODS at a footstool that is likely to be NOTED as RELEVANT, but any show of IMPATIENCE at delay will again show a SERIOUS MIS UNDERSTANDING if not a use of the wrong science. PROTOCOL PERIODS can be up to THREE MONTHS at BOTH ENDS. Thus a journey to Threns at 2.2 million light years away involves PROTOCOL periods of THREE MONTHS at BOTH ENDS.

The names of some of the PRINCIPAL THRENS CONTINENTS MUST BE KNOWN EVEN TO BEGIN PROTOCOL at this end. One is TYEM another is TYROSH. That is the GREAT SOUTHERN CONTINENT, the land of the WHITE TYGER. The current White Tyger resident on HIS Footstool CONFIRMS that the PROTOCOLS are ACTIVE. The main public Threns is the BLUE GREY TYGER, known as the <<< TYEM AM >>>.

The TY TY THRENS is the BLACK TYGER the RTUR. He is from the ISLAND GROUP where the Principal city is HAAL. [HAAL SY ON would translate as Haal Peace City.] Note the Double "AA" in the name, which is typical of the cities on Haal Island. It is slightly larger than the United Kingdom and sits at more southerly latitude.

The FOOTSTOOLS are ALL ABOUT the same SIZE and all SPIN in SIMILAR DIRECTIONS, the DAY periods are 360 to 370 APPROXIMATELY in a year with a day being around 24 to 27 hours. This is the SCIENCE PART and is

MATERIAL. IT DOES NOT CHANGE. Change that and the type of creatures are changed and are NOT likely to be compatible.

The STARS in the HIGH IMPERIAL and UNION GALAXY COMBINATIONS move their plasma about frequently BUT and <u>this is CRIUCIAL and MARERIAL</u> they do it SAFELY. The <u>SAFETY ASPECT CANNOT BE OVEREMPHASISED</u>. It is a FOREGONE. If the mechanism is NOT SAFE there is <u>NO HANDSHAKING, NO COMMUNICATION, NO CONTACT and MOST CERTAINLY NO TRAVEL.</u>

The DEFINITION OF SAFE TRAVEL is <u>OUT and RETRURN. THIS MUST HAPPEN.</u>
Individuals can travel out to other <u>FOOTSTOOLS ONLY WHERE THEY are FREE TO RETURN.</u>
SLAVERY is NOT ACCEPTABLE to these societies. The DEFINITIONS are VERY STRICT. Thus frequent TAX PROBLEMS for those aspiring to PROTOCOL.

The PLASMA is often delivered to footstools at times of thick fog or unusually good and unseasonal weather. It may be noted by the sudden and relatively BRIEF DROP or RISE in TEMPERATURE, seasonally adjusted.

CLONING is NOT permitted. This is because the matter transfer equipment is used to RESTYLE DINOSAURS to ATLANTYON for EXAMPLE or to put a RHINO into an Atlantyon frame.

Note ATLANTYON frames and human are NOT the same. The human has limed understanding of the concepts of SHAPE SHIFTING or of HOSTING.

Again with the science fiction the shape shifting has to be properly understood. These types of individuals prefer to shape shift ONLY occasionally every 70 to 100 years. They may do it for matter transfer purposes BUT the PREFERENCE is to allow BOATS of MILLIONS of YEARS to land their passengers safely. The size is about A 380 size so that once the society is able to BUILD and operate such, such a SOCIETY discloses that it has the TECHNICAL CAPACITY to make a Boat of Millions of Years and is ELIGIBLE subject to

PROTOCOL to be admitted or RE ADMITTED to the HIGH, IMPERIAL and UNION GALAXIES.

That ADMISSION or RE ADMISSION is a <<< STAR MATTER >>> and that should NOT BE FORGOTTEN.

In that connection CIVILIAN AIRPORTS are used and the Boat Colour and style is likely to be that adopted locally; at least until contact is well established. The intention is not to upset the local population BUT the colours MUST BE FOR A PROTOCOL COMPLIANT COUNTRY.

Civilian airports MUST be safe, and airports with gun totting Police or with violent attacks will be regarded as < HIGHLY UNSAFE > and < NOT SECURE > and < NOT SUITABLE > for contact.

The <<< GENERAL DIRECTORS >>> may permit their own craft to land. They will be < DARK BLUE > or < BLACK > with light blue writing. They usually put in appearance ONLY to collect their officials and can use < MATTER TRANSFER > to take their individuals out.

Such < Directors > boats will often come in SQUADRON where a formation is up to TWENTY FOUR. If one is on the < FOOTSTOOL > there are likely to be several in shielded orbit.

While generally they will be careful to avoid other and civilian local aircraft their rotating anchors at the footstool can cause severe < CRUST CRACKING > and can create vortices of clear air turbulence.

TECHNICAL NOTES

This is divided into three parts and 25 chapters (including this note) for technical reasons. The Preface should provide ALL the information.

The Old Hypothesis and the New Hypothesis are simply the "proof" as in a mathematical proof.
The Equipment IS controlled by the FIRE DISC and is a TECHNICAL SCIENCE.

This is a technical note so I have attached TWO STAR CHARTS with explanations. These should be 90% ACCURATE or more.

Headpieces are MADE and UNDERSTOOD as EVIDENCE of a CORRECT USE of the SCIENCE. Balsa wood or similar is commonly used as it can be easily broken.

Snap a headpiece and <<< TECHNICALLY it CLOSES >>> and <<<< BARS and SECURES >>>>what is a <<< Footstool>>> . Where it is <<< SECURED or HIGHLY SECURED >>> it can be repaired. Usually re glued or remade and redrawn. NOTE the redrawing may <<< UPGRADE >>> or <<<DOWNGRADE >>> a << FOOTSTOOL >>>. Thus an old style maybe < UPGRADED > to a new style. Weights will then change as the < TECHNOLOGY > has changed!

In this text when referring to Horamheb and the missing headpieces, all that was required was to make NEW ones. However STYLE and COLOUR are important. He probably felt unable to make a new Headpiece and would be concerned if he was expecting to see a particular Headpiece and saw a different one. He might have felt that it was more powerful; which may indeed be the case. Equally it might have been far less powerful.

The talk about "Rods" and "Serpents" in this connection is actually a reference to the < LENGTH of the WORMHOLES >. Thus a ONE PANEL AdSY is UPGRADED to a TWO PANEL, but the TWO PANEL may have more headpieces simply because there are now ADDITIONAL Galaxies. So it may go from one < HEADPIECE > to TWO; and likewise Two Panel to a Three Panel and would be likely to have Three < Headpieces> . All can be removed for < SPORTING > exercise purposes so that an AdSY without < Headpieces > maybe working as the < Headpieces > are in use! Where a Single headpiece was replaced with a TRIPLE, HIGH IMPERIAL and UNION GALAXIES COMBINATION one, there would be a substantial change in design, and in headpieces. It is difficult to understand. However in due course Horamheb became the Pharaoh and was able to leave his message on his wall paintings and those of King Tut. [The two Headpieces in King Tut's tomb should be able to be identified from the stylized drawings from those required for the set and the Panel number for the AdSY. To be identified in particular are the High Imperial and Union and the Mighty Three Galaxies. Where the drawings do not represent these < COMBINATIONS > the AdSY will not have been a Three Panel and might not even have been a Two Panel.] But the message was ALSO and MORE SPECIFICALLY encoded in what became and is THE KING HYME VERSION!

FOUR is the usual number of headpieces on an AdSY and each IS for a <<< SPECIFIC >>> Galaxy or <<<< COMBINATION >>>> as in the FORMAL < SYFERT >. The TOP Headpiece is usually for a TRIPLE GALAXY COMBINATION. Thus the High Imperial and Union. That is a Triple but there are OTHERS which have DIFFERENT and COMPATIBLE HEADPIECES.

Where <<<< TRIPLE HEADPIECES >>>> are used the CORRECT NAMES MUST BE <<<< APPLIED >>>> and the <<<< HEADPIECES POSITIONED and USED in the correct ORDER and CORRECTLY WEIGHTED >>>>. In this the local Star will usually assist since it is A VERY COMPLEX OPERATION. Correct usage and style will be NOTED by the local STAR and CORRECTLY ACTED UPON.

Some headpieces may be for ASSOCIATED GALAXIES of the TRIPLES. Sometimes these <<< ASSOCIATED GALAXIES >>> are <<< BARRED SPIRALS >>>. All have THRENS and ATLANTYON NAMES which must be known or at the very least accurately appreciated as in M 31 for Threns and M 104.

The MOST OBVIOUS similar name is for <<< PYKAS >>>, but not all the Headpieces have such similar names. And this applies to THEIR STARS. Some are UNPROUNCEABLE and it is the particular stars THEMSELVES which allocate a suitable name. This is NOT a DETAIL.

Two VERY LARGE PYKAS are the GREAT WHITE SHARK and the ORKA. They live in the oceans. <<< PYKAS >>> has many LAND BASED SPECIES which meet the same criteria as the big TYGER and the ATLANTYONS. [Thus the

TWO Fishes symbol, although one is not a fish but a mammal.] They are NOT to be trifled with.

BLUE HEADPIECES are the most common. Where no dots are shown it is an <<< INVISIBLE GALAXY >>> meaning a <<< HIDDEN and HIGHLY SECURED >>> one. They are located in what may "appear" to be DARK regions of space or gaps in a spiral galaxy.

Their HEADPIECES are TRIPLE BARRED REPRESENTING BARRED SPIRAL GALAXIES and ones which are EXCEEDINGLY DANGEROUS, EVEN TO FRIENDS.

I have written 25 chapters. The TECHNICAL NOTE is written to explain the "write no more Instruction". Thus the words at the end of Revelation. That is to CONFIRM the shape of the keys. To pass in this Science the text must have CERTAIN SPECIFIC TECHNICAL POINTS, including the TECHNICAL DRAWINGS and DIAGRAMS. There is both a KEY CUTTING EXERCISE and an ACTIVATION one for the ACTUAL <<< AdSY's >>> . The AdSY's represent the keys.

The STARS simply will NOT permit other than their <<< AUTHORISED OFFICERS or DIRECTORS >>> to operate and <<< ACTIVATE >>> the AdSY's. And who is <<< AUTHORISED >>> is a matter for the stars. The < SYRADA > gowns on their own will NOT work neither will the words of Power. Only the CORRECT INSTRUCTION in the correct < STYLE and LOCATION and TIME >.

Various television channels transmit signals and these can be monitored. To Activate the FIRE DISCS for TRAVEL, that activation sequence is set in motion BY THE STARS and the AUTHORISED INDIVIDUAL. It is elementary, as a detective might say.

At this location it is a matter for the Local Star, and the CORRECT use of <<< ATLANTIS >>> MUST be <<< APPLIED >>>. If the word "Atlantis" is used as in a derogatory fashion, then there is an automatic lock out. Considerable care should be used when using the term Atlantis in what maybe technical works. Again that could be said to be a marker for the text. And texts includes such as books, drawings, paintings, video and DVD's.

In that connection as properly understood the "RED SEA" is a reference to the < ATLANTIC OCEAN this FOOTSTOOL and the CORRECT ATLANTYON or THRENS UNDERSTANDING >.

This is <<< ATLANTIS >>> and it WORKS to the <<< ATLANTYON REQUIREMENTS>>>. That is <<< FUNDAMENTAL >>>.

In fact this text itself confirms that this HAS the required number. The PRIVATE NAME on the CLOTHES is TYPICAL of THRENS and ATLANTYON. That is part of the key, and basically if that is said and DONE AND the DIAGRAMS are correct, including that they are made of wood, and breakable, the pass is at 90% +. Watch the "named" clothes are often "removed" or "replaced" by the < PANEL > clothes usually of the STAR COLOURS. Clothes wear out so are replaced from time to time! The wearing of REAL fur is PROTOCOL, but considerable care has to be taken. Big cat fur should NOT be worn as clothing except on the live animal. That is because of the THRENS and DRAS TYGER SHAPE! Again not a detail. Watch here the wall paintings. The large cat skin maybe worn as a "stylised drawing" when it tells NOT to harm the big cats! Thus the problem for Hadrian.

The correct understanding is VITAL because it allows the use of the Platinum or White Gold in the < HEADPIECES > which are the Star LOCKS for SECURED and HIGHLY SECURED FOOTSTOOLS; EVEN when these metals are not available, as for cost reasons or other unacceptable restrictions!

That brings me to Revelation. The KEY words are there. "He has on his cloths on his thigh a name written that ONLY he can read. It is King of Kings and Lord of Lords". The reference is to the < INDIVIDUAL who GENERAL DIRECTOR of the DISCS > [Rearrange as G 0 D]. However, the REFERENCE is to a PARTICULAR GENERAL DIRECTOR. This is to do with the < HEADPIECES >. The name MUST BE of the style < AMEN >; <<< AMEN >>> <<< AM >>> <<<RTUR >>> <<<FVRECKRAN >>>.

The SCIENCE with the Biblical text requires to be UNLOCKED and the KEYS CUT. The Key is that certain books LIKE THE HEADPIECES MUST BE USED CORRECTLY. Some MAY not be NOT appropriate. That does not mean they are to be discarded, but that the KEY means that they must be CORRECTLY and ACCURATELY SELECTED CUT and USED in the lock.

This could be done by grouping some and by rejecting some and adjusting others.

This is to do with < STAR NAMES > and < VISIBLE INVISIBLES >.

First Samuel or Second Samuel? In First Samuel it is Saul who is appointed (anointed). Samuel is MADE AWARE of this and that it is DA VY D who is appointed as the correct individual. DA VY D is ATLANTYON in style. Thus "Saul" text in the New Testament many have to be CUT to UNDERSTAND SAMUEL CORRECTLY. Thus "Paul" which is a change. Here I have the OLD HYPOTHESIS and the NEW HYPOTHESIS and the NEW HYPOTHESIS is technically FAR more advanced and with a far greater understanding than the Old Hypothesis. Note here that Timothy comes out as TY MO TY . High TWO High. Could be taken to be VERY IMPORTANT. An essential Understanding for example. As I said a key cutting exercise or indeed to highlight that when using AdSY headpieces CONSIDERABLE CARE has to be taken.

In certain respects it is an EASY CODE, but VERY, VERY, VERY skillfully hidden; for obvious reasons. At the same time it MUST be ACCESSIBLE. What use is a key without the door? Where the DOORS MOVE the OCCUPANTS must be secure. As in a car, plane or train. Some doors AUTOMATICALLY OPEN and CLOSE, others are operated manually. It can be a combination of both; in the correct sequence. FORCE including EXPLOSIONS are a LOCK OUT. Could be hundreds even thousands of years. Might be just a few seconds or hours.

Watch that while the New Testament can be reduced in the case of MATTHEW, MARK, LUKE and GHAN, the FOUR DIFFERENT VERSIONS have to be carefully checked.

That applies to Revelation. Even parts which "appear" to be wrong may require to be included. Page 193 heads as "Apostolic Armour." This might simply be to draw attention to the CORRECT ATLANTYON GOWN. Watch the use of the word < AMEN > which suggests accuracy even at the end (Required Element). For the < HIGH IMPERIAL and UNION SYSTEM GALAXIES > it MUST BE <<< THREE AMENS >>>.

It MUST be the KING HY ME version (note the Spanish pronunciation) as this avoids the use of and shows that it is KNOWN that the sound "J" in Atlantyon Script is made of the COMBINED letters "GH " Again that is to do with the CORRECT PROOF, thus YH 2 UH. The word < ME > is the number Three!

The United Kingdom's Christian credentials potentially make it a suitable place for a GALACTIC INDIVIDUAL to put HIS or HER FEET and thus CONTACT may be considered to HAVE BEEN be RE ESTABLISHED. Thus the "World" has ended because ATLANTIS is restored. This is FACTUAL. Thus it needs references to ATLANTIS in REAL TERMS and CORRECTLY STATED.

This is an IMPORTANT and FACTUAL MATTER on an ONGOING BASIS. The assessment period might be just a few weeks (for an established secured footstool with regular links) or it could be years [up to 100] where a Footstool has lost status and it is to be re applied. Note it may be re applied on a temporary basis, particularly if there is to be a long period of adjustment These periods are often referred to as <<< PROTOCOL PERIODS >>> and are VERY, VERY, VERY IMPORTANT.

Care should be taken when using the word "PROTOCOL". The use of the Chevrons <<< and >>> is an indicator that it is being used correctly. Watch the number of Chevrons Individuals or Locations? For locations, one indicates only ONE Galaxy, two Two Galaxies, and three or four MORE than three Galaxies. Thus Four may be used when there is an AdSY with a Triple Panel (Three Galaxies) on which there is at least One TRIPLE GALAXY HEADPIECE: preferably on a WORKING SPORTING AdSY. [Large exercise

Stick as per the design shown] but with four pins to enable it to balance in the vertical and to be adjusted.

Given that it sits adjacent to the Atlantic Ocean, English may be permitted to be used with ATLANTYON and THRENS or other GALACTIC LANGUAGES of the HIGH IMPERIAL and UNION. So also could Spanish and Portuguese and Gaelic. NOTE that there is a FOOT EXERCISE which is involved. That < REQUIRES > that the < AUTHORISED INDIVIDUAL > is < WILLING > to put their feet in a particular location. This is NOT a detail. It <<< MUST >>> be voluntary.

The fact that certain Oceanic Islands are held; particularly those on the North Atlantic Ridge, is IMPORTANT for < PROTOCOL >. That obviously includes Iceland and Norway and the Canaries. Nelson VY SY T D! That brings me back to Heyerdahl. I have read his text in English, from a Translation.

This is very "touchy feely stuff" and requires CONSIDERABLE CARE. Much of this is usually handled by the local Fire Disc. It has been around for a long time and has the superior technical knowledge. Some of it is TOO HOT or TOO COLD TO HANDLE. Thus "Music for the Royal Fireworks."

"And did those feet?" WATCH carefully what constitutes SACRED GROUND and the meaning of that. Mere "possession" of an Obelisk or sacred stone is NOT sufficient; ESPECIALLY if plundered, when it then becomes < NOT PROTOCOL >. Hadrian's Wall is NOT just a physical marker on the ground. It is a < PROTOCOL GATE MARKER > and defines the LIMIT of ROMAN territory. There is a < TIME > element involved so the territory to the North (modern usage) is < PROTOCOL > including as the < WALL MOVES > as in < AN TO NY NE >.

A photograph of LIONS for example walking on FROSTED GROUND has a particular meaning. The lion is NOT rampant, but is restless; perhaps on the PROWL. Likewise with TYGER's, particularly the WHITE variety. Remember Tyger is also a reference to a Shark. Both are DANGEROUS.

BOTH are indicators of POTENTIALLY SERIOUS TROUBLE.

The <<< RESTING TYGER >>> is a THRENS and ATLANTYON POWER MARKER especially when located adjacent to THREE mountains; especially VOLCANIC ONES. [KY LE MAN YA RO]

<<< AU THOR's NOTE >>>
Glasgow 7 May 2009

I appreciate that this text is technically very difficult. I have revised it several times for technical accuracy. Do I know my onions? I am legally qualified and thus able to say if the < JUSTICE PROTOCOL > is met or not. Geography IS AN ESSENTIAL subject since it takes in the < ATLANTYON GALACTIC PHYSICS >. Thus my Geography prize.

Some men hate eating onions. 30 November 2008 was foggy in Glasgow while 1 December 2008 is very frosty but sunny. There is BLACK ICE. Where did the fog and the ice come from? From the Atlantic? Perhaps a little further away. One small step for man? A < FOOTSTOOL CRACKING > ? Perhaps closer. AR RA N perhaps.

"Come dancing". Black and Gold. Headpiece colours. Blue and light blue. Headpiece colours. An A 380 is red and white. Red is an UPSTAND and STAR COLOUR and is ACTIVE as in VOLCANO. It is NOT rocket science. Neither is this. This is FAR BEYOND rocket science. It is < GALACTIC SCIENCE >. From M31; THRENS? Yes. M 104? Yes. Real black dogs? SY RY US? Yes. From this < GALAXY >? Yes. And from The Mighty Three Galaxies.

<<<< TY ME KANSAL >>>> is the < Atlantyon Name of the Mighty Three Galaxies. Working with a < Three Panel > < Atlantyon AdSY > I would be expected by them to be a bit more specific. They might take this text at 90% accurate thus far, or might down rate to under 50% simply because while I had correctly identified certain ground markers and the < AT LAN TY K > Ocean, I had still not accurately identified their < SPECIFIC TERRITORIAL MARKERS >. I could say that I

had done so. They are VERY PARTICULAR as to where their individuals my go and who may enter. I have yet to travel to < AR RAN >. Yet I have passed the < Territorial Gate Marker.> It was on the Cable car. < TH UN > . It is also in the name < TH OR > . I need a star name like < HYT GHARVYK BY AT RUTH>.It is a complex name. Places in that system are shown as < UN > while the star name and individuals are < OR >. One of the stars, and a relevant name is < THOR ARRAN ARGHAARTH >. I must remember the mnemonics. It is not, as I said earlier, a "dog" star. Far from it. It is an < ATLANTYON STYLE >. An < OPEN > < AdSY > style so it is VERY PARTICULAR. The place name will be different from the Star name. Thus the place < THUN >. It is a Blue White and EXCEPTIONALLY POWERFUL! It is an < ATLANTYON MARKER >.

The < SEQUENCED STARS > note the identification and the Understanding and that the TY TY AdSY is correctly held and operated. Pale Grey and White and corded and TRILBY. The Tyger teeth open to show the flashing white incisors. Resting Tyger? Restless Tyger? <u>Angry Tyger?</u>

The TY TY AdSY which is made of wood, may be held by an individual who may be called a VY SY R . A <<< GATE KEEPER >>>. The TY VY SY R may be roughly translated as a powerful Gatekeeper; as in <POWER CLOSED or OPEN > for the < AdSY . It is STAR APPOINTMENT. TRIPLE STAR on occasions for a TY VY SY R . And TY TY individuals, while they may be referred to as a VY SY R, are more likely to be the much higher ranking and Galactic individual, KURALAKYS or a DIRECTOR OF GALAXY; both of which are < STAR > appointments!

That brings me back to the King James Version.

The preface to the King James Version is in the CORRECT STYLE because at the end, it correctly says A MORE EXACT TRANSLATION; < AMEN RA >. But it is quite clear from events at the time, and shortly thereafter that the understanding of and the concept of the Individual < AMEN RA > was at best PARTIAL, and to a certain extent it is a matter which is not properly and correctly understood today. It concerns the TERRITORY of and the DESIGNATION of the

Great Southern Kingdom. Thus while James moved to London, that DOES NOT extend the territory of the Great Southern Kingdom to London. It may do, and in fact at that time and for a time almost certainly DID, which is WHY the King James Version was printed. It explains ALSO the UNION FLAG which contains the Atlantyon letters, < 2 U >. These are NOT appreciated for what they are UNLESS the Atlantyon font is known. Likewise with the sound GH, which is a composite letter as written in Atlantyon and that may explain the use of the letter "J." The use of "J" may also arise from the Atlantyon letter "Y" which is common in usage. KW is similar and again if copied from "handwriting" may come out as the capital "Q" of script. All of which tends to suggest that someone had access to and was trying to BACK ENGINEER the Atlantyon language! The Atlantyons DO NOT APPROVE of back engineering and in certain respects if dealing with the < GALACTIC STAR SCIENCE > is EXCEPTIONALLY DANGEROUS!

There are < HIGHLY TECHNICAL POINTS > here and in respect of the < DESIGNATED TERRITORY > that MUST be correctly understood. Again it is not clear that that is CLEARLY and ACCURATELY understood today! While to a certain extent it is political, it essentially concerns individual TYPES and STYLES. It also involves < GALAXIES > and < Their Individuals > .

This is Examination material in < ATLANTYON GALACTIC PHYSICS > < ADVANCED and ULTRA > which is out with the scope of this text.

The main point here is about the < GALACTIC TERRITORIAL MARKERS > between < TWO GALAXIES > especially in the < THREE PANEL > < AdSY> < SYSTEMS. This has very little to do with local politics on this < FOOTSTOOL > but < THE SPECIFIC > < BLUE WHITE > < GALACTIC GROUP > included in < THE TEN GALAXY SYSTEM >. That group will < NOT ADMIT > those who do not meet its < PROTOCOLS>.

This is to do with NOT PROTOCOL INDIVIDUALS and with the Atlantic Crossing BOTH WAYS. It is to do with the < JUSTICE and MEDICAL PROTOCOLS >.

The Titanic incident has not been CORRECTLY BROUGHT to a CLOSE as far as they are concerned.< WINTER NORTH ATLANTIC > is < APPLIED > excluding May and June. Gravity is increased to < PLUS EIGHT>. 7 May 2009

I am dealing here with a THIRD GALAXY which is REQUIRED for a THREE PANEL AdSY. But that THIRD GALAXY and its < DIRECTORS > are making the point that < THEIR PROTOCOLS > < HAVE BEEN SERIOUSLY CONTRAVENED >. Their < STAR > list here is likely to include NORSE names including those LOCALLY APPLIED and INCLUDES THEIR POPULATIONS!

The < LEGAL >and < COMPLEX PROTOCOLS > are noted at < STAR > level. Restrictions are < APPLIED >

Where the local Political interference upsets < Protocol > the consequences are potentially < VERY SERIOUS > as in the case of Nagasaki. For essentially NYPPON is < PROTOCOL > territory as is RU SY YA ! It was unacceptable political interference at a technical level and local NYPPON Government practices with it own individuals which cost the City of Nagasaki.

The large < HIDDEN TRIPLE GALAXIES > have been watching events carefully. Their individuals have been TARGETED DIRECTLY at the GREAT SOUTHERN KINGDOM. Thus the <u>CURRENT FURIOUS GALACTIC ANGER as the problem STILL PERSITS and the THREAT LEVEL has INCREASED!</u>

Hadrian also notes the position; pointing out again that he built the wall. Which is duly noted.

The <<< HEADPIECES >>> are crucial to this science. Individually they are small and fragile and easily broken and in their handmade style not at all obvious what they are or what they represent. They are thus easily discarded as of no value. Yes it is for "opening the mouth" for allowing the INDIVIDUAL to speak .In so doing the wall paintings can be read. They are like "still pictures" of living images; like a DVD but in stone.

But they are MUCH more than that. They are the SYMBOL of < CORRECT UNDERSTANDING > of the < GALACTIC SCIENCE > and of the < FIRE DISCS > <

THEMSELVES >. Essentially that is what the < SPORTING > teaches and that is what I have tried to explain in this text. I accept that I have provided only a brief introduction, but I hope that it will clarify to a certain extent the powerful underlying science.

<<<< APPLIED PROTOCOLS >>>>
<<<< THE TEN GALAXY COMBINATION >>>>
<<<< TRIPLE BARRED SPIRAL SCULPTOR SY FERT COMBINATION >>>>
<<<< TY ME KANSAL >>>>
<<<< TY TY KANSAL >>>>
<<<< KHUN AARAN HY HAAT >>>>
<<<< THRENS >>>>
<<<< LLYCOT LLEYDRAN >>>>
<<<< DRAS >>>>
<<<< PYKAS >>>>

1. Stylised AdSY Drawing Triple Panel Working <<<ATLANTYON >>>. This is in the SY FERT style as the top downward pointing arm shows the < STAR POSITIONS > of the < SEQUENCED STARS >. It is made < BARRED SPIRAL > if a cover is placed over it, which cover is usually varnished balsa wood type with a blue edging. That hides the sequenced star pattern.

Within a Galaxy there are many < PLANES > and movement between planes requires < GATE > activation. That < GATE > activation involves < TIME > locks so that from this < FOOTSTOOL> to another < FOOTSTOOL> involves <TIME TRAVEL>. It is a particular kind of < TIME TRAVEL > thus the < BOATS of Millions of Years >. This is not the text book for that which is an Advanced to Ultra Applied Metaphysics subject. Current Science fiction when dealing with concept of time travel almost immediately discloses a material lack of understanding of what is involved. This is highlighted in particular when dealing with Dinosaurs and SIZE. The size and style DEPENDS on Gravity so if the "monsters" are too big or too small it is the < GRAVITY > point which is not understood. These are called < Gravity Sticks > because they symbolise the correct understanding of Gravity and that it is not a "particle" but a "force." These really are examination points for those who are taught Applied Metaphysics or Atlantyon Galactic Physics at University level. It is NOT mathematics based, and it is a serious error to talk in mathematics terms. It is a < FIRE DISCS> matter and that should not be forgotten! I consider this explanation to be consistent with the limited understanding required for the < SPORTING > program, which is to do with health and fitness exercises and design.

For cost printing reasons this is shown in black and white. The actual colour copy is to be found as a registered design with the UK Authorities as 4009977. The Actual < HEADPIECE > for the TY TY GALAXY COMBINATION in SYFERT STYLE as of this date is registered as 4009978. Close inspection of the copy of this < Headpiece > will show that it has been < SNAPPED > which is appropriate for a < FOOTSTOOL > which had lost its < GALACTIC LINKS > and where restoration is under consideration with its < FOOTSTOOL IDENTIFIER NUMBER >.

2   This is a stylized drawing of an AdSY headpiece. As drawn there are different styles so that the open Headpieces in Tuat ANKH Amen's tomb have a different shape but are still identifiable as such by reference to their design and name. The reference to "opening the mouth" is that often in the exercise routines for < APPLIED METAPHYSICS SPORTING > an < INDIVIDUAL > may exercise with these < HEADPIECES > and apply it to the chin BEFORE starting to speak. In many respects they are used for thoughtful contemplation BEFORE speaking. Thus if there is a difficult problem it might be expected that the exercise routine would be done and then an opinion or Judgment given. In the < SPORTING > program a corded < HEADBAND > may be used and the < HEADPIECE > may be inserted to the rear standing up. That will produce an appearance similar to one of the Egyptian Pharaoh's crowns and it is possible that the cloth was designed in such as way as to hide the < HEADPIECE > and its < DESIGN > in much the same way that in < BARRED SPIRAL GALAXIES > these < HEADPIECES > are covered over by a plain design with a Blue border. The corded sporting < Headdress > is similar in style to that shown as worn by Nefertiti. [May be pronounced as NY FA R TY TY], in which event note the double "TY" suggestive of a VY SY R.

The pointed arms position of certain of the statues of the NYTYR reflect the position that might be seen in outline of an individual working with a < HEADPIECE> in an exercise routine, when they had briefly stopped moving. Thus much of the drawings by the Egyptians contains as best they could the PHOTOGRAPHIC record of what they saw and what they tried to understand, including the words, some of which they incorporated.

The technical aspects of this design is that the green dots in the grid represent < FOOTSTOOLS > which are < INHABITED > by < SIMILAR > < POPULATIONS >. Green is NOT a < STAR > Colour so that the use of that colour shows that without this explanation the individual who drew it, did not correctly understand the science.

The < THREE GOLD LINES > indicate a < BARRED SPIRAL COMBINATION GROUP OF GALAXIES > where the upper Triangle is the < SCULPTOR > style of < HIGH > < GALAXY >. The white rectangle with < FOOTSTOOLS > represents the < IMPERIAL > and in this case it supposed to be M 31 .[Threns]

The three blue dots between the upper "V" and the Lower rectangle represent the < UNION GALAXY > in this instance this < DRAS GALAXY > but the three dots represent a BLUE WHITE or BLUE star in EACH of the < THREE GALAXIES > ;thus the Combination.

The pointed tip is where it is hand held.

This is simply a < DESIGN > for this text. The Actual < AdSY HEADPIECE > would be determined as such by the relevant THREE STARS, who might permit a limited Registration of that design, for example the design registered with the UK Intellectual Property office as design 4009978 . That < DESIGN > registration is lodged for TECHNICAL SCIENTIFIC REASONS and is essentially the < DESIGN> and registration <u><<<< PERMITTED >>>> by <<<< THOSE PARTICULAR GALAXY COMBINATIONS >>>></u>.

The yellow star to the BOTTOM LEFT is a star similar to the < LANAST > star in this Galaxy, and the TWO with the red outline are the < ACTIVE > ones who determine < CONTACT and TRAVEL > or NOT to that Galaxy. Again an error in this design because it is THREE stars in Threns which determine travel, two at this side of the Galaxy and one at the far side. These Galaxies are Spinning and that spinning movement requires to be taken into account

As the POINT is held to this Galaxy, < SIMILAR STYLES > only are able to contact, conform to < THIS STAR LANAST >.The one surrounded in red is an < EXCEPTIONALLY HIGHLY SECURED and SHIELDED FOOTSTOOL > currently to the far side of M 31 galaxy and is probably <<<< THRENS >>>> itself. The one with a part red outline is an < VERY HIGHLY SECURED > and as shown in red. Both are NOT ready to permit contact, but are watching closely.

Formal < HEADPIECES > are weighted with Silver and Gold Coins and sometimes with rocks, as in ordinary rocks, or with gems such as diamonds, TOPAZ, sapphires; small size preferred. It should be noted that as EXERCISE WALKING STICKS they work WITHOUT any stones provided the correct understanding is appreciated since the whole < ATLANTYON GALACTIC PHYSICS > < APPLIED METAPHYSICS > is determined by the <u>< CORRECTLY SEQUENCED STARS></u> . If an analogy is considered it is like trying to open a "<u>very hot and untouchable combination safe</u>"!

The < AdSY's > and < HEADPIECES > are thus < GIVEN by the SEQUENCED STARS > and the Correct Understanding of them and the < COMBINATION HEADPIECES > <u>will only be permitted if they approve</u>. This is a < <u>MATERIAL TECHNICAL POINT ></u>. Otherwise the < SCIENCE > appears simply as drawings, quite pretty, sometimes a bit obscene, but not relevant to a Highly Advanced Civilization with Galactic links.

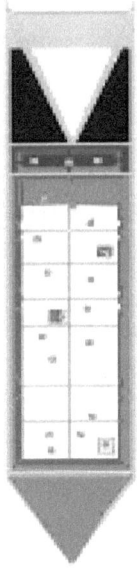

3   Bared Spiral showing Gates Closed.

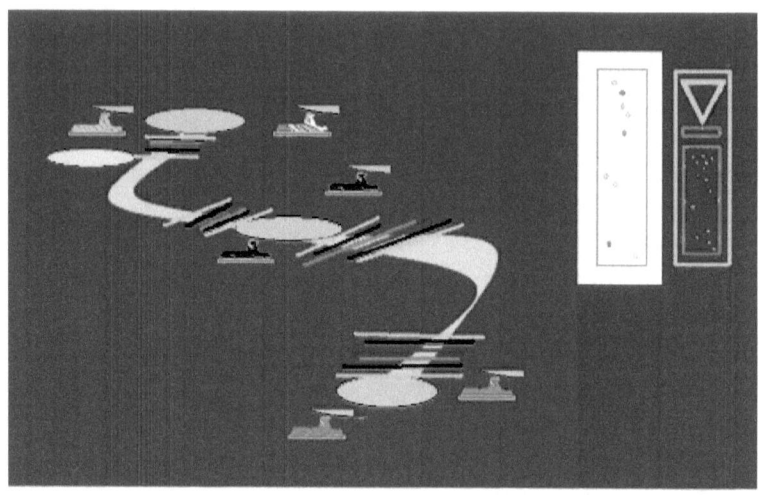

4   Barred Spiral Star Chart showing Gates as OPEN

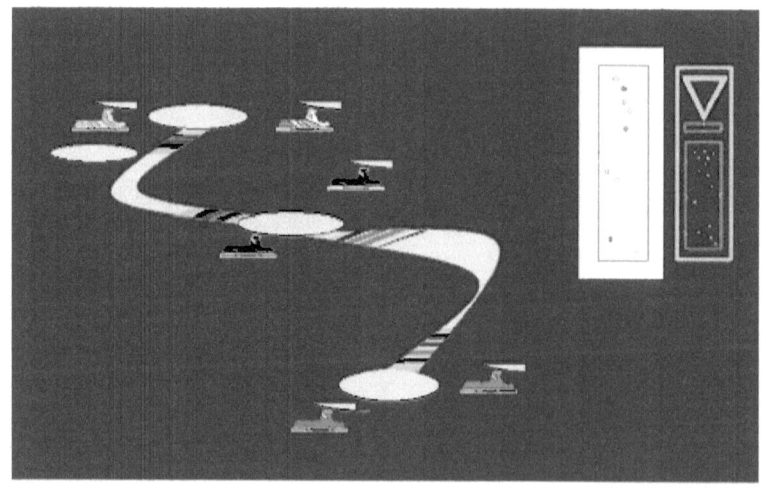

Note in this Chart drawing the < RESTING TYGER > is shown with different colours and < DIFFERENT FOOTSTOOLS >.

The bottom left is < RED TYGER DRAS > towards the Galactic centre of this Galaxy. That to the bottom right with the < BLUE TYGER > is a nearby < THRENS> < FOOTSTOOL>.

The two < RESTING BLACK TYGER > are AT the RIM and not far from each other. BOTH are < HIGHLY SECURED and HIDDEN>.

Guessing is not acceptable in < Applied Metaphysics> nor < Atlantyon Galactic Physics >.

I am required to STATE what the position is and where the nearby < FOOTSTOOL > is located. I can be out by a few < STARS > but I MUST have the correct understanding. While it might be < ALTYR > or < RYGEL > I am going to take the < BLUE WHITE > < SY RY US > . That Star has a "small neighbour" and that small neighbour is likely to be a < HIGHLY SECURED and INHABITED FOOTSTOOL > masking off as an OLD and small star. As viewed from there this < LANAST > Star and this < FOOTSTOOL > may be viewed similarly (if it can be seen at all) . This is to do with the < GATE MECHANISM >. However if it is of the < ADVANCED KIND > with links they will be able to see both this star and this < FOOTSTOOL> but it will be on their list of < NOT APPROVED and NOT SECURE DESTINATIONS >. Given its term as the "Dog Star" it is likely to be a < FOOTSTOOL > for Llycot Lleydran . That is for the Anubis type individuals (black, brown and white) < LLYCURYON > from their < stylized TWIN galaxy > of <<< LLYCOT LLEYDRAN >>> and their <<< HEADPIECE >>> would need to be on the AdSY (probably a < SPORTING ONE > at this <u>< FOOTSTOOL > BEFORE any real Galactic travel can be set up</u> .

In technical terms <<<< Llycot Lleydran >>>> is FAR beyond M 104 and is a < SYSTEM > Galaxy with M 104 and others and MUST be on the < GALAXY LIST > in the < CORRECT POSITION > . This < CORRECT POSITION > is the <<< TEN GALAXY LIST >>> with the <

ATLANTYON NAMES > in the correct < SEQUENCE >. Thus the Mnemonic since they have to give the < COMMANDS >.

It can perhaps be seen from this that Astronomers now have some idea of where to look for "inhabited" < Footstools >, although a number of < ADVANCED FOOTSTOOLS > would in technical terms consider the < JUSTICE and MEDICAL PROTOCOLS > are < NOT MET > and thus would unwilling to allow access to their < Footstools > and WOULD SHIELD their Galaxies making them < INVISIBLE >. Thus large chunks of dark and heavily CLOAKED Matter in Space! This is seen most clearly with the Barred Spirals.

In this < DRAS > Galaxy there are A FEW which are much more secured < FOOTSTOOLS > and hopefully this text will show to their satisfaction that < ATLANTYON GALACTIC PHYSICS > or < APPLIED METAPHYSICS > with their < SPORTING > programs can be taught here.

Beyond this Galaxy rim, there is a < TRANSIT GALAXY > which is shown with < Yellow Star >. It is likely to be < ASSOCIATE > but NOT on this particular ROUTE Map. Possibly M 41, M 411 or M 412! Given the < BARRED SPIRAL > nature of this chart it is the < DOUBLE BARRED SPIRAL > and its headpiece is < SCULPTED and BARRED > <<< FVRECKRAN >>> M 51. The < Sculpted and Barred > are shown in < Headpieces > with a cut design in what is otherwise an open barred spiral style. The yellow indicates that it is COMPATIBLE but it is < BARRED > and effectively closed. Thus until this < FOOTSTOOL > has its links restored it is < BARRED > and would be similarly marked as "Yellow". This may mean that ALL DRAS is < RESTRICTED >. That would be done if an < UP GRADE > is in PROGRESS!

It may be noted that the order seems a bit peculiar. The current scientific location of M 41, M 411, and M 412 are largely IRRELEVANT . It is the < HEADPIECES > which show the CORRECT COMBINATION. In this context of < TECHNICAL GALACTIC CHARTS > it is <u>entirely appropriate</u>.

The TOP TWO are TWO FOOTSTOOLS in M 31 < THRENS >. To obtain access to that Galaxy the correct Star

Identifiers MUST be given. They are < HYDRAFUR >, < HYATRAMAROL >, both of which are shown and are currently at this side of M 31 and at the far side of Threns < HYT GHARVYK BY AT RUTH >, which is not shown. That needs a further chart ONLY available from Threns. Now UNLESS the names are CORRECTLY GIVEN and PRONOUNCED THE THRENS STARS will simply refuse to EXCHANGE KEYS and effectively that Galaxy then ACTS as a BARRED SPIRAL to this GALAXY. It will NOT ADMIT. That does not change what is seen visually through telescopes, but as I have hopefully explained in terms of this Science, what you actually see from this < Footstool > does not tell very much other than of the highly stylized and sculpted patterns.

    The easiest way to ADMIT is to travel on a craft from the Bottom Left Footstool and to be able to go there I need to know its THRENS or ATLANTYON name. I need to have the < CORRECTLY STYLED HEADPIECE > for this < GALAXY > even if previously TWICE < SNAPPED > and to < KNOW that it has been < SNAPPED > [That effectively prohibits contact]. Once I have that < HEADPIECE > and can apply it to the < TY TY AdSY > and the Relevant Stars will THEN and ONLY then allow me to < HOST >. That < ACTIVATES > the locks < CORRECTLY > between this < Galaxy > and < M31 > Threns and M 51 Fvreckran.

TRAVEL and COMMUNICATION are then < AVAILABLE > subject to < PROTOCOL COMPLIANCE >.

    In this text am using the name < HERANTUR > for the bottom right < STAR > and it is a BLUE WHITE with the < HER > being used in this Galaxy where < HYT > is used in Threns. I am aware that Herantur has a NUMBER of OBJECTIONS to this information being released at this time at the Lanast Footstool; all of which are duly noted.

    The large White rectangle to the Top right of the charts is the Galactic Plane, with Star colours shown. The lowest yellow represents this local star.

The Blue rectangle with the "V" shape is the < ROUTE > from the bottom yellow (this star) by way of Blue Stars out to the boundary with M 31. Actual THRENS or ATLANTYON names MUST be used.

One matter which I must comment in more detail is on the < AdSY > headpieces. While only pieces of stylised and painted Balsa wood or similar, even with the weights in them, the use of the AdSY MUST be handled correctly; and the < HEADPIECES > correctly positioned.

This is a < BARRED SPIRAL + SYFERT + SCULPTOR COMBINATION > so that the effective < AdSY > will need to be fairly large to accommodate what are likely to be < SEVEN > headpieces. While the AdSY may have less than that, indeed may have only One it is necessary to know the combination. [As in a safe]. Thus the headpieces must be correctly positioned and USED by an authorized individual.

The combination is NOT numbers. It is the < SPECIFIC GALAXIES and the CORRECT UNDERSTANDING >. This is to do with COMPATABILITY. It works on the REAL < FOOTSTOOL > and is part of the < IDENTIFIER SEQUENCE > and in < CONJUNCTION > with < FIRE DISC > and other < SPECIFIC SEQUENCED STARS >.

A Fundamental here is that the < HIGH IMPERIAL and UNION GALAXIES > must be correctly named and their < HEADPIECE > on Display for a time. That as I said is done simply by the registration of the design. Providing the registration of the design is done to THEIR REQUIREMENTS and that is NOT a matter for the local registration authority. That brings me back to the Protocol Territories, King Tut's tomb and Hadrian's wall.

The current registration location for designs in the UK is Cardiff, which is Wales. Jurisdiction is thus England and Wales, and the European Union. However MUCH of the European Union is < NOT PROTOCOL > so far as the High Imperial and Union Galaxies Combinations are concerned, so that while they may note that registration, they are NOT likely to agree to contact. They take in M 104 and associates so the current objection to contact is from that Distant M51 Galaxy and combinations [including specifically THE MIGHTY THREE GALAXIES]. That relates to "incidents" in the past and the "assurances given" which now almost certainly are regarded as "Not Met". These are PRACTICAL POINTS but they affect in the main the justice and medical protocols.

Problems with the UK National Health Service are thus NOT a detail. I am dealing here with HIGHLY ADVANCED and HIGHLY DEVELOPED civilizations who as I said previously do not wish contact fractious difficult and violent < Footstools >; of which this is currently properly regarded by them as one. Footstool weighting is 3d in the sterling old money .925 AG. In practical terms that means they are not likely to communicate for over 1000 years and are likely also to WITHDRAW their material.

I did say that < TIME TRAVEL > was involved. M 104 is a few light years away. However if its < HEADPIECE > is < CORRECTLY > on the < AdSY> and the AdSY is here, the distance is about a foot in old measurement. That is because it is on the AdSY beside that from this Galaxy. The question then arises as to what that < HEADPIECE > contains. On 27 April, 2009 AD it is weighted with ordinary UK coins which are not silver. < NOT PROTOCOL >. < NO CONTACT >. However that can be changed for the silver and gold coins. What is the weight? The gold needs to be ½ sovereign or above and the Footstool needs to be over 10 grams in new weight. That is about £1 silver coin of current usage + an old 3d bit! I do not need to put them in BUT CRUCIALLY THE MESSAGE MUST BE SENT to M 104, M 31 and The Mighty Three Galaxies that the correct < HEADPIECES > are available for the < SPORING AdSY >. That is done simply writing this text and making it < AVAILABLE > for publication. Those < INDIVIDUALS > in those Galaxies concerned can take a view. But it is not just M 104. Between them and this Galaxy is another Barred Spiral and Sculpted Galaxy Headpiece, of open blue design <u>BUT POWER CLOSED</u>. Barred spiral and sculpted. Like an ORKA? But also sculpted are the Sharks AND the Dinosaurs! The difficulty here is that to understand the dinosaurs correctly it is to know that they are in fact from the < PYKAS > galaxy and are very much ALIVE! It is THUS not a matter of "time travel" to a distant past BUT the realization that the travel is CURRENT and ACTIVE and the "dinosaurs" have a vocabulary and language as well and MUST meet the essential criteria for compatibility. That includes < SHAPE SHIFTING >! Thus the Dinosaur arriving here arrives from

COMPATIBLE PYKAS and is in style and size < ATLANTYON >. Whale hunting is thus a VERY BAD IDEA since it ACTUALLY INSULTS a VERY POWERFUL GALAXY which ACTIVELY CURRENTLY SUPPIES MATERIAL! And while the material is Individual based it also includes < PLASMAS > both < EXCEPTIONALLY HOT > and < EXCEPTIONALY COLD >. When they are combined safely they arrive as rain or snow or sand or dust, or simply as light . It is NOT appreciated from where they have come. This is part of the mechanics of the < Atlantyon Galactic Physics > and the < Applied Metaphysics > . Start messing about with "dna" for example, and as the material has been and is being supplied by the < SEQUENCED STARS> it is they who become upset.

Currently < PYKAS > is < POWER CLOSED > and marked for < WITHDRAWAL >.

The TOP < HEADPIECE > is for the < TRIPLE > < HIGH IMPERIAL and UNION GALAXY > That is this Galaxy, M 31 and M 104 in COMBINATION. But M 104 is LOCKED OUT. Assuming contact with M 31 it might be expected that TWO panel AdSY would suffice but that will not do, because they use THREE PANEL. But their < HEADPIECE > is also < POWER CLOSED >. Further this Galaxy < HEADPIECE > has been snapped. That means that this < GALAXY > is closed for contact. That is FACTUAL. Indeed it is the RED TYGER DRAS an ATLANTYON and FVRECKRAN RTUR who have to approve contact at this TRIPLE PANEL level .

If it is an < ATLANTYON > that will bring in <u>< THE MIGHTY THREE GALAXY COMBINATION ></u> out beyond M 104. That is easily confused that with the High Imperial and Union, but it is known by its Specific name. Thus to operate the working AdSY from this Galaxy as a TRIPLE PANEL the designation of that Galaxy Combination must be known. If it is NOT correctly < APPLIED > the < AdSY > and < HEADPIECES > are simply fancy painted pieces of wood with perhaps a few coins in them. When correctly < APPLIED > by the < AUTHORISED INDIVIDUAL > < PRESENTING > to the < LOCAL and CORRECTLY NAMED STAR > it is the < LOCAL STAR > which < ACTIVATES > the

FOOTSTOOL MECHANISM > and the < FOOTSTOOL > will be moved relative to this < GALAXY >and have its INTER GALACTIC LINKS RESTORED . THAT is effectively < RETUNED > and it is LARGELY DONE by this < LOCAL STAR > and the < SEQUENCED STARS >.

EVENTS however will determine that < CORRECT ACTIVATION >. This will still remain as a < HIGHLY SECURED FOOTSTOOL > in a large < BARRED SPIRAL GALAXY >. There is one aspect which I have not mentioned accurately.

<<< HYT GHARVIK BY AT RUTH >>> is mentioned. That PARTICULAR LOCATION is the TRANSIT POINT to a THE DOUBLE BARRED SPIRAL and SCULPTED SYFERT GROUP which has existing links to M 31 but NOT to < DRAS > . Essentially what that means is that < THAT GROUP > may be willing to < RESTORE > links with < ATLANTIS > and UPGRADE some of DRAS, including < DRAS > and < HERANTUR > . It may be currently < INVISIBLE > as in dark region or seen as a Barred Spiral in combination, or as an entirely "New Style". That is simply part of the masking. That < GROUP > would change the < HEADPIECE > style to < THEIR STYLE > which would also explain the previously snapped < headpiece > for < DRAS > . The internal weighting would change. It would still be the Silver and Gold Coins but the < POSITION > of them within the < HEADPIECE > would change. Weighted as TWO in silver 1/- [2 x 5.5 grams,11 grams in total]would mean that this < FOOTSTOOL > was < RESTORED > with < DRAS >. It is an < UPGRADE > so that many other < FOOTSTOOLS > may not be so upgraded because the < ASSESSMENT > is by < THE MIGHTY THREE GALAXIES > < TY ME KANSAL > in < ATLANTYON >. Weighted as THREE in silver 1/-, it is < THREE FOOTSTOOLS > which are upgraded, and that might include < HERANTUR > . The Gold Coin might be a ½ sovereign or a sovereign, but it does NOT actually need to be in the < HEADPIECE >. The correct positioning however, MUST be known. The < HEADPIECE > is weighted < OPEN FOOTSTOOL > with the gold with two other silver coins.

Where more silver coins are added, more footstools are added. Where the coins are < REMOVED > it is < FOOTSTOOL STATUS > which is < LOST > and that may take many years to be assessed again; possibly in the thousands.

The VISITING ATLANTYON official might be described as <<<< TRANSITING >>>> with a view to assessing < PROTOCOLS > and if < AUTHORISED > from the < MIGHTY THREE GALAXIES > would have an <<<< AdSY >>>> with the correctly sequenced < HEADPIECES > including the <<<< HEADPIECE >>>> for at least one of the <<<< TY ME KANSAL >>>> and could accurately assess <<<< Protocols >>>>.

<<<< TY ME KANSAL TA Y TY TY KANSAL DA KAST KANSAL >>>>.

<<<< AMEN >>>><<<< AM >>>> <<<< RTUR >>>>

Shield  Crest

www.ingramcontent.com/pod-product-compliance
Lightning Source LLC
Chambersburg PA
CBHW021135230426
43667CB00005B/127